Renaissance Literature

TITLES IN THE
GREENHAVEN PRESS COMPANION TO LITERARY
MOVEMENTS AND GENRES SERIES:

American Humor
American Modernism
American Realism
American Romanticism
Children's Literature
Elizabethan Drama
English Romanticism
Fairy Tales
Greek Drama
Renaissance Literature
Slave Narratives
Victorian Literature

THE GREENHAVEN PRESS COMPANION TO
Literary Movements and Genres

Renaissance Literature

Stephen P. Thompson, *Book Editor*

David L. Bender, *Publisher*

Bruno Leone, *Executive Editor*

Bonnie Szumski, *Editorial Director*

Stuart B. Miller, *Managing Editor*

David M. Haugen, *Series Editor*

Greenhaven Press, Inc., San Diego, CA

Every effort has been made to trace the owners of copyrighted material. The articles in this volume may have been edited for content, length, and/or reading level. The titles have been changed to enhance the editorial purpose. Those interested in locating the original source will find the complete citation on the first page of each article.

Library of Congress Cataloging-in-Publication Data

Renaissance literature / Stephen P. Thompson, editor.
     p.   cm. — (The Greenhaven Press companion to literary movements and genres)
   Includes bibliographical references and index.
   ISBN 0-7377-0418-7 (pbk. : alk. paper) —
ISBN 0-7377-0419-5 (lib. : alk. paper)
   1. European literature—Renaissance, 1450–1600—
History and criticism. I. Thompson, Stephen P., 1953-   .
II. Series.

PN715 .R46 2001
809'.024—dc21
                                       00-045470
                                          CIP

CONTENTS

Foreword   9

Renaissance Literature: Aspiration and the Individual   11

Chapter 1: Italian Renaissance Literature

1. Italian Humanism: Recovering the Past
by Gloria K. Fiero   32

The birthplace of the Renaissance was Florence, Italy, where affluent merchants began to patronize the arts, including sculpture, painting, and architecture. Artists and scholars alike, led by the scholar and poet Francesco Petrarch, began to study the achievements of the ancient world. Petrarch's passionate enthusiasm inspired a movement known as humanism.

2. The Achievement of Petrarch
by Charles G. Nauert Jr.   39

The first great "Renaissance man" was Petrarch, whose devotion to classical writers, especially the Roman writer Cicero, led to the recovery of classical Latin as the language of eloquence throughout Europe. In his essays, his letters, and his poetry, Petrarch engaged in a kind of self-examination that influenced European writers for generations.

3. Princes and Courtiers: The Writings of Machiavelli and Castiglione *by E.R. Chamberlin*   47

The early sixteenth-century Italian writers Machiavelli and Castiglione present contrasting visions of the behavior of the all-powerful princes of Renaissance Italy. Machiavelli depicts these princes as they are, obsessed with keeping power. Castiglione presents an idealized portrait, based on an actual Italian court, of how civilized and cultured princes could be.

Chapter 2: The Northern Humanist Movement and Its Influence

1. Beginnings of the Northern Renaissance
by Robert E. Lerner   54

Due in part to long and destructive wars, the Renaissance did not come to Northern Europe until around 1500. With the advent of the printing press to help spread their ideals,

Christian humanist writers such as Erasmus and Sir Thomas More inspired Northern Europeans to embrace the study of the ancient world as a way to improve their own.

2. Erasmus's *The Praise of Folly* and the Humanist Reform Agenda *by Clarence H. Miller*   62

No other work of the sixteenth century so fully espouses the educational, religious, and political ideals of Christian humanism as *The Praise of Folly* by the Dutch scholar Erasmus. The work mounts a sustained attack, through the humor of satire, against stale ideas and hypocritical practices in the Catholic Church, in governments, and in the universities of Europe.

3. Sir Thomas More and His *Utopia* *by Burton A. Milligan*   70

The *Utopia* of Sir Thomas More is a fictitious travel dialogue in two parts. The first part critiques the economic and social evils of contemporary European societies, while the second depicts the ideal society on the newly discovered island of Utopia, a place where values and practices closely resemble the ideals of such classical writers as Plato.

4. The Comic Vision of Rabelais *by M.A. Screech*   78

In typical Renaissance fashion, the comic works of Rabelais reflect a wide range of classical sources and inspirations, many of which are unfamiliar to modern readers. But the underlying values behind his satire and mocking jests are fundamentally Christian and humanist values, mixed with a healthy dose of skepticism inspired by the Roman satirist Lucian.

Chapter 3: The Forms of Renaissance Poetry

1. The Conventions of Petrarchan Poetry *by Leonard Forster*   88

The dominant approach to love poetry in the earlier Renaissance, the Petrarchan style of poetry, remained potent throughout the period, influencing poets from Chaucer to Thomas Wyatt to Shakespeare and John Donne. In its conventional formula, the poet praises the beauty of his beloved while also lamenting her unattainable distance from the poet.

2. Edmund Spenser's *The Faerie Queene:* Educating the Reader *by Russell J. Meyer*   98

In *The Faerie Queene*, Edmund Spenser seeks to "fashion a gentleman or noble person in vertuous and gentle discipline," and to accomplish this, he will employ allegory as a strategy to involve his readers in the dilemmas of his characters. By this approach, Spenser wants the reader of Book I to participate in the trials and tribulations of a Christian knight wandering in a world full of hypocrisy and vice.

3. **John Donne and the Metaphysical Poets**
   by Richard Willmott   107
   The three most prominent English metaphysical poets,
   John Donne, George Herbert, and Andrew Marvell, were
   well-educated public figures (all were Members of Parliament) who wrote poetry on the side. Their poetry is characterized by ingenious analogies, witty arguments, and unusual imagery, all designed to convey a particular moment
   and its emotion.

4. **The Epic Sensibility of Milton's *Paradise Lost***
   by Merritt Y. Hughes   116
   Through its extensive use of dialogue and conversation,
   Paradise Lost approximates drama, but it is best thought of
   as "an epic built out of dramas," for it is deeply embedded
   in the epic tradition of Homer and Virgil. Some readers
   have thought that Satan has the highest heroic stature in
   the poem, but this view misses the deep and devastating
   irony that undercuts Satan's posturing.

Chapter 4: Renaissance Prose

1. **Renaissance Women Writers**
   by Katharina M. Wilson   125
   The women who benefited most from the Renaissance
   revolution in education were women of the upper classes.
   Though restricted in their choice of genres by their social
   roles, female writers of the period did compose eloquent
   and popular stories, poetry, tracts, and translations.

2. **Montaigne and His Readers** *by Richard L. Regosin*   136
   During the latter half of his life, Montaigne wrote essays,
   short pieces on a particular topic which invariably involved
   some dialogue with one or more ancient writers. But Montaigne's purpose in these essays was never didactic; he was
   not so much trying to teach his reader as to involve his
   reader in the intimate process of self-understanding.

3. **The Educational Writings of Sir Francis Bacon**
   by Brian Vickers   141
   The lifelong goal of Sir Francis Bacon in his writing was to
   improve the quality of human knowledge and so to benefit
   mankind. The topics of his writings span most realms of
   human knowledge, including natural and social sciences,
   the life sciences, psychology, and communications theory,
   but they all share distinctive literary qualities and strategies.

Chapter 5: English Renaissance Drama

1. **Shakespeare's Predecessors: Lyly, Greene, Kyd,
   and Marlowe** *by David Bevington*   152
   In the years just before Shakespeare's glory years, the successful and innovative plays of Robert Greene and John

Lyly opened new territory in romantic comedy and drama inspired by Greek romance. Also inspiring Shakespeare were Thomas Kyd and Christopher Marlowe with their innovations in dramatic tragedy.

2. **Marlowe's *Dr. Faustus* and Renaissance Aspiration** *by Roma Gill*   161

In an age when the new learning—both of the classical past and of the world around—was a dominant force in society, Christopher Marlowe produced a play that epitomizes the contradictions involved in the quest to go beyond the traditional limits of human knowledge. Dr. Faustus is a Renaissance man whose aspirations lead him to forbidden knowledge and into tragedy.

3. **Shakespeare's Earlier Plays: History and Romantic Comedy** *by Derek Traversi*   171

All of Shakespeare's early plays are characterized by a very innovative approach to genre as they combine comedy with history and history with tragedy. The early history plays provide a sustained meditation on the nature of kingship, while the early comedies are focused on the experience of romantic love.

4. **Shakespeare's Later Plays: The Achievement in Tragedy** *by Philip Edwards*   179

The heroes of Shakespeare's tragedies all suffer from moral deficiencies and weakness of character, but these are not the cause of the heroes' fall. Rather, Shakespeare's heroes engage in defiance of the status quo in their societies, and it is their bid for liberation that leads them into tragedy.

5. **Ben Jonson and the Sensational Jacobean Drama** *by Eugene P. Wright*   193

The English plays of the early seventeenth century demonstrate overall the demise of romantic comedy and the rise of a more skeptical and satiric kind of comedy. In tragedy, the revenge genre continues to thrive with even more sensational situations and graphic violence.

Chronology   204

For Further Research   209

Index   213

FOREWORD

The study of literature most often involves focusing on an individual work and uncovering its themes, stylistic conventions, and historical relevance. It is also enlightening to examine multiple works by a single author, identifying similarities and differences among texts and tracing the author's development as an artist.

While the study of individual works and authors is instructive, however, examining groups of authors who shared certain cultural or historical experiences adds a further richness to the study of literature. By focusing on literary movements and genres, readers gain a greater appreciation of influence of historical events and social circumstances on the development of particular literary forms and themes. For example, in the early twentieth century, rapid technological and industrial advances, mass urban migration, World War I, and other events contributed to the emergence of a movement known as American modernism. The dramatic social changes, and the uncertainty they created, were reflected in an increased use of free verse in poetry, the stream-of-consciousness technique in fiction, and a general sense of historical discontinuity and crisis of faith in most of the literature of the era. By focusing on these commonalities, readers attain a more comprehensive picture of the complex interplay of social, economic, political, aesthetic, and philosophical forces and ideas that create the tenor of any era. In the nineteenth-century American romanticism movement, for example, authors shared many ideas concerning the preeminence of the self-reliant individual, the infusion of nature with spiritual significance, and the potential of persons to achieve transcendence via communion with nature. However, despite their commonalities, American romantics often differed significantly in their thematic and stylistic approaches. Walt Whitman celebrated the communal nature of America's open democratic society, while Ralph Waldo

Emerson expressed the need for individuals to pursue their own fulfillment regardless of their fellow citizens. Herman Melville wrote novels in a largely naturalistic style whereas Nathaniel Hawthorne's novels were gothic and allegorical.

Another valuable reason to investigate literary movements and genres lies in their potential to clarify the process of literary evolution. By examining groups of authors, literary trends across time become evident. The reader learns, for instance, how English romanticism was transformed as it crossed the Atlantic to America. The poetry of Lord Byron, William Wordsworth, and John Keats celebrated the restorative potential of rural scenes. The American romantics, writing later in the century, shared their English counterparts' faith in nature; but American authors were more likely to present an ambiguous view of nature as a source of liberation as well as the dwelling place of personal demons. The whale in Melville's *Moby-Dick* and the forests in Hawthorne's novels and stories bear little resemblance to the benign pastoral scenes in Wordsworth's lyric poems.

Each volume in Greenhaven Press's Companions to Literary Movements and Genres series begins with an introductory essay that places the topic in a historical and literary context. The essays that follow are carefully chosen and edited for ease of comprehension. These essays are arranged into clearly defined chapters that are outlined in a concise annotated table of contents. Finally, a thorough chronology maps out crucial literary milestones of the movement or genre as well as significant social and historical events. Readers will benefit from the structure and coherence that these features lend to material that is often challenging. With Greenhaven's Literary Movements and Genres in hand, readers will be better able to comprehend and appreciate the major literary works and their impact on society.

RENAISSANCE LITERATURE: ASPIRATION AND THE INDIVIDUAL

The literature of the Renaissance consists of an extremely diverse set of works. From allegorical Christian epics to revenge tragedies with themes of incest and murder to emotional love poetry of great purity and beauty—the Renaissance had it all. Few periods of history have witnessed as much rapid change and radical experimentation in literature as the Renaissance. Readers of medieval literature were fondest of short, bawdy, comic tales, or longer tales of chivalry, in which knights in armor—often from the court of King Arthur—accomplished heroic deeds in service to a lady. Also popular were epic romances about heroes of old, such as Roland, who saved, or tried to save, their civilizations from destructive outside forces. The well-established conventions of these powerful literary traditions dominated European culture for hundreds of years and remained popular into the early stages of the Renaissance. However, under the influence of a group of Italian scholars and poets, European writers began to experiment radically with subject matter, genres, and language itself. Paradoxically, the fruit of this experimentation, the creative body of Renaissance literature, owes its deepest debt to the literature and culture of societies—ancient Rome and Greece—that flourished a thousand years before. The story of this literary revolution begins in late-fourteenth-century Italy.

In the later decades of the 1300s, Italian scholars who became known as humanists began to recover from musty archives the original texts of the great writers and thinkers of ancient Greece and Rome, especially Plato and Cicero. The best works of these and other classical writers had lain virtually unread, except in piecemeal form, for centuries. As Sir Francis Bacon wrote, these texts had "long time slept in libraries."[1] The Italian humanists, led by the scholar and poet Francesco Petrarch (1304–1374), began to advocate the recovery and dissemination of these classical texts as a means of improving Italian society. Their project was to restore to Italy the lost wisdom, art, and literature of these ancient cultures as a way of reinstating the legacy of Italians, the greatness of their past civilization. As scholar J.R. Hale has observed:

> It is difficult to imagine the excitement that attended this unearthing of new and purer texts, this tuning in on voices that spoke with such joy and conviction about the noblest, most triumphant age that Italy has ever known. Above all, since most of the ancient writers studied were Roman, it was an intensely personal excitement. The Italian humanists were discovering their own ancestors, finding buried treasure in their own house. To Petrarch, Cicero was not just a dusty sage, but a real person to whom he could write a letter—and did.[2]

When Petrarch wrote his letter to Cicero, he consciously tried to imitate Cicero's elegant style; this kind of imitation was to be replayed throughout Europe for the next three centuries. For the earliest humanists, the first phase of their new education focused on popularizing the ideas of the ancients, such as the ideas of Plato, as well as imitating the eloquence of their expression in Latin.

THE ASPIRATIONS OF ITALIAN HUMANISM

Under the influence of Petrarch, Giovanni Boccaccio (1313–1375), and other humanists, enthusiastic Italian writers and artists began first to imitate and then to emulate the classical past. They reasoned that if their ancient ancestors were capable of such achievements, then they too could accomplish great things. The mood of the early Renaissance in Italy was exhilarating and contagious. As the humanist scholar Matteo Palmieri wrote from Florence in the 1430s: "Now indeed, may every thoughtful spirit thank God that it has been permitted to him to be born in this new age."[3] Ninety years later, the excitement of the so-called New Learning led Ulrich von Hutten, poet laureate of the German Empire to exclaim: "What a century! What genius! It is sheer joy to be alive, even though not yet in tranquility. Learning flourishes, men are spiritually quickened. O Barbarism, take a rope and prepare for extinction!"[4] This enthusiasm spread steadily among the ranks of European scholars, and expanded to all levels of society in the decades after the invention of the moveable-type printing press in 1455. The exu-

berant optimism of the humanists was fueled by the belief 15
that they were players on a new stage of history, witnesses to
a new era of unlimited possibility.

The significance of Italian humanism to Renaissance literature is broad and deep, but two fundamental contributions stand out. The Italian humanists gave to Europe the
concept of Renaissance itself, the idea of a rebirth of culture
based on classical values and ideals after a long period of
cultural stagnation. The humanists also established the first
educational system based on the study of the recovered texts
of Rome and Greece. This new view of history and the educational system inspired by it spread throughout Europe
over the next two and a half centuries, culminating in the
English Renaissance, which flourished into the early 1600s.

A NEW SENSE OF HISTORY

The power and appeal of the Italian humanist agenda was
due in large part to the conviction of the humanists that they
were on the verge of a new era of human history. The medieval world saw itself as part of a long tradition, an ongoing
story involving commentary, synthesis, and the extraction of
nuggets of wisdom from all that had been written before. But
as Petrarch strove to understand the ancient writers in their
historical context, he tried to envision the cultures of ancient
Rome and Greece as a whole. From this perspective, he developed a radically different understanding of European history. As scholar Charles G. Nauert Jr. explains:

> As [Petrarch] looked at conditions in his troubled century, he
> concluded that the modern age was worthless. Indeed, he de-
> fined the whole period of history since the decline of Rome as
> a 'dark age'. When Petrarch defined this postclassical or 'mod-
> ern' age, the age we now call medieval, as a dark age, he
> meant an age of barbarism, ignorance, low culture. . . . His fel-
> low humanists fully shared his opinion. They also shared his
> conviction that their own classical scholarship was bringing
> that darkness to an end, and that high civilization, which had
> flourished in ancient Greece and Rome, was being reborn in
> their own time and through their own efforts. In short, they
> claimed that after the centuries of 'darkness', they were bring-
> ing about a cultural rebirth: a Renaissance. . . . The humanist
> intellectuals of the Renaissance were the first to define, and
> even to name, the preceding centuries as a distinct historical
> period, a Middle Age lying between the high culture of Antiq-
> uity and the incipient high culture of reborn Antiquity.[5]

After studying the brilliant classical works of art, literature, and philosophy, admiring Italians aspired to emulate and even surpass these achievements in the new era. But to Petrarch and his fellow humanists, great achievement would be possible only after the establishment of a classically oriented system of education.

A CLASSICAL EDUCATION

To that end, Petrarch borrowed from the great Roman statesman and philosopher Cicero the idea of the liberal arts, or *studia humanitatis*, which focused on grammar, rhetoric, poetry, history, and moral philosophy. The humanists emphasized rhetoric and eloquence in place of the logic that had come to dominate scholastic philosophy in medieval universities. In the decades after Petrarch's death, Italian humanists continued to advance his agenda, especially the ability to read, write, and speak classical Latin as the centerpiece of the new educational model. The teaching of classical Latin as the one indispensable tool of the Renaissance is one of the greatest legacies of Italian humanism to the rest of Europe. Later generations of northern humanists embraced the Italian agenda, placing the study of Latin at the heart of their educational paradigm as well. Like Petrarch, the northern humanists, led by Desiderius Erasmus (1466–1536), believed that education was not merely a matter of style or eloquence, but essentially a moral enterprise. As scholar Euan Cameron says:

> The intention behind the elegance, however, was thoroughly moral. Erasmus, and other humanists to some degree, believed passionately that the educated person would be a morally good person, and that only such education as made a person more upright was worthy of the name. . . . The humanists had an almost infinite faith in the liberalizing and improving power of a classical education.[6]

This perception remained a guiding force behind the classical educational system throughout the Renaissance.

The widespread study of the Latin language and culture led to more extensive cultural unification and cross-currents in Europe than had ever been known before, lasting several centuries. In fact, the most notable continuity between the Renaissance in fifteenth-century Italy and the Renaissance nearly two hundred years later in England is the prominence of classical Latin as the common language of politics and education in European societies. For example, the influential treatise *The Courtier* by Castiglione was translated from Italian into English in 1561 and went through two more editions by the time of Queen Elizabeth's death in 1603. But during that same period in England, a translation of *The Courtier* from Italian into Latin went through five editions. In other words, *The Courtier* was read by educated English readers more often in Latin than in English.

The fundamental legacy of Italian humanism is its radical reinterpretation of history and its influential paradigm of a classical education. But the debt of Renaissance literature to Italian humanism extends to two additional pervasive, highly optimistic attitudes. First, much of Renaissance literature reflects and even embodies the concept of aspiration: that powerful urge to create something worthy of this new age, something as good or even better than the ancients. The Italian humanists are also largely behind the Renaissance fascination with individual personality, the focus on the mind, morality, dignity, and creative potential of individuals. About manifestations of individuality in the later Italian Renaissance, historian Richard Tarnas has written:

> This new value placed on individualism and personal genius reinforced a similar characteristic of the Italian Humanists, whose sense of personal worth also rested on individual capacity, and whose ideal was similarly that of the emancipated man of many-sided genius. The medieval Christian ideal in which personal identity was largely absorbed in the collective Christian body of souls faded in favor of the more pagan heroic mode—the individual man as adventurer, genius, and rebel.[7]

These related concepts, aspiration and individuality, are central to many different kinds of Renaissance literature and some of its greatest works.

RENAISSANCE ASPIRATION

The Renaissance attitude toward human potential and creativity can be summed up in the concept of aspiration, the desire to go beyond what has been known before, what has been done before, to go beyond in all human endeavors. It originated as the attempt to imitate the great writers of Greece and Rome, but it evolved into the attempt to surpass even the ancients. The British poet and playwright Ben Jonson had this in mind about Shakespeare when he wrote that Shakespeare's only equals in tragedy were the greatest Greek and Roman tragedians, and that in writing comedies, he surpassed "all that insolent Greece or haughty Rome sent forth, or since did from their ashes come."[8] High praise indeed from a rival playwright!

The explorers searching the seas, the astronomers searching the heavens, the scholars searching ancient cultures, and the religious reformers searching for authentic religious models—all were involved in the quest to discover what had been previously hidden and unknown. If a whole new continent had existed all these centuries unknown to Europeans, what other secrets and mysteries could be uncovered? Writers began to imagine the world in new ways. In his *Utopia*, for example, the English humanist Sir Thomas More wrote of a society with radically different political institutions and social arrangements than those prevailing in sixteenth-century Europe. He dared to depict a society that did not depend on the seemingly timeless institutions of kingship and the Catholic Church, but rather was founded on human reason, a society reminiscent of Plato's ideal in *The Republic*. But it was often recognized that aspiration, the attitude that human beings can uncover all mysteries and solve all problems, bordered on hubris, or excessive pride, and that unchecked aspiration for anything was dangerous. After all, Renaissance writers were quite familiar with the story of the fall of Lucifer, who aspired to God's power, and the story of Adam and Eve, who aspired to the forbidden knowledge of good and evil. The story of Icarus, who made waxen wings to fly to the heavens but crashed when he flew too close to the sun, was a well-known classical version of the dangers of aspiration.

Still, the idea of aspiration, with its rewards and dangers, continued to fascinate Renaissance writers. It is a recurrent theme in Renaissance literature, from the musings of Petrarch on his own aspirations, to the historical aspirations of princes in Machiavelli's *The Prince*, to the cosmic aspirations of Satan in Milton's *Paradise Lost*. But it is the play *Dr. Faustus* (c. 1588) by Christopher Marlowe that most vividly dramatizes the dangers of unbridled aspiration, in this case the search for the power of secret knowledge. The character of Faustus achieves advanced scholarly degrees in medicine, law, philosophy, and theology, but he remains unsatisfied. His profound academic knowledge has made him skeptical of conventional religion. "Come, I think hell's a fable," he says at one point. So he turns to magic, selling his soul to the devil for the promise of hidden knowledge. In Marlowe's version of the story, Faustus suffers from self-deception and gains only illusory powers, powers on the level of a parlor magician. For his bargain, Faustus achieves only lasting damnation, for the world depicted in the play is still governed fundamentally by the Christian scheme of salvation. What makes the play so powerful is its dramatization of the labyrinth of Faustus's inner turmoil and afflicted conscience as he wrestles with the competing claims of classical beauty (represented by Helen of Troy in the play) and repentance leading to salvation.

INDIVIDUAL CONSCIOUSNESS IN RENAISSANCE LITERATURE

The concept of the individual personality unifies a wide range of Renaissance literature. From Petrarch to Michel de Montaigne to Shakespeare, one can see recurring attempts to depict inner states of consciousness, attempts that place a high value on what is felt and thought by an individual. As scholar J.R. Hale notes:

> This new vision of man sprang from a heightened awareness of self. Medieval men had been preoccupied with searching their souls, but Renaissance men were much more intrigued with exploring, and indeed parading, their personalities. Petrarch is a perfect example. Although his serious interests centered on his work in discovering and editing ancient texts, Petrarch was also interested in himself. In his letters, designed for posterity as well as his friends, he left a record of his reactions to love affairs and friendship, to mountains and the flowers in his garden. They are an intellectual and emotional self-portrait, the first since antiquity.[9]

Certainly there were classical and medieval precedents for this approach—the *Confessions* of St. Augustine is one prominent example—but in the Renaissance this mode of introspective self-analysis became common. Introspection is central to both Petrarch's confessional essays and his very personal love poetry in which his emotions seem to be all on display.

Introspection is also the hallmark of the essays of Montaigne, in which the writer skeptically examines his own thought processes and challenges his own reliance on tradition or the ideas of others instead of his own. In the words of British scholar Margaret Aston:

> After so much refashioning, of self-fashioning, through the imitation of classical models, it was eventually possible to discover more about both the world and the ancient past by turning inwards, taking the self as the object of study. 'I study myself more than any other subject. That is my metaphysics,

that is my physics.' It was Montaigne, trying (assaying) himself in his *Essaies*, who established this new department of knowledge. Here was an inescapable book to illuminate every library, 'the only book of its kind in the world.'[10]

Though put to different uses, an introspective attitude also characterizes the intensely personal poetry of John Donne, as he seeks, for example, to capture a moment of love joyfully awaking with his wife one morning. Another of the metaphysical poets, George Herbert, also tries to express the innermost experience of religious faith in his devotional poetry. These writers all take themselves, their feelings, and their states of inner consciousness as the legitimate subject matter of literature. This emphasis on individual personality and interior consciousness reached a peak of sorts in Elizabethan drama, in the tormented anguish of Doctor Faustus, the guilty conscience of Macbeth, and the haunted soliloquies of Hamlet, but is evident in all forms of the newly developing literature of the Renaissance, in prose and poetry as well as drama.

THE HUMANIST INFLUENCE ON RENAISSANCE PROSE

The prose of the Renaissance takes many different forms, some unrecognizable to modern readers as literature. But what unifies most of these works of prose is their reflection of the ideals and values of Renaissance humanism, including the affirmation of human dignity for all individuals. Either directly or indirectly, these works promote the notion that deep engagement with the thought of the classical past is essential to the improvement of both individuals and societies. It is not a matter of knowledge for knowledge's sake, but the idea that engagement with the ideals and values of the classical past improves character and instills morality, the idea that education promotes self-reflection and authenticity in place of sterile adherence to tradition.

Modern readers of literary prose are accustomed to a plot or story line. But Renaissance prose takes such diverse forms as: the formal speech, such as Erasmus's *The Praise of Folly*; the treatise, such as Machiavelli's *The Prince;* and the essay, such as those of Montaigne and Sir Francis Bacon. What makes these prose efforts literary is their eloquence and their use of literary and rhetorical devices and strategies to achieve effect. *The Praise of Folly*, for example, achieves its humor through the personification of the speechgiver,

Folly, and through the sustained satire made possible by this literary device.

The treatise form, in which the writer discourses at length on a given topic, using hundreds of examples, both classical and biblical, was a long-recognized, popular literary genre. *The Courtier* by the Italian writer Castiglione may be described best as a treatise in dialogue form. It achieves its literary quality by its use of setting and lively, dramatic conversation, influenced by the dialogue form of Plato. In content, *The Courtier* is also an extremely popular argument for humanist values and manners. In place of the values of chivalry that had dominated European court life for centuries, Castiglione provides a humanist model of courtly behavior, involving study, engagement with the fine arts, and courtly manners based on respect for individual achievement and talent rather than social status. Some English examples of the treatise, both heavily influenced by Castiglione, are Sir Thomas Elyot's *The Book Named the Governor* and Roger Ascham's *The Schoolmaster*, both of which advocate classical education as the key to the morality of individuals and the overall health of society.

Other prose efforts of the Renaissance are difficult to categorize. Renaissance writers were continually experimenting with received forms and genres; they were familiar with medieval and classical precedents, but they insisted on going their own way. In *Don Quixote*, for example, Cervantes uses the basic form of the medieval romance, in which a wandering knight on a quest for a lady encounters strange and wondrous adventures. But Cervantes is, of course, not serious. He is using the form to parody the values of chivalry and to depict in a humorous, more realistic style the lower strata of Spanish society.

The *Utopia* of Sir Thomas More is also difficult to categorize. It is a travelogue in some respects, a story reported to others by the fictitious traveler Raphael Hythloday. But satire arises in the contrast between the ideal achievements of Utopia and the shortcomings of European societies in More's day. Reflecting the humanist values of its author, *Utopia* begins with a thinly veiled critique of contemporary British society, attacking the idle rich, injustices in the legal system, and the uses of war by European princes. The latter part of *Utopia* also exposes the social ills of European society, but does so indirectly through comparison to the wonderful accomplishments of the Utopians. The comic prose of the French writer Rabelais is hardest of all to categorize, and it is one of the more difficult Renaissance texts for modern readers. His *Gargantua* and *Pantagruel* combine satire, folklore, fabliaux, carnival values, and other elements, though the underlying values of these works are firmly grounded in the Christian humanist tradition.

WOMEN AND LITERATURE

Another notable genre of Renaissance prose, which also reflects humanist ideals about human dignity, is the treatise about the status of women. Around 1380, the humanist writer Boccaccio composed his treatise *Concerning Famous Women*, which was modeled after the Roman writer Plutarch's similar work. Boccaccio attempted to refute many late medieval misogynistic tracts attacking women. The next two hundred years saw numerous tracts on both sides of the issue, but few voices were as influential as that of the Dutch humanist scholar Erasmus. Erasmus was a leading advocate of the education of girls and women in the Renaissance, while his friend Sir Thomas More actively educated his daughters in the full humanist tradition.

As more women began to benefit from their inclusion in humanist education, the result was a steady increase in literature by women and literature for women. This output was enhanced by the power and stature of a number of prominent women, such as Queen Elizabeth, whose accomplishments encouraged women writers. Elizabeth had received a strong humanist education and could read and write Latin, French, Italian, and, to a lesser degree, Greek. Other prominent women became powerful patronesses of the arts, particularly in Italy and France. Women writers continued to feel excluded from certain genres of writing, such as playwriting, but embraced other kinds of writing wholeheartedly, especially translations, poetry, and essays. In the sixteenth century, defenses of women and their capacity for learning proliferated, most written by men in the humanist tradition.

As women became more educated and active in the affairs of society, they were more frequently attacked by men for transgressing the "natural" order of things. This resulted in a long public debate throughout the sixteenth century and into the seventeenth century about the proper roles of women in public life and literature. Scholar Margaret L. King characterizes the attacks on women in this way:

> The possibility of the reversal of sexual roles threatened the Renaissance men who wrote books, governed cities, and guided social behavior. The man ridden by a woman—as Phyllis humiliated the philosopher Aristotle—was the butt of jokes and the subject of the popular village carnivals called *charivari*, so characteristic especially of the sixteenth century. . . . The English *Hic-Mulier*, or *The Man-Woman*, crystallizes the hatred felt by men for women who aspired to literary or public roles. . . . The pages of Renaissance books bristle and thunder with armed and dangerous women, the personifications, both fearful and admirable, of inverted sexual order.[11]

This debate, both literary and political, crossed national boundaries and epitomizes both the impact of humanist ideals and the cross-cultural European world made possible by its common educational heritage based on the classics. It also reflects the power of the humanist ideal that education is the key to individuals' attaining their full human potential.

THE FORMS OF RENAISSANCE POETRY

As does Renaissance prose, the poetry of the era reflects wide experimentation in subject matter and genre, as well as the period's enthusiasm for the depiction of inner conflict and nuances of consciousness. The most prevalent forms of Renaissance poetry are the sonnet, the romantic epic, pastoral poetry, lyric (or song) poetry, and satire. In early-sixteenth-century France, the most important writers and poets, led by Joachim du Bellay and Pierre Ronsard, reflected a wide range of forms and influences, including Petrarch and the Italian humanists, but especially Cicero, Virgil, and Plato. Ronsard aspired to conquer all the classical genres of poetry, but he is best remembered today for his sonnets. Poets in various countries experimented broadly with poetic form and style, but two forms of poetry can be said to have yielded the most lasting results: the sonnet form of love poetry and the romantic epic. In both forms, the pervasive Renaissance drive to express inner states of consciousness in new and intricate ways is evident.

The most recognizable and influential poetic style of the Renaissance belonged to the Italian poet Petrarch. His imitators were legion, and even later poets who sought to go beyond Petrarch often used his conventions and preferred poetic devices and figures to make their points. Petrarch's love poetry typically takes the sonnet form, characterized by a set of conventions about how love should be described. Petrarch, as scholar Gary Waller explains,

> sees love as a frustrating though inspiring experience, characterized by a melancholy yet obsessive balance between desire and hopelessness, possibility and frustration. Its fundamental characteristic is conflict, or—the key term in Petrarchism— 'paradox', usually expressed as a balance of powerful opposites, forces in or outside the lover which simultaneously move him on or hold him back.[12]

These conventions, especially the figure of paradox, allowed great flexibility in how a poet could express the experience of love. Most Renaissance poets at some point attempted love sonnets in this vein, including such luminaries as the artist Michelangelo, who spent years writing more than three hundred Petrarchan love poems. In the English tradition, the poets Sir Thomas Wyatt, Sir Philip Sidney, Shakespeare, and John Donne all engage the Petrarchan tradition, through translations, imitation, and even parody. At its best, Petrarchan poetry enabled poets to speak their innermost thoughts and emotions, though within a highly controlled form and set of conventions.

The romantic epic tradition in the Renaissance begins with the Italian poets Tasso and Ariosto, but it comes to its highest fulfillment in *The Faerie Queene* of Edmund Spenser, published between 1590 and 1596. *The Faerie Queene* is an allegorical epic poem that uses the knight-on-a-quest motif to illustrate the adventures and challenges facing the Christian soul as it navigates the temptations and dangers of the world. Spenser's poem draws heavily from classical epics, as well as from chivalric romances and the Italian romantic epics. Levels of allegory in the poem illustrate such events as the political-religious struggles of Protestantism in mid-sixteenth-century England. But the most fundamental level of allegory in the poem is the moral allegory of each individual Christian's quest for salvation. Like the sonnets of Petrarch, the poem seeks to engage readers on a very personal level.

This brings us to the last great Renaissance poet, John Milton. Though Milton wrote his greatest works after the Renaissance in England had largely run its course, his achievement places him squarely in the Renaissance tradition of epic poetry. His passion for ancient Greek and Roman authors, along with his deep involvement in the religious and political controversies of his day, make Milton a prime example of the well-rounded "Renaissance man." In *Paradise Lost*, Milton achieves an unsurpassed fusion of classical poetic form, derived squarely from Homer and Virgil, and Christian content, derived from Milton's deep familiarity with the Bible and Christian theology. One of the highest achievements of the poem is Milton's detailed depiction of inner conflict in the psychological rationalizations and self-deception of Satan, along with the psychology of sin, guilt, and repentance in Adam and Eve. *Paradise Lost* was first published three hundred years after the poetry of Petrarch; it is helpful here to trace the development of the northern Renaissance from seeds sown so many years before.

THE RENAISSANCE IN NORTHERN EUROPE

The ideals and the educational program initiated by the Italian humanists came to England and the rest of northern Europe after some delay. One obvious reason for this was the Hundred Years' War between England and France, which preoccupied those countries from 1337 to 1453. Partially overlapping this conflict was the civil conflict in England called the War of the Roses, which finally concluded in 1485. That same year, the first printing press in England was established, and the publication of books, including the works of many important Roman and Greek writers, increased exponentially from that year forward. In this same decade, the Aldine Press in Switzerland began its systematic publication of the best editions of classical texts, many unpublished to this date. Thus the great Latin and Greek texts became available for study in northern Europe to an extent undreamed of in the early stages of the Italian Renaissance. Around 1500, John Colet and other English humanists undertook the reform of the educational system in London to focus on a classical curriculum; by the mid–sixteenth century that agenda had expanded to include Stratford and other regional towns. Once the new system was in place, such pupils as the shoemaker's son, Christopher Marlowe, the bricklayer's son, Ben Jonson, and the glove maker's son, William Shakespeare, could acquire a deep and wide-ranging familiarity with classical culture unknown before that time.

The educational curriculum at Shakespeare's grammar school in Stratford provides a window into the long-lasting, powerful ideal of a classical education. Shakespeare's main years of education were the decade of the 1570s, from ages six to sixteen. During those ten years, Shakespeare, along with the other middle-class sons of Stratford, studied ten hours a day, six days a week, under a university-educated teacher. The vast majority of each day's study was Latin grammar and literature; in fact, in the upper forms the boys were required to speak only Latin, and were censured for speaking English in the classroom. There are suggestions in Shakespeare's plays that such a system was a dreary and unsatisfying way to spend one's boyhood. Yet the evidence of Shakespeare's classical education is everywhere in his plays, from his early borrowings from the Roman playwrights Plautus and Seneca, to the inspirational influence of the Roman poet Ovid, to his heavy reliance on the historian and philosopher Plutarch in the creation of his plays *Julius Caesar, Antony and Cleopatra*, and others.

Thus, the later Renaissance in northern Europe, especially in England, was grounded in the study of the classics, yet it was shaped by other intellectual and cultural forces as well. The northern Renaissance shared with the Italian Renaissance a passionate love of ancient Greece and Rome; in this regard, Plato and Cicero were just as influential in England and France as they were in Italy. But the northern Renaissance, as already noted, had a broader access to a wider range of classical texts than did the Italians, and it also had full knowledge of the Italian humanists themselves, from Petrarch, Pico, and Ficino to Castiglione and Machiavelli. In addition, the Renaissance in England drew inspiration from many native literary and cultural traditions, including folklore, festive traditions, English history, and a long tradition of popular drama.

THE IMPACT OF THE REFORMATION

The northern Renaissance also took shape during and after the Reformation, which began in Germany in 1517 and created religious divisions both within and between nations. Germany adopted the Lutheran reforms of the church quickly, while Italy remained steadfastly Catholic. After considerable turmoil and some bloodshed, England settled on a Protestant version of its church in 1560, while France, also after much turmoil, remained Catholic. The Reformation movement forged a new kind of self-consciousness among many Europeans. The questions and issues raised by the Reformation challenged many northern Europeans to take a hard look at their faith, to figure out what they personally believed. In newly Protestant countries, the reading public had an insatiable desire to understand the implications of their new faith. Thus more than half of all books printed in England during the sixteenth century were on religious topics. This popular, Protestant literature focuses extensively on self-examination of readers' "afflicted conscience," or troubled consciousness, as they attempt to ascertain the state of their own salvation.

As with the Italian humanists, the responsibility for one's destiny in the Protestant scheme lies with the individual, not with institutions such as the church. The Reformation stressed not what an individual does, but what he or she believes, as the key to salvation. Its significance in English Renaissance literature is the widespread cultural endorsement of introspection and the examination of the interior lives of individuals, an emphasis that engaged the popular mind throughout the later sixteenth and early seventeenth century. This same self-questioning, introspective mode infuses much of the poetry and popular drama of this period, and it contributed to some of the most profound explorations of personality and consciousness found in the literature of any period.

THE RISE OF THE ELIZABETHAN PUBLIC THEATER

The most powerful and significant form of literature to arise in the northern Renaissance was the drama of Elizabethan England, which featured such writers as Marlowe, Shakespeare, and Jonson. Long before the achievements of these playwrights, though, English drama consisted primarily of the traditional mystery plays and morality plays, all of which had religious themes and characters. In the mid–sixteenth century, though, university graduates familiar with the body of classical drama began to experiment with new forms of drama, and the older forms went out of fashion. A major turning point in the history of British theater occurred in 1576 when the first important public playhouse, the Theatre, was erected in London. Prior to that time, popular plays were performed on a transient basis, on portable platform stages in courtyards or innyards. Two other relatively large theaters were built soon after the Theatre, notably the Curtain in 1577 and the Rose in 1587, each of which held perhaps two thousand spectators. By the time Shakespeare came to town in the late 1580s, these theaters had become a popular and central part of London cultural life.

The most important figures of Elizabethan drama before Shakespeare were Thomas Kyd and Christopher Marlowe, who were actually roommates in 1592. Kyd is the author of the very influential revenge play *The Spanish Tragedy* (c. 1587), which initiated a vogue for revenge tragedy that carried into the seventeenth century. That play exerted a significant influence on Shakespeare's *Hamlet*. Marlowe mastered an approach to dramatic writing called blank verse, which eliminated the sing-song of end rhyme in favor of the driving rhythms of conversational speech within the iambic pentameter (or five-beat) line. Shakespeare embraced and successfully emulated this mode of writing in most of his plays. Marlowe wrote five well-received tragedies, including *Doctor Faustus* (c. 1592), the single best work of tragedy before Shakespeare's tragedies. Unfortunately, both these playwrights died young, soon after Shakespeare's rise to prominence in London. Marlowe was killed in a tavern brawl in 1593, at the height of his success, and Kyd died in poverty the following year.

THE CAREER OF SHAKESPEARE

What brought Shakespeare his first serious public notice, in the early 1590s, was the production of his first four history plays about the Wars of the Roses. The onstage depiction of the rulers and power struggles of this conflict caused a minor sensation and made Shakespeare a celebrity. In an age before public libraries, not to mention movies, television, and videotape, Londoners were absolutely amazed to see these historical events "live" on stage. Because of his success in depicting the events of these wars, Shakespeare turned to the earlier wars between France and England for the subject matter of his next round of plays, *Richard II, 1 Henry IV, 2 Henry IV,* and *Henry V*. Among those enjoying Shakespeare's early plays was Queen Elizabeth herself, who was reportedly much amused by the character of Falstaff in *1 Henry IV*. Supposedly the queen requested a new play from Shakespeare in which she could see Falstaff in love, and the result was the comedy *The Merry Wives of Windsor*.

Also during these early years in London, Shakespeare published his only attempts at highbrow literature, the long narrative poems *Venus and Adonis* (1593) and *The Rape of Lucrece* (1594). In the fashion of the day, both poems were dedicated to a powerful patron, the Earl of Southampton. Shakespeare's accomplishments by 1594 were already so notable that he was invited to become a member (and resident playwright) of the newly formed Lord Chamberlain's Men, which by virtue of its powerful patron, its accomplished actors, and its highly proficient playwright became the premier acting company of its day. During the 1590s, Shakespeare concentrated on history plays and on romantic comedies. Around the turn of the century, Shakespeare returned to tragedies, including *Julius Caesar* and *Hamlet*, followed a few years later by *Othello, Macbeth, King Lear,* and *Antony and Cleopatra.* When Queen Elizabeth died in 1603, her successor King James immediately took over patronage of Shakespeare's company, renaming it the King's Men. During and after his greatest tragedies, Shakespeare turned to experimentation in terms of genre and subject matter, and not all his later plays are successful. But in two of his last plays, *A Winter's Tale* and *The Tempest*, he turned to classical romance for genre and Christian reconciliation for subject matter, and they remain two of his most appealing plays.

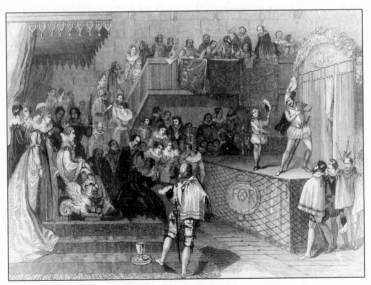

Shakespeare's acting company, the Lord Chamberlain's Men, performed frequently before Queen Elizabeth I and her court.

Like Christopher Marlowe before him, Shakespeare was fascinated by the depiction of interior consciousness and the delineation of individual character onstage. His unique characters are some of the most famous in the history of drama: Richard II, Falstaff, Othello, Cleopatra, Hamlet. There is of course no way to tell how much Christopher Marlowe personally shared in the anguish of his character Faustus, or how much Shakespeare shared in Hamlet's tortured states of mind, and attempts to ascertain such insight are fruitless. But through the use of such devices as the tormented, soul-searching soliloquy, these writers succeeded in depicting inner consciousness on the public stage as never before. This is a far cry from medieval drama in which the dramatization of the conflicted conscience was accomplished by allegorical good and bad angels standing on either side of the protagonist. The character Hamlet is probably the supreme Renaissance depiction of personality onstage. As British scholar George Holmes has written:

> Whatever one thinks about Hamlet's place in European history as a whole, Shakespeare in creating him quite clearly made a massive innovative leap. He lifted the portrayal of character onto a new level of increased sophistication. *Hamlet* has been the most admired of Shakespeare's plays since 1599, though recently yielding to *King Lear*, and the reason has been that Hamlet's character reveals a conception of the human personality of an altogether new complexity. He was invented at a time when the English language was emerging into its fullest richness and produced by the possibilities open to genius in the late Renaissance which had stimulated literary interest in individual personality.[15]

In this regard, English Renaissance writers provided some of the most lasting achievements of the Renaissance. This focus on the depiction of the inner self and the introspective conscience, in essays, in poetry, and in drama, is one of the most important legacies of Renaissance literature. It anticipates similar concerns both in the Romantic movement and in most branches of modern literature, where the introspective individual is also valued over the rules and demands of tradition and the institutions of society.

The drama produced during Shakespeare's later career and after his death shared the interest of earlier playwrights in the depiction of individual personality onstage, but the focus shifted strongly toward the depiction of what we would call deviant personalities. Some scholars see this de-

velopment as a reflection of the breakdown of values elsewhere in the culture, especially in the royal court of King
James, the successor to Queen Elizabeth:

> 'Horror waits on princes.' This phrase by the Jacobean play-
> wright John Webster (?1580–?1625) suggests the claustro-
> phobic world of moral confusion, lust, revenge, and blood-
> shed characteristic of many of Shakespeare's contemporaries
> and successors in tragedy. While these motifs had been fun-
> damental to the genre from the time of Kyd, they were fre-
> quently given an added force in the work of later writers by
> their relation to what was widely seen as the profligate and
> corrupting power of the Jacobean court.[14]

As do some of Shakespeare's tragedies, some of the greatest
Jacobean plays explore the psychology of evil. This, too, is a
logical outgrowth of the Renaissance concern for all that is
human, and for the intricacies of individual personality,
whatever may be revealed by such exploration. In this endeavor, Jacobean playwrights also reflect the fundamental
Renaissance attitude of aspiration, assaying to go in drama
where none had gone before, to map out boundaries and aspects of the human condition that had previously never been
fully depicted.

NOTES

1. Quoted in Euan Cameron, "The Power of the Word: Renaissance
and Reformation," in *Early Modern Europe: An Oxford History.* Ed.
Euan Cameron. Oxford: Oxford University Press, 1999, p. 69.

2. J.R. Hale, *Renaissance Europe: The Individual and Society, 1480–
1520.* Berkeley and Los Angeles: University of California Press,
1977, p. 16.

3. Quoted in Margaret Aston, *The Panorama of the Renaissance.*
New York: Henry N. Abrams, 1996, p. 11.

4. Quoted in Lewis W. Spitz, *The Renaissance and Reformation
Movements,* vol. 1. Rev. ed. St. Louis: Concordia, 1987, p. 5.

5. Charles G. Nauert Jr., *Humanism and the Culture of the Renaissance.* Cambridge: Cambridge University Press, 1995, pp. 19–20.

6. Euan Cameron, "The Power of the Word," p. 72.

7. Richard Tarnas, *The Passion of the Western Mind.* New York: Harmony, 1991, p. 227.

8. Ben Jonson, "To the Memory of . . . William Shakespeare," in *Seventeenth Century English Poetry.* Ed. John T. Shawcross and Ronald
David Emma. Philadelphia: J.P. Lippincott, 1969, p. 133.

9. Hale, *Renaissance Europe,* p. 18.

10. Aston, *The Panorama of the Renaissance.* p. 28.

11. Margaret L. King, *Women of the Renaissance.* Chicago: University of Chicago Press, 1991, pp. 188–89.

12. Gary Waller, *English Poetry of the Sixteenth Century.* 2nd ed. London: Longman, 1993, p. 75.

13. George Holmes, *Renaissance.* New York: St. Martin's, 1996, p. 263.

14. Stephen Coote, *The Penguin Short History of English Literature.* London: Penguin, 1993, pp. 154–55.

CHAPTER 1

Italian Renaissance Literature

Renaissance Literature

Italian Humanism: Recovering the Past

Gloria K. Fiero

The Renaissance in Europe originated in late-fourteenth-century Italy as an intellectual and educational movement that came to be called humanism. The leading figure of this movement, Francesco Petrarch, was also one of the most important Renaissance poets. According to Professor Gloria K. Fiero of the University of Southwestern Louisiana, Petrarch led the way in the recovery of writings from ancient Rome and Greece, and he also popularized the poetic form known as the sonnet. Following in Petrarch's footsteps, the Italian writers Pico, Ficino, and Alberti also popularized classical ideas and writers, while their own writings became widely influential in Renaissance Europe.

The Renaissance designates that period in European history between roughly 1300 and 1600, during which time the revival of classical humanism spread from its birthplace in Italy throughout Western Europe. Italy was the homeland of Roman antiquity, the splendid ruins of which stood as reminders of the greatness of classical civilization. The least feudalized part of the medieval world and Europe's foremost commercial and financial center, Italy had traded with Near and Middle Eastern cities even in the darkest days of the Dark Ages. Italy also had maintained cultural contacts with Byzantium, the heir to Greek culture. The cities of Italy, especially Venice and Genoa, had profited financially from the Crusades and—despite the ravages of the plague—continued to enjoy a high level of commercial prosperity. In fourteenth-century Florence, shopkeepers invented double-entry bookkeeping to maintain systematic records of transactions in what was the soundest currency in the West: the Florentine gold *florin*.

From Gloria K. Fiero, *On the Threshold of Modernity: The Renaissance and the Reformation* (Dubuque, IA: Wm. C. Brown, 1992). Reprinted by permission of the McGraw-Hill Companies.

The pursuit of money and leisure, rather than a preoccupation with feudal and chivalric obligations, marked the lifestyle of merchants and artisans who lived in the bustling city-states of Italy. Here especially, the Avignon Papacy and the Great Schism[1] had produced a climate of anticlericalism and intellectual skepticism. Middle-class men and women challenged canonical sources of authority that frowned upon profit-making and the accumulation of wealth. In this materialistic and often only superficially religious society, the old medieval values no longer made sense, while those of pre-Christian antiquity seemed more compatible with the secular interests and ambitions of the rising merchant class. The ancient Greeks and Romans were indeed ideal historical models for the enterprising citizens of the Italian city-states.

Politically, Renaissance Italy had much in common with ancient Greece. Independent and disunited, the city-states of Italy, like those of ancient Greece, were fiercely competitive. As in Golden Age Greece, commercial rivalry among the Italian city-states led to frequent civil wars. In Italy, however, such wars were not always fought by citizens (who, as merchants, were generally ill prepared for combat), but by *condottieri* (professional soldiers) whose loyalties, along with their services, were bought for a price. The papacy, a potential source of political leadership, made little effort to unify the rival Italian communes. Rather, as temporal governors of the Papal States (the lands located in central Italy), Renaissance popes joined in the game of power politics, often allying with one group of city-states against another.

Italian Renaissance cities were ruled either by members of the petty nobility, by mercenary generals, or—as in the case of Florence and Venice—by wealthy middle-class families. In Florence, some one hundred families dominated political life. The most notable of these was the Medici, a wealthy banking family that rose to power during the fourteenth century and proceeded to take over the reins of state. Partly because the commercial ingenuity of the Medici enhanced the material status of the Florentine citizens, and partly because strong, uninterrupted leadership guaranteed local economic stability, the Medici ruled Florence for four generations. The Medici merchant-princes, especially Cosimo (d. 1464) and

---

1. In 1378 the Christian church split and two rival popes (Urban VI and Clement VII) were elected. Clement reigned in Avignon while Urban remained in Rome.

Lorenzo "the Magnificent" (d. 1492), supported scholarship and patronized the arts. Affluence coupled with intellectual discernment and refined taste inspired the Medici to commission such artists as Brunelleschi, Botticelli, Verrocchio, and Michelangelo, who produced some of the West's most brilliant works of art. In Florence, the birthplace of the Renaissance, scholars, poets, painters, and civic leaders shared common interests, acknowledging one another as leaders of a vigorous cultural revival.

PETRARCH: FATHER OF HUMANISM

The most famous of the early Florentine humanists was the poet and scholar Francesco Petrarch (d. 1374). Often called the Father of Humanism, Petrarch devoted his life to the recovery, copying, and editing of Latin manuscripts. In quest of these ancient sources of wisdom, he traveled all over Europe, hand-copying manuscripts he could not beg or buy from monastic libraries, borrowing others from personal friends, and gradually amassing a private library of more than two hundred volumes. Petrarch was a tireless popularizer of classical studies. Reviving the epistolary (letter-writing) tradition that had practically disappeared since Roman times, he wrote hundreds of letters describing his admiration for antiquity and his enthusiasm for the classics, especially the writings of the Roman statesman Cicero. In his letters, Petrarch eulogized and imitated Cicero's polished prose style, which stood in refined contrast to the corrupt Latin of his own time.

The intensity of Petrarch's passion for antiquity and his eagerness to rescue it from neglect come across powerfully in a letter addressed to his friend, Lapo da Castiglionchio. Here, he laments the scarcity and incompetence of copyists, bemoans the fact that books that are difficult to understand have "sunk into utter neglect," and defends his ambition to preserve them, despite the inordinate amount of time it takes to copy them. (Such fervor, shared by his successors, surely motivated the invention of print technology within one hundred years of his death.) In the letter to Lapo . . . Petrarch vows to sacrifice the precious hours of his old age to the pleasures of copying Cicero (whom he calls fondly by his middle name—Tullius).

Nothing in the letter to Lapo suggests that Petrarch was a devout Christian; yet, in fact, Petrarch's affection for Cicero was matched only by his devotion to Saint Augustine and his writings. Indeed, in their introspective tone and their expression of intimate feelings and desires, Petrarch's letters reveal the profound influence of Augustine's *Confessions,* a work that Petrarch deeply admired. Torn between Christian piety and his passion for Classical Antiquity, Petrarch experienced recurrent psychic conflict. Yet this conflict did not prevent him from pursuing worldly fame. At Rome in 1341, he proudly received the laurel crown for outstanding literary achievement—the tradition, which looks back to the ancient Greek practice of honoring victors in the athletic games with wreaths made from the foliage of the laurel tree, survives in our modern honorary title "poet *laureate.*" But Petrarch remained, in part, a medieval man. In his writings we detect a gnawing and unresolved dissonance between the dual imperatives of his Western heritage: the Judeo-Christian will to believe and the classical will to reason. This inner conflict between spiritual and secular claims is particularly evident in Petrarch's poetry, over three hundred examples of which make up the *Canzoniere* (*Songbook*).

The object of Petrarch's physical passion and the inspiration for the *Canzoniere* was a married Florentine woman named Laura de Sade. To Laura, Petrarch dedicated more than three hundred love lyrics, many of which were written after she died of bubonic plague in 1348. While Petrarch used Latin, the language of learning, for his letters and essays, he wrote his poems and songs in vernacular Italian. His favorite poetic form was the sonnet, a fourteen-line lyric poem. The sonnet form originated among the poets of Sicily, but it was Petrarch who brought it to perfection. Influenced by the "sweet style" of his Italian forebears and, more generally, by troubadour songs and Islamic lyric verse, Petrarch's sonnets are a record of his struggle between flesh and spirit. In their self-reflective and even self-indulgent tone, they are strikingly modern, especially where they explore Petrarch's passion for Laura—and for love itself. In the . . . sonnet written "to Laura in death," Petrarch pictures himself adrift in a ship tossed by the tempest of his emotions.

In his own time, Petrarch was acclaimed as the finest practitioner of the sonnet form. His sonnets were translated by Chaucer and set to music by Landini. During the sixteenth century, Michelangelo Buonarroti in Italy and the English poets Thomas Wyatt, Edmund Spenser, and William

Shakespeare all wrote sonnets modeled on those of Petrarch. Petrarch's influence as a classical humanist was equally significant: He established the standards for the study of the Latin classics and helped form the modern concept of the educated individual. Although Petrarch never learned to read Greek, he encouraged his contemporaries and friends (including Boccaccio) to master the language of the first philosophers. Petrarch's passion for classical learning initiated something of a cult, which at its worst became an infatuation with everything antique, but which at its best called forth a diligent examination of the classical heritage.

THE HUMANISM OF FICINO AND PICO

The effort to recover, copy, and produce accurate editions of classical writings dominated the early history of the Renaissance in Italy. By the middle of the fifteenth century, almost all of the major Greek and Latin manuscripts of antiquity— the bounty of devoted textural scholarship—were available to scholars. Among the humanists of Italy, these writings kindled new attitudes concerning the importance of active participation in civic life. Aristotle's view of human beings as "political animals" and Cicero's glorification of duty to the state encouraged Renaissance humanists to perceive that the exercise of civic responsibility was the hallmark of the cultivated individual. Such civic humanists as Leonardo Bruni (d. 1444) and Coluccio Salutati (d. 1406), who served Florence as chancellors and historians, defended the precept that one's highest good was activity in the public interest.

After the fall of Constantinople in 1453, Greek manuscripts and Greek scholars poured into Italy. Encouraged by the availability of Greek resources and supported by his patron Cosimo de Medici, the humanist philosopher Marsilio Ficino (d. 1474) translated the entire corpus of Plato's writings from Greek into Latin, making them available to Western scholars for the first time since antiquity. Ficino's translations and the founding of a Platonic Academy in Florence (financed by Cosimo) launched a reappraisal of Plato and the neoplatonists that had major consequences in the domains of art and literature. Plato's writings—especially the *Symposium,* in which love is elevated as a divine force—advanced the idea, popularized by Ficino, that "platonic" (or spiritual) love attracted the soul to God. Platonic love became a major theme among Renaissance poets and painters, who held that such love was inspired by physical beauty.

While Ficino was engaged in popularizing Plato, one of his most learned contemporaries, Giovanni Pico della Mirandola (d. 1494), undertook the translation of ancient literary works in Hebrew, Arabic, Latin, and Greek. Humanist, poet, and theologian, Pico sought not only to bring to light the entire history of human thought, but to prove that all intellectual expression shared the same divine purpose and design. This effort to discover a "unity of truth" in all philosophic thought—similar to but more comprehensive than the medieval quest for synthesis and so dramatically different from our own modern pluralistic outlook—dominated the arts and ideas of the High Renaissance.

Pico's monumental efforts to recover the past and his reverence for the power of human knowledge influenced Renaissance *individualism*—the assertion of the uniqueness of the human being. In Rome, at the age of twenty-four, Pico boldly challenged the Church to debate some nine hundred theological propositions. The young scholar did not get the chance to debate his theses, which blatantly challenged the institutional Church; indeed, he was persecuted for heresy and forced to flee Italy. As an introduction to the disputation, Pico had prepared the piece that has come to be called the *Oration on the Dignity of Man.* In this preface, Pico boldly affirms the perfectibility of the individual. The Renaissance idea of rational man at the center of a rational universe is nowhere better described than in . . . Pico's *Oration.*

ALBERTI AND RENAISSANCE VIRTÙ

Although Pico's *Oration* was not circulated until after his death, its assertion of free will and its acclamation of the unlimited potential of the individual came to symbolize the collective ideals of the Renaissance humanists. In words hauntingly reminiscent of Sophocles, Pico gave voice to the optimistic view of the individual as free and perfectible. This view—basic to so much Renaissance literature—is especially evident in the life and thought of the Florentine humanist Leon Battista Alberti (d. 1474). A mathematician, architect, engineer, musician, and playwright, Alberti's most original literary contribution (and that for which he was best known in his own time) was his treatise *On the Family.* Published in 1443, *On the Family* is the first sociological inquiry into the structure, function, and responsibilities of the family. It is also a moralizing treatise that defends the importance of a classical education and hard work as prerequisites for worldly success. In Alberti's view, skill, talent, fortitude, ingenuity, and the ability to determine one's destiny—qualities summed up in the single Italian word *virtù*—are essential to human enterprise. *Virtù*, Alberti observes, is not inherited; rather, it must be cultivated. Not to be confused with the English word *virtue*, *virtù* describes the self-confident vitality of the self-made Renaissance individual.

In *On the Family*, Alberti warns that idleness is the enemy of human achievement, while the performance of "manly tasks" and the pursuit of "fine studies" are sure means to worldly fame and material fortune. Pointing to the success of his own family, he defends the acquisition of wealth as the reward of free-spirited *virtù*. The buoyant optimism so characteristic of the Age of the Renaissance is epitomized in Alberti's statement that "man can do anything he wants." Alberti himself—architect, mathematician, and scholar—was living proof of that viewpoint.

The Achievement of Petrarch

Charles G. Nauert Jr.

In the following essay, Charles G. Nauert Jr., professor of history at the University of Missouri-
Columbia, suggests that Francesco Petrarch was a
revolutionary whose contributions to Renaissance
literature can hardly be overstated. His passionate
scholarship concerning ancient authors and his radical rejection of medieval values and perspectives led
to a new historical perspective influential throughout Europe. From the ancients, Petrarch derived his
focus on eloquence and morality, issues that remained central to the literature of Europe for centuries following. As Petrarch's love poetry was also
extremely influential, the range of his endeavors certainly qualifies him as one of the first and most important "Renaissance men."

The truly important point about Renaissance humanism is
not its enthusiasm for the classics but its new conception of
history, which was the source of the overpowering new interest in the classics. As we have already seen, interest in ancient Greek and Roman culture was always present in the
Middle Ages, and at some times and places, notably in
France during the twelfth century, a lively study of ancient
books arose and had a major impact on thought and literature. Although some important works of Latin literature
were little known during the Middle Ages and became
widely known only during the Renaissance, the "rediscovery" of Roman literature consisted more in a new outlook on
the ancient texts than in the literal findings of books previously unknown. There were some significant new finds, but
it is hard to regard this filling out of the corpus of Latin lit-

From Charles G. Nauert Jr., *The Age of Renaissance and Reformation* (Lanham, MD:
University Press of America, 1981). Reprinted by permission of the publisher.

erature as truly decisive in cultural history, considering how
much was already well known. . . .

PETRARCH AND THE "DARK AGES"

Humanism involved more than demands for minor adjust-
ments in the university curriculum. The humanists were
claiming that their mission in life was nothing less than the
restoration of "true" civilization in place of the "barbarous"
civilization that prevailed in their own time. Such a notion
implied definite ideas of historical value, implying above all
the worthlessness of the whole medieval heritage—of everything, including the Gothic cathedrals and the scholastic
theological books.

These ideas of history were radically new, and as much as
any set of ideas can be attributed to any one person, they
were the creation of [Francesco] Petrarch himself. During
his long and active literary career, Petrarch [1304–1374] became convinced that ancient Greek and Roman civilization
had reached the highest level ever attained by any society.
But this great civilization declined during the fourth, fifth,
and subsequent centuries, simultaneously with the power of
the Roman empire which had protected it. Europe was
flooded by Germanic barbarians whose dominance completed the almost total loss of ancient art and literature. For
a thousand years thereafter, European society lived through
a "Dark Age"—a term by which Petrarch meant an age that
had lost the light of ancient civilization and had achieved
nothing of value on its own. This worthless, barbarous civilization, characterized by Gothic architecture and scholastic
thought, survived down to his own time. In his terminology,
it was "modern."

HISTORICAL DISCONTINUITY

Whereas medieval thinkers had regarded their own age as a
mere extension of Roman times, Petrarch drew a sharp distinction between two separate historical periods, an "ancient" period characterized by light, by high civilization, and
also by the domination of the whole world by the Italians;
and a "modern" period characterized by crude barbarism,
by cultural darkness, and by the degrading disunity and
weakness of the Italians. At least in germ, Petrarch's thought
also contained the idea of a third major period in the history
of civilization, a future age of cultural revival (rebirth, or

"renaissance") in which there would be a rediscovery of the sources of Greek and Roman cultural power, so that a new civilization would grow up, not identical with the ancient but inspired and guided by its best elements.

There is some evidence that Petrarch himself realized that once this new historical age had developed, it would be called "modern," and that the Dark Age lying between the old and the new ages of high civilization would seem a sort of middle period, an unhappy gap in the growth of civilization. Although Petrarch himself never used the exact phrase "Middle Ages" for that worthless age, his followers within a generation did. Indeed, not only the term "Middle Ages" but also the whole concept of distinct cultural periods in history, and the conventional and still useful division of history into ancient, medieval, and modern periods, was the invention of Petrarch and his followers, the humanists.

The modern student of history is often irritated by the wrong-headedness and unfairness of this attack on medieval civilization. We know, and even Petrarch, Boccaccio, and their followers should have known, that the Middle Ages had already attained a high level of culture. The negative attitude of the humanists toward medieval civilization was not a scientific and scholarly judgment. It can be understood only in terms of the severe breakdown in late medieval civilization. Not in a social or a political sense but certainly in a cultural sense, the Renaissance humanists were rebels against the heritage of the immediate past. The idea of medieval barbarism and Renaissance rediscovery of true civilization is indeed false concerning the Middle Ages, but it is very profoundly true concerning the Renaissance. The denigration of the Middle Ages and the rhapsodic idealization of Antiquity were devices through which a new age of creative thinkers defined their goals and justified their abandonment of prevailing traditions.

What the humanist rebels against medieval culture found in the Latin classics was not primarily new factual knowledge about the classical past, but a new appreciation of classical civilization as a whole. Classical Antiquity gave them a yardstick by which they could measure their own age and find it wanting, thus justifying their hostility to medieval tradition. In a more positive sense, it gave them new inspiration, confidence that a better civilization, a more wholesome society, and even a stronger Italy could be created. It also offered

ENRICHMENT OF THE HUMAN SPIRIT

Francesco Petrarch would be a major figure of the Renaissance if all he had written was his love poetry in the sonnet form. But in addition to his poetry, Petrarch initiated a tradition of scholarship that sought to read and understand classical authors on their own terms. Literary scholar Richard Tarnas believes this led to the widespread desire not only to imitate the best qualities of the ancients, but also to emulate and even surpass their achievements.

It was a pivotal moment in Western cultural history when Petrarch looked back on the thousand years since the decline of ancient Rome and experienced that entire period as a decline of human greatness itself, a diminishment of literary and moral excellence, a "dark" age. In contrast to this impoverishment, Petrarch beheld the immense cultural wealth of Greco-Roman civilization, a seeming golden age of creative genius and human expansiveness. For centuries, medieval schoolmen had been gradually rediscovering and integrating the ancient works, but now Petrarch radically shifted the focus and tone of that integration. Instead of Scholasticism's concern with logic, science, and Aristotle, and with the constant imperative of Christianizing the pagan conceptions, Petrarch and his followers saw value in all the literary classics of antiquity—poetry, essays, letters, histories and biographies, philosophy in the form of elegant Platonic dialogues rather than dry Aristotelian treatises—and embraced these on their own terms, not as needing Christian modification, but as noble and inspirational just as they stood in the radiance of classical civilization. Ancient culture was a source not just for scientific knowledge and rules for logical discourse, but for the deepening and enrichment of the human spirit. The classical texts provided a new foundation for the appreciation of man; classical scholarship constituted the "humanities." Petrarch set about the task of finding and absorbing the great works of ancient culture—Virgil and Cicero, Horace and Livy, Homer and Plato—not just to inculcate a sterile imitation of the past masters, but to instill in himself the same moral and imaginative fire that they had so superbly expressed. Europe had forgotten its noble classical heritage, and Petrarch called for its recollection. A new sacred history was being established, a Greco-Roman testament to be placed alongside the Judaeo-Christian. Thus Petrarch began the reeducation of Europe.

Richard Tarnas, *The Passion of the Western Mind.* New York: Harmony Books, 1991, p. 209.

practical guidance in the achievement of these goals. This conviction that current problems could best be solved by conscious imitation of the ancients was a powerful force throughout Renaissance civilization. It was not confined to idealistic poets like Petrarch, but was still powerful a century and a half later in the thought of the hard-bitten and politically experienced Machiavelli, who thought that the foundering Italian society of the early sixteenth century could be saved only if it reconstructed on the Roman model everything from its basic political institutions to its manner of recruiting and arming troops.

MORAL REFORM

In the opinion of Renaissance humanists from Petrarch to Machiavelli and beyond, the true secret of Rome's greatness was not some trick of military organization or even of constitutional structure, but its success over a long period in producing great leaders who were truly devoted to the welfare of their city. The moral grandeur that made the best and ablest men of Rome dedicate their lives to public service rather than to amassing private fortunes or seeking private enjoyment was the key to Rome's mastery of the whole world. As the Roman ruling classes became corrupted by the desire for personal advantage in the late Republic and the Empire, both the physical power and the culture of Rome declined. The spirit that made Rome great might today be called patriotism, but the men of the Renaissance commonly called it *virtù*. For this term the modern English word *virtue,* with its connotations of straitlaced adherence to a negative and puritanical moral code governing mainly individual and private acts, is a poor equivalent. The Italian *virtù* implied "strength of character" and "public-spiritedness." It dealt more with one's ethics in public life than with private life. In order to undo the political, moral, and cultural degeneracy that humanists saw in their own society and regarded as typically medieval, what was needed was a recovery of this sense of "virtue" or public spirit—in other words, a moral reform, in the broadest sense of the word *moral.*

This emphasis on the need for a moral reorientation explains many aspects of Italian humanism that otherwise fit into no rational pattern. For example, the humanists attacked scholastic education and scholarship, dismissing these flippantly as mere trifling. They did so because they

believed that scholasticism, with its cold, orderly rational-
ism and its apparently deliberate avoidance of literary artifice, was too narrowly intellectual, too concerned with abstract speculation about metaphysical, logical, and scientific
matters, to stimulate the kind of emotional commitment to a
life of virtue (that is, devotion to public service) which they
felt necessary for the recovery of ancient greatness. In a similar vein, the constant stress on character formation, on the
reading of Roman texts on ethics, politics, and history, and
even the stress on Christian piety that marks the educational
reforms of the Renaissance, are closely linked with this desire to regenerate the morals of society and to graduate
young men whose outstanding trait would not be their deft
mastery of logical disputation but their wholehearted devotion to the general welfare.

THE NEED FOR ELOQUENCE

Finally, the constant harping of humanists on the need for an
elegant and eloquent literary style and their apparently superficial dismissal of brilliant scholastic thinkers because
they wrote inelegant and nonclassical Latin are directly related to their emphasis on moral regeneration. Eloquent
form and the deliberate, artistic application of stylistic devices in speaking and writing were very important to the humanists. But this stress on eloquence, on effective use of
rhetorical devices learned from ancient Roman examples,
was no mere accidental peculiarity of the humanists. In order to make men virtuous, they argued, more is needed than
subtle, logical argumentation. Men are not purely intellectual beings, and hence their behavior will not be revolution-
ized by something so coldly rational as a scholastic disquisi-
tion on virtue and political obligation. The real springs of
human action are more emotional than rational. Thus the
man who is being educated for a career of public service and
leadership must himself be personally committed to the
common good by nonrational as well as rational influences,
and he must be taught to use the oratorical and literary devices that will allow him to appeal to the emotions of the
people and carry them along with him. The growing conviction that humanistic study of Latin literature did in fact make
men more effective at persuading their fellow citizens is precisely why in the closing fourteenth century more and more
heads of Florentine families, men who themselves were

more interested in political power and wealth than in intellectual matters, sought a humanistic education for their sons.

The humanists' professional skills as masters of rhetoric (the art of eloquence) were intended to be instrumental in bringing about a moral regeneration. In their opinion, humanistic studies—grammar, rhetoric, ethics, and history (which they regarded chiefly as a source of concrete illustrations of moral principles)—were to be preferred above all others mainly because they were eminently practical, dealing as they did with the study of man in his social and moral setting and with the arts of modifying human behavior through oratory and writing. The humanists from the time of Petrarch onward challenged the scholastic assumption that the main purpose of man is to understand the world of God and the world of nature. Rather, they believed, the main purpose of man is to understand and control himself and the whole complex web of relationships that bind him to other men. Thus their deliberate preference for rhetoric over philosophy, for eloquence over truth, does not mean that as a class they were "mere" rhetoricians, spineless time-servers who sold their skills to the highest bidder. Their devotion to rhetoric springs partly from their view of man as a being who is not just a disembodied intellect but much more a creature of passion and partly from their conception of themselves as moral reformers struggling to regenerate society and of moral reform itself as the key to solving the many problems of their age. . . .

THE CULT OF FAME

The humanists' ideal of regenerating the world, and opening up a whole new age of human history through "the recovery of classical antiquity" (that is, through the use of classical eloquence to recreate in modern times a sense of public morality comparable to that of Rome at her best) is linked to another humanistic trait that has elicited much attention and some amusement: their constant concern about their own fame among future generations. The humanists did seek fame. Men like Petrarch may have had some qualms about this desire, but usually they concluded, as he did, that desire for fame was a noble motive, that it had been one of the sources of patriotism and self-sacrifice among the heroes of Antiquity. The notion of fame was inseparable from the humanists' conception of themselves as the men who were initiating simultaneously a new age in history and a profound moral regeneration of modern society. In all modesty, Petrarch could hardly say, "With me there begins a third age in the history of human civilization." And yet in a very real sense, that is what he must have believed, and it was to that goal that he and his followers devoted their most serious efforts. Such men did value themselves highly, but only because they valued their purposes highly.

Princes and Courtiers: The Writings of Machiavelli and Castiglione

E.R. Chamberlin

Written and published within four years of each other in the early sixteenth century, *The Prince* by Niccolo Machiavelli and *The Courtier* by Baldassare Castiglione are two of the most influential Renaissance books. In the view of British historian E.R. Chamberlin, *The Prince* was intended as an explanation of how successful Renaissance princes actually behave, depicting a set of political values that were widely interpreted as amoral and corrupt. *The Courtier*, on the other hand, was intended to reflect the cultural practices and values already in place at the court of Urbino, Italy, and its highly idealized depictions influenced by several generations of European courtiers.

At the peak of Renaissance society stood the prince, the single, powerful man who, by a combination of political skill and hereditary authority, virtually ruled absolute over his state. It seems a curious contradiction that this period, which stressed, above all, the freedom of the individual, should have accepted the concept of the single ruler. There was good reason for it. In Italy, where the prince achieved his most brilliant and characteristic form, he was born of the fierce and endless tumults between factions in the cities. Despairing of ever finding peace except under the rule of one man, cities deserted the republican ideal, placing power freely in the hands of a leading citizen. Theoretically, that power was merely lent, not given, but once having enjoyed it few men intended to yield it back. Elsewhere in Europe, similar causes were at work in every country which did not

From E.R. Chamberlin, *Everyday Life in Renaissance Times* (London: Batsford, 1965). Reprinted by permission of Salamander Books.

possess a strong, central monarchy. . . .

Renaissance society, having perforce accepted the single
ruler, did not thereby accept him as a natural phenomenon to
be endured or adored. His office was analysed, as it had never
been before, in an attempt to explain its growth and function,
to prepare a blue-print of a piece of political machinery which
was to drive Europe for nearly three hundred years. The machinery was 'political' in the fullest sense, for it governed in
some degree every aspect of the lives of men gathered together in communities, decreeing how they should be judged,
how they should earn their bread, refresh their minds and
bodies, protect themselves from enemies within and without
the State. Two books appeared in the early years of the sixteenth century which placed the prince and his court under
the microscope, *The Prince* by Niccolo Machiavelli and *The
Courtier* by Baldassare Castiglione. They appeared within
four years of each other, in 1528 and 1532 respectively, but
both had been written, quite independently, many years
before—testimony to the fact that the phenomenon of the
prince was beginning to engage European attention.

THE PRINCE

Machiavelli's intention was to dissect the mechanics of state-
craft in terms of its effectiveness. Morality was irrelevant: if
a strategy worked, it was good; if it failed, it was bad. There
have been few writers so grossly misjudged as this Florentine republican who produced the classic textbook for the
practice of tyranny. It is as though a doctor, having diag-
nosed a disease, were to be accused of inventing it. Machiavelli was well aware of the construction likely to be placed
upon his work and went out of his way to stress that this was
the picture of things as they were—that, given that the prince
was necessary in civil life, then it was best that he should
learn how to conduct himself in the most perilous craft in
the world. He should indeed be a wise and virtuous man, but
'the manner in which men now live is so different from the
manner in which they should live that he who deviates from
the common course of practice and endeavours to act as
duty dictates, necessarily ensures his own destruction'.
Every man has a price, every seemingly disinterested action
can be shown to be rooted in self-interest. A prince should
keep his word—but few successful men actually do so. Is it
better for a prince to be loved or feared? It depends, Machi-

avelli replies; circumstances alter cases but, on the whole, it is safer to be feared, for most men are fickle and timid and will abandon in the hour of need those who have favoured them and have no other call upon them than the claims of gratitude. A prince as a commander of troops should always be feared, never worrying about a reputation for cruelty, for this was the only possible way to keep cruel men in order. It was a jaundiced view of the world; none knew better than Machiavelli that men could, and did, die for no other price than love of their country. But such love presupposed freedom; where there was no longer freedom the only incentives were self-interest or fear.

Machiavelli's prince was the first among men but was still a man; the Latin mind declined to invest him with that tinge of divinity which, in the north, came to infuse the idea. In Burgundy, the concept of the duke as being the personification of the State, and therefore as being something greater than a common man, was erected into a principle and a ritual. . . . Such adulation would have astonished the Italians. Lorenzo de' Medici, popular and competent though he was, came under heavy and sustained criticisms for his pretensions: 'He did not want to be equalled or imitated even in verses or games or exercises and turned angrily on any one who did so'. No one would have dared even attempt to be the equal of a duke of Burgundy. The excess was to bring its reaction: a king of England lost his head through too much devotion to the Divine Right and the monarchy of France ultimately collapsed in bloody ruin.

Niccolo Machiavelli

THE COURTIER

Machiavelli's *Prince* was a cold exercise in logic; Castiglione's *Courtier* was a warm, living portrait of the ideal man. 'I do not wonder that you were able to depict the perfect courtier', a friend wrote to him, 'for you had only to hold a mirror before you and set down what you saw there'. The graceful compliment was essentially true for Castiglione possessed most of the qualities he praised: piety, loyalty, courage, an easy learning and wit. Indeed, his life was almost a demonstration of Machiavelli's opinion that a virtuous man was at a disadvantage. As envoy between Pope Clement VII and the Emperor Charles V during the perilous days which culminated in the Sack of Rome in 1527, he was deluded by both, failed in his mission and died a discredited man. The Emperor, who so sorely tried him, said sadly, 'I tell you, one of the finest gentlemen in the world is dead'. Castiglione would have been proud of the epitaph and history, too, remembers him, not as diplomat but as gentleman.

The Courtier was the outcome of four brief years spent at the little court of Urbino. Afterwards, Castiglione was to mix with the truly great and powerful. As representative of the duke at the Papal Court, he came into intimate contact with Raphael, Michelangelo, Bembo; later he was Apostolic Nuncio to the Emperor's court. But always he looked back with nostalgia to the little court set among the hills of the northern Marches. He left Urbino in 1508, but for twenty years thereafter he lovingly polished and repolished his account of a civilised society, creating a monument to his own Golden Age. The duchy of Urbino owed its foundation to Federigo da Montefeltro, a professional soldier who yet managed to create a court in which the new humanist values were dazzlingly embodied. Piero della Francesca's portrait of him shows a man in whom strength is combined with tolerance, who would be surprised by nothing, expected nothing and was well able to defend his own rights. . . . He was a man who made a fortune from soldiering, played off his enemies one against the other and so kept inviolate the 400-odd hill villages and towns which acknowledged him as prince. But he was also a man who, in childhood, had been schooled by Vittorino da Feltre, the greatest humanist teacher in Europe, who infused in his pupils the new view of man. The great library at Urbino was Federigo's work. 'He alone had a mind to do what had not been done for a thousand years and more; that is, to create the finest library since ancient times'. Not for him was the common product of the new printing press; he employed thirty or forty scribes so that all his books should be 'written with the pen, not one printed, that it might not be disgraced thereby'.

In 1450 he began the construction of the palace which

Castiglione knew and which attracted travellers on the Grand Tour long after the brief life of the duchy had passed. 'It seemed not a palace but a city in the form of a palace', Castiglione affirmed, 'and [he] furnished it not only with what is customary such as silver vases, wall hangings of the richest cloth of gold, silk and other like things but for ornament he added countless ancient statues of marble and bronze, rare paintings'. . . . In this twofold role, admirer of ancient art and patron of modern painters, Federigo was essentially of the Renaissance. He died in 1482 and the dukedom passed to his son, Guidobaldo, who maintained the intellectual atmosphere of the court although he proved himself unable to hold back the militant world outside. It was his court which Castiglione described in the process of building up the portrait of the courtier. It is the picture of a group of brilliant minds, familiar with each other and therefore at ease, who have turned aside briefly from the cares of state and seek refreshment in conversation. There are feasts and entertainments of wide variety; during the day the members go about their business but each evening they meet again, under the presidency of the duchess (for the duke is grievously afflicted by gout and retires early). They talk into the small hours, pursuing each topic informally but with sobriety and order—and merriment too—fashioning between themselves the perfect man. So vividly did the memory stay with Castiglione that he could describe the end of one of these sessions with the poignancy of a paradise lost.

> Then every man rose to his feet . . . and not one of them felt any heaviness of sleep. When the windows were open then upon the side of the Palace that looks towards Mount Catri, they saw already risen in the east, a fair morning, rose coloured, and all stars gone save only Venus, from which seemed to blow a sweet blast that, filling the air with biting cold, began to quicken the notes of the pretty birds among the hushing woods of the hills nearby. Then they all, taking their leave with reverence of the Duchess, departed toward their lodging without torch, the light of day sufficing.

After Castiglione's day, the image of the courtier suffered a decline, becoming either the image of a fop or an intriguing social climber; even the Italian feminine of the word—'*la cortegiana*' or courtesan—became a synonym for a high-class harlot. But for Castiglione, the courtier was the cream of civilised society. He did not have to be nobly born; admittedly, he usually was, for only those born into the upper classes had the leisure or the opportunities to practise the arts, but this recognition that 'courtesy' was a quality of mind, and not of class, went far to explain the wide influence of the book. The courtier must be able to acquit himself in all manly exercises—wrestling, running, riding, but should be equally at home with literature, able to speak several languages, play musical instruments, write elegant verse. But everything should be done with a casual air so that his conversation, though sensible, was sprightly; he was even enjoined to study the form and nature of jokes. In love, he was to be discreet and honourable; in war, courageous but magnanimous. Above all, he was to be a man of his word, loyal to his prince, generous to his servants. He was altogether far removed from that other ideal man, the knight, with his fantastic code of personal honour. In modern language, Castiglione's courtier would be described as a well-educated, 'decent' man, with a strong code of personal morals but tolerant of the weakness of others. It was an ideal by which most men probably measured their lapses, for the standard demanded was high. But that the book filled a void is well shown by the speed with which it entered other languages and how long it maintained its influence. It was translated into French in 1537, into Spanish in 1540, into English in 1561, and, 200 years after Urbino ceased to exist as a state, Samuel Johnson gave his benediction to the book which enshrined its memory. 'The best book that ever was written upon good breeding, Il Cortegiano, by Castiglione, grew up at the little court of Urbino and you should read it'.

CHAPTER 2

The Northern Humanist Movement and Its Influence

Renaissance Literature

Beginnings of the Northern Renaissance

Robert E. Lerner

The literary Renaissance in northern Europe, including England, was made possible by the intellectual
movement Christian humanism and the educational
reforms it brought to northern Europe. As historian
Robert E. Lerner observes, northern humanists like
Erasmus and Sir Thomas More were inspired by the
earlier Italian humanists, but their writings were
also influenced by powerful religious traditions. The
three most enduring literary accomplishments of the
earlier northern Renaissance were works of fantasy,
humor, and satire by Erasmus, More, and the French
writer Rabelais. All three writers attacked the shallow hypocrisies of their day, and they shared an impulse to improve society by going beyond the con-
straints of received tradition.

It was inevitable that after about 1500 the Renaissance,
which originated in Italy, should have spread to other European countries. Throughout the fifteenth century a continuous procession of northern European students went to Italy
to study in Italian universities such as Bologna or Padua,
and an occasional Italian writer or artist traveled briefly
north of the Alps. Such interchanges helped spread ideas,
but only after around 1500 did most of northern Europe become sufficiently prosperous and politically stable to provide a truly congenial environment for the widespread cul-
tivation of art and literature. . . .

Simply stated, the northern Renaissance was the product
of an engrafting of certain Italian Renaissance ideals upon
preexisting northern traditions. This can be seen very
clearly in the case of the most prominent northern Renaissance intellectual movement, *Christian humanism.* Agreeing

with Italian humanists that medieval Scholasticism was too ensnarled in logical hair-splitting to have any value for the practical conduct of life, northern Christian humanists nonetheless looked for practical guidance from purely biblical, religious precepts. Like their Italian counterparts, they sought wisdom from antiquity, but the antiquity they had in mind was Christian rather than pagan—the antiquity, that is, of the New Testament and the early Christian fathers. Similarly, northern Renaissance artists were moved by the accomplishments of Italian Renaissance masters to turn their backs on medieval Gothic artistic styles and to learn instead how to employ classical techniques. Yet these same artists depicted classical subject matter far less frequently than did the Italians, and inhibited by the greater northern European attachment to Christian asceticism, virtually never dared to portray completely undressed nudes.

THE INFLUENCE OF ERASMUS

Any discussion of northern Renaissance accomplishments in the realm of thought and literary expression must begin with the career of Desiderius Erasmus (c. 1466–1536), "the prince of the Christian humanists." The illegitimate son of a priest, Erasmus was born near Rotterdam in Holland, but later, as a result of his wide travels, became in effect a citizen of all northern Europe. Forced into a monastery against his will when he was a teenager, the young Erasmus found there little religion or formal instruction of any kind but plenty of freedom to read what he liked. He devoured all the classics he could get his hands on and the writings of many of the Church fathers. When he was about thirty years of age, he obtained permission to leave the monastery and enroll in the University of Paris, where he completed the requirements for the degree of bachelor of divinity. But Erasmus subsequently rebelled against what he considered the arid learning of Parisian Scholasticism. In one of his later writings he reported the following exchange: "Q. Where do you come from? A. The College of Montaigu. Q. Ah, then you must be bowed down with learning. A. No, with lice." Erasmus also never entered into the active duties of a priest, choosing rather to make his living by teaching and writing. Ever on the lookout for new patrons, he changed his residence at frequent intervals, traveling often to England, staying once for three years in Italy, and residing in several different cities in the Netherlands before settling finally toward the end of his life in Basel, Switzerland. By means of a voluminous correspondence he kept up with learned friends he made wherever he went, Erasmus became the leader of a northern European humanist coterie. And by means of the popularity of his numerous publications, he became the arbiter of "advanced" northern European cultural tastes during the first quarter of the sixteenth century. . . .

But although Erasmus's urbane Latin style and wit earned him a wide audience for purely literary reasons, he by no means thought of himself as a mere entertainer. Rather, he intended everything he wrote to propagate in one form or another what he called the "philosophy of Christ." The essence of Erasmus's Christian humanist convictions was his belief that the entire society of his day was caught up in corruption and immorality as a result of having lost sight of the simple teachings of the Gospels. Accordingly, he offered to his contemporaries three different categories of publication: clever satires meant to show people the error of their ways, serious moral treatises meant to offer guidance toward proper Christian behavior, and scholarly editions of basic Christian texts.

In the first category belong the works of Erasmus that are still most widely read today—*The Praise of Folly* (1509), in which he pilloried Scholastic pedantry and dogmatism as well as the ignorance and superstitious credulity of the masses; and the *Colloquies* (1518), in which he held up contemporary religious practices for examination in a more serious but still pervasively ironic tone. In such works Erasmus let fictional characters do the talking, and hence his own views can only be determined by inference. But in his second mode Erasmus did not hesitate to speak clearly in his own voice. The most prominent treatises in this second genre are the quietly eloquent *Handbook of the Christian Knight* (1503), which urged the laity to pursue lives of serene inward piety, and the *Complaint of Peace* (1517), which pleaded movingly for Christian pacifism.

Despite this highly impressive literary production, however, Erasmus probably considered his textual scholarship his single greatest achievement. Revering the authority of the early Latin Fathers, Augustine, Jerome, and Ambrose, he brought out reliable editions of all their works, and revering the authority of the Bible most of all, he applied his extraordinary skills as a student of Latin and Greek to producing a reliable edition of the New Testament. After reading Lorenzo Valla's *Notes on the New Testament* in 1505, Erasmus became convinced that nothing was more imperative than divesting the text of the entire New Testament of the myriad errors in transcription and translation that had piled up during the Middle Ages, for no one could be a good Christian without being certain of exactly what Christ's message really was. Hence he spent ten years studying and comparing all the best early Greek biblical manuscripts he could find in order to establish an authoritative text. Finally appearing in 1516, Erasmus's Greek New Testament, published together with explanatory notes and his own new Latin translation, was one of the most important landmarks of biblical scholarship of all time.

THE CAREER OF THOMAS MORE

One of Erasmus's closest friends, and a close second to him in distinction among the ranks of the Christian humanists, was the Englishman Sir Thomas More (1478–1535). Following a successful career as a lawyer and as speaker of the House of Commons, in 1529 More was appointed lord chancellor of England. He was not long in this position, however, before he incurred the wrath of his royal master, King Henry VIII, because More, who was loyal to Catholic universalism, opposed the king's design to establish a national church under subjection to the state. Finally, in 1534, when More refused to take an oath acknowledging Henry as head of the Church of England, he was thrown into the Tower, and a year later met his death on the scaffold as a Catholic martyr. Much earlier, however, in 1516, long before More had any inkling of how his life was to end, he published the one work for which he will ever be best remembered, the *Utopia*. Creating the subsequently popular genre of "utopian fiction," More's *Utopia* expressed an Erasmian critique of contemporary society. Purporting to describe an ideal community on an imaginary island, the book is really an indictment of the glaring abuses of the time—of poverty undeserved and wealth unearned, of drastic punishments, religious persecution, and the senseless slaughter of war. The inhabitants of Utopia hold all their goods in common, work only six hours a day so that all may have leisure for intellectual pursuits, and practice the natural virtues of wis-

REJECTION OF MEDIEVAL TRADITIONS

At first, the instigators of the northern Renaissance, the Christian humanists, saw the recovery of the classical past and the reform of the Christian Church as parts of the same project, the restoration of "good letters," or literate culture to Europe. Their embrace of the original fountains or sources of Christian doctrine led many Christian scholars of the Renaissance into a highly critical stance toward the medieval inheritance of the Catholic Church. In their quest for authenticity in religion, these Christian humanists were appalled at abuses such as those encountered by Erasmus and John Colet in the following account.

Sometime between 1511 and 1513, two of Europe's leading scholars paid a visit to the shrine of St Thomas à Becket at Canterbury. One was John Colet, Dean of St Paul's and founder of its new grammar school; the other was the Dutchman Erasmus, author of the leading spiritual handbook for Christian laymen, and of a much-admired satire on the Church, *In Praise of Folly.* In one of his later *Colloquies,* Erasmus left an account of their visit, and it would be hard to conceive of a more poignant little episode, on the eve of the Reformation, than this confrontation between the shrine of the martyred clerical triumphalist, and the two earnest apostles of the New Learning. Both the scholars were pious men, and their visit was reverent. But Erasmus's account makes it clear they were deeply shocked by what they saw. The riches which adorned the shrine were staggering. Erasmus found them incongruous, disproportionate, treasures 'before which Midas or Croesus would have seemed beggars'; thirty years later, Henry VIII's agents were to garner from it 4,994 ounces of gold, 4,425 of silver-gilt, 5,286 of plain silver and twenty-six cartloads of other treasure. Colet infuriated the verger who accompanied them by suggesting that St Thomas would prefer the whole lot be given to the poor. He added insult to injury by refusing to give a reverential kiss to a prize relic, the arm of St George, and by treating an old rag supposedly soaked in St Thomas's blood with 'a whistle of contempt'. Two miles from the town, outside the Harbledown almshouse, the Dean's impatience with 'mechanical Christianity' was further tested when a licensed beggar showered them with holy water and offered St Thomas's shoe to be kissed: 'Do these fools expect us to kiss the shoe of every good man who ever lived?' he asked furiously. 'Why not bring us their spittle or their dung to be kissed?' After this memorable encounter, the two men rode back to London.

Paul Johnson, *A History of Christianity.* New York: Simon & Schuster, 1976, p. 267.

dom, moderation, fortitude, and justice. Iron is the precious metal "because it is useful," war and monasticism are abolished, and toleration is granted to all who recognize the existence of God and the immortality of the soul. Although More advanced no explicit arguments in his *Utopia* in favor of Christianity, he clearly meant to imply that if the "Utopians" could manage their society so well without the benefit of Christian Revelation, Europeans who knew the Gospels ought to be able to do even better. . . .

But despite a host of achievements, the Christian humanist movement, which possessed such an extraordinary degree of international solidarity and vigor from about 1500 to 1525, was thrown into disarray by the rise of Protestantism and subsequently lost its momentum. The irony here is obvious, for the Christian humanists' emphasis on the literal truth of the Gospels and their devastating criticisms of clerical corruption and excessive religious ceremonialism certainly helped pave the way for the Protestant Reformation initiated by Martin Luther in 1517. But . . . very few Christian humanists were willing to go the whole route with Luther in rejecting the most fundamental principles on which Catholicism was based, and the few who did became such ardent Protestants that they lost all the sense of quiet irony that earlier had been a hallmark of Christian humanist expression. Most Christian humanists tried to remain within the Catholic fold while still espousing their ideal of nonritualistic inward piety. But as time went on, the leaders of Catholicism had less and less tolerance for them because lines were hardening in the war with Protestantism and any suggestion of internal criticism of Catholic religious practices seemed like giving covert aid to "the enemy." Erasmus himself, who remained a Catholic, died early enough to escape opprobrium, but several of his less fortunate followers lived on to suffer as victims of the Spanish Inquisition.

Yet if Christian humanism faded rapidly after about 1525, the northern Renaissance continued to flourish throughout the sixteenth century in primarily literary and artistic forms. In France, for example, the highly accomplished poets Pierre de Ronsard (c. 1524–1585) and Joachim du Bellay (c. 1522–1560) wrote elegant sonnets in the style of Petrarch, and in England the poets Sir Philip Sidney (1554–1586) and Edmund Spenser (c. 1552–1599) drew impressively on Italian literary innovations as well. Indeed, Spenser's *The Faerie Queene,* a long chivalric romance written in the manner of Ariosto's *Orlando Furioso,* communicates as well as any Italian work the gorgeous sensuousness typical of Italian Renaissance culture.

THE SATIRE OF RABELAIS

More intrinsically original than any of the aforementioned poets was the French prose satirist François Rabelais (c. 1490–1553), probably the best loved of all the great European creative writers of the sixteenth century. Like Erasmus, whom he greatly admired, Rabelais was educated as a monk, but soon after taking holy orders he left his monastery to study medicine. Becoming thereafter a practicing physician in Lyons, Rabelais from the start interspersed his professional activities with literary endeavors of one sort or another. He wrote almanacs for the common people, satires against quacks and astrologers, and burlesques of popular superstitions. But by far his most enduring literary legacy consists of his five volumes of "chronicles" published under the collective title of *Gargantua and Pantagruel.*

Rabelais' account of the adventures of Gargantua and Pantagruel, originally the names of legendary medieval giants noted for their fabulous size and gross appetites, served as a vehicle for his lusty humor and his penchant for exuberant narrative as well as for the expression of his philosophy of naturalism. To some degree, Rabelais drew on the precedents of Christian humanism. Thus, like Erasmus, he satirized religious ceremonialism, ridiculed Scholasticism, scoffed at superstitions, and pilloried every form of bigotry. But much unlike Erasmus, who wrote in a highly cultivated classical Latin style comprehensible to only the most learned readers, Rabelais chose to address a far wider audience by writing in an extremely down-to-earth French, often loaded with the crudest vulgarities. Likewise, Rabelais wanted to avoid seeming in any way "preachy" and therefore eschewed all suggestions of moralism in favor of giving the impression that he wished merely to offer his readers some rollicking good fun. Yet, aside from the critical satire in *Gargantua and Pantagruel,* there runs through all five volumes a common theme of glorifying the human and the natural. For Rabelais, whose robust giants were really life-loving human beings writ very large, every instinct of humanity was healthy, provided it was not directed toward tyranny over others. Thus in his ideal community, the utopian "abbey of Thélème," there was no repressiveness whatsoever, but only a congenial environment for the pursuit of life-affirming, natural human attainments, guided by the single rule of "do what thou wouldst."

Erasmus's *The Praise of Folly* and the Humanist Reform Agenda

Clarence H. Miller

The Praise of Folly by Desiderius Erasmus was a
best-seller across Europe for many years after its
first printing in 1511. As scholar Clarence H. Miller
points out in this brief introduction to the work, *The
Praise of Folly* is heavily indebted to Greek and Roman literature for its form and for many of its satiric
strategies. It serves as a critical examination of
hypocrises and vices in European society of the early
sixteenth century, including failures within the
Catholic Church. Yet, as Miller observes, the *Folly*
contains serious affirmations of Christian values
alongside the humor and the satire.

Fortunately Erasmus himself has given us some detailed in-
formation about the genesis, composition, and publication of
his masterpiece. In the summer of 1509 he was on his way to
England from Italy, where he had been stimulated by his contact with Italian humanism, disgusted by secular and ecclesiastical corruption, and exhausted by his prodigious labors on
the *Adagia*, an enormous, profusely annotated collection of
Greek and Latin proverbs published by Aldus at Venice in
1508. Riding on horseback over an Alpine pass, he conceived
the notion of writing a mock-encomium on folly—Folly's oration in praise of herself—partly because he was thinking of
his friends in England, particularly of his closest friend there
Thomas More, whose family name resembles the Greek
word for folly. After a journey of about two months, he ar-
rived at More's house in London, the Old Barge in Bucklers-
bury, where he was confined for a while with a kidney ail-
ment. Whether he was delivered of a kidney stone we do not

know, but he did bring Folly into the world, smiling and eloquent from her first breath. When he had written part of Folly's speech, he showed it to his English friends to let them share the fun, or (as we can easily imagine) he read them what he had written, taking on the role of Folly himself. Thoroughly delighted, they urged him to go on with it. Within about a week, Folly, though not quite full grown, was essentially complete and ready to begin her brilliant career as one of the most popular and controversial prima donnas of Western literature. . . .

That *Folly* was conceived on the great watershed of Europe, poised between the urbanity of the Italian Renaissance and the earnestness of Northern Humanism, has seemed significant to some critics in moments of lofty speculation. That it was written in More's house and dedicated to him may suggest affinities with the genial wit of the author of *Utopia*, but it should also serve to remind us that during an earlier stay in London in 1505 and 1506 More and Erasmus had collaborated and competed in translating from Greek to Latin some dialogues of Lucian, whose caustic and brilliant satire provided one important model for the *Folly*. That it was composed in England also has a broader significance in that it was only after his first visit to England in 1499 that Erasmus finally fixed his sights firmly on the great goal of his life: to edit, translate, and annotate the Greek New Testament—a work which he largely executed in England, especially during his five years at Cambridge (1509–14), and which finally appeared in print at Basel in 1516. Finally, that the *Folly* was first printed in Paris may seem fitting, since the Sorbonne [Parisian university] was the very stronghold of the reactionary theologians whose hairsplitting arrogance and exegetical ineptitude are so often the butts of Folly's wit.

The Humanist Reform Agenda

In fact, no other brief, integral work of Erasmus condenses the humanists' program for educational, religious, and theological reform better than the *Folly*. . . . During the three centuries before Erasmus wrote, logic had gained a commanding position in the university arts curriculum, casting the pale survivals of grammar and rhetoric, the dominant studies during classical antiquity, into the shade. The enormous and intricate structure of scholastic philosophy and theology rested on the revival (about 1200) of Aristotle's logical works, the *Organon* or great "instrument" of human learning, and on the subtle, dazzling (not to say dizzying) refinements of them made by medieval logicians, especially Peter of Spain (about 1250). The humanist revival, which gained increasing momentum during the fifteenth century, especially in Italy, might be simplistically described as an attempt to regain and restore the rightful roles of grammar and rhetoric. Grammar was no longer to be the mere mastery of the ordinary rules of Latin syntax but the establishment and explication of sound texts through linguistic and historical studies, a movement which culminated in nineteenth-century classical philology. Grammar in this larger sense was made possible and necessary because of the rediscovery of many works by ancient Greek and Latin writers. Rhetoric was no longer to be lists of ornamental figures of speech, the medieval flowers and "colors" of rhetoric, but the art of speaking and writing Latin persuasively, with coherence and fluency, articulation and copiousness. The new rhetoric was based largely on the rediscovered rhetorical works of Aristotle, Cicero, and Quintilian—especially the last two. We should remember that the new grammar had as its province not merely what we think of as literature, but also philosophy (especially Plato, Cicero, and Seneca), history, politics, medicine, law, geography, astronomy, architecture, and even military strategy. And the new rhetoric was not merely an academic pursuit or the elegant entertainment of a leisured elite, but the key to many important ecclesiastical, governmental, and diplomatic posts.

Needless to say, the pillars of the educational and ecclesiastical establishment, especially the old-fashioned theologians and monks, were not very eager to be reformed. It is hard for us to conceive of a time when anyone could deny that the New Testament should be studied in the original Greek and explicated in the light of the Greek and Latin fathers. But Erasmus' *New Testament* was repeatedly and bitterly attacked, and so was his *Folly*, especially after the Lutheran outburst dashed the hopes of moderate reformers and Erasmus found himself caught between Scylla and Charybdis, between the Protestant revolt and the Catholic reaction. As Erasmus' prefatory letter shows, he fully expected the *Folly* to be attacked. . . .

CLASSICAL INFLUENCES ON *THE PRAISE OF FOLLY*

One reason why the *Folly* was persistently misunderstood and attacked was the novelty of its literary form. It was a spectacular revival of a classical genre which had been practically extinct for a thousand years, the paradoxical encomium. Arthur Pease has defined such an encomium as a declamation "in which the legitimate methods of the encomion are applied to persons or objects in themselves obviously unworthy of praise, as being trivial, ugly, useless, ridiculous, dangerous, or vicious." Among the precedents for the *Folly* cited by Erasmus in his preface are a number which do not strictly belong to the genre. But when Folly herself, with involuted irony, defines the form she is following by dissociating herself from it, she mentions only examples which fit the genre exactly: many orators, she says, "have spent sleepless nights burning the midnight oil to work out elaborate encomia of Busiris, Phalaris, the quartan fever, flies, baldness, and other dangerous nuisances." The form was continuously cultivated in both Greek and Latin from the fifth century B.C. to the fourth century after Christ and included among its practitioners such luminaries as Plato, Isocrates, and Lucian, but very few examples have survived from classical times. . . .

Classical sources for the arguments, allusions, sayings, and proverbs in the *Folly* are numerous indeed, as the footnotes will testify. Few have been able to savor its finer bouquet without the help of notes, to catch the wit on the wing rather than in the taxidermy of annotation. As Sir Thomas Chaloner, the first English translator (1549), remarked, Erasmus turned out his whole scholarly knapsack for the *Folly*, and it was crammed full in 1509 because he had just finished listing and commenting at length on 4,500 Greek and Latin proverbs and sayings in his *Adagia*. Tags from Virgil and Homer are sprinkled generously, especially in the first part, to lend a dash of mock-heroic elevation. Horace is frequently cited and quoted throughout to provide a comfortable aura of urbane common sense. Gellius and Pliny are exploited for useful anecdotes or "scientific" evidence. With sophistical ease, Folly often distorts, almost unnoticeably, the classical authorities she cites to support her arguments. At one point she even boasts of her sophistical prowess in distorting evidence. Since Plato was among the most important and influential of the Greek writers rediscovered by the humanists, it might be helpful to notice how she uses (and abuses) him.

The major ideas drawn from Plato are: (1) the distinction between two kinds of madness, modelled on Plato's distinction between two kinds of love; (2) the Sileni of Alcibiades; (3) the myth of the cave; and (4) the higher kind of love leading from the impermanent world of flux to the stable realm of the one, true, and beautiful. The distinction between the two kinds of madness is structurally important because it allows Folly to describe various beneficent obsessions (hunting, building, gambling, and so on). But her analogy between madness and love, however convenient, is merely superficial and sophistical. She exploits the myth of the cave in two quite inconsistent ways. In the first part, when she is trying to prove that foolish illusions enable us to lead a happy life, she praises the fools who contentedly watch the shadows in the cave and contemptuously dismisses the wiseman who perversely insists on seeing the reality outside. But in the third part, when she claims as her own devout Christians who reject the world and the flesh for the things of the spirit, she praises this same wiseman as an exemplary Christian fool. . . .

From start to finish Folly is simplistic and sophistical. Folly, but not necessarily Erasmus, defines Christianity narrowly as the irrational pursuit of mystical ecstasy and the utter repudiation of the material world. The last part of Folly's speech is completely inconsistent with the first part, but it is equally ironical. When she argues that folly is the only source of comfort, joy, and happiness, our first reaction is "certainly not," but we are gradually forced to admit "yes, too often." When she argues that the true Christian must act like a fool in the eyes of the world, we are forced to admit "yes, certainly," but we find ourselves continually wishing to interject "no, there's more to it than that." The experience of the book is to play off one irony against the other, not to imagine that Erasmus is simply propounding straightforward Platonism. . . .

A THREE-PART STRUCTURE

As for the literary structure of Folly's speech, most critics have begun to take a tripartite plan as their starting point:

(1) Folly provides the illusions necessary to render life in this world tolerable or even pleasant.

(2) Folly makes the professional leaders of church and state blind enough to be happy in their vicious irresponsibility.

(3) Folly enables the Christian fool to renounce the world in favor of Christian joy in this life and the beatific vision in the next. . . .

The first section is devoted to the ironical thesis that the happiest life is a fool's life. The wise man is not only inept and ineffective in the practical affairs of everyday living, but his harsh truths would also destroy the illusions and deceptions necessary to keep up the stage play of life. Sexual pleasure, the propagation of the human race, the pleasures of the table, friendship and marriage, the glories of warfare, the investigations of science, the inventions of technology, the harmony of civil society all depend on illusions, self-deception, and vainglorious aspirations. Natural fools are among the happiest of men. Even madness, as long as it is not violent, can make people far happier than wisdom. Protected by benevolent euphoria, fanatics of all sorts—hunters, gamblers, alchemists, superstitious worshippers of saints—can maintain the illusion of happiness. Self-love and flattery oil the wheels of society and keep it running smoothly. All life is dual, like the Sileni of Alcibiades—ugly or beautiful according to the viewer's angle of vision. The comedy of life is a play that can be entertaining only so long as its basic illusion is kept up. To strip away disguises ruins the play and leads only to disillusionment, futility, despair, or even suicide. The ironic double vision of this first part has been most frequently analyzed, admired, and related to the outlook of other great writers of the Renaissance, such as Ariosto, Rabelais, Cervantes, or Shakespeare. As in the *Utopia* the reader is piquantly poised between seemingly contradictory views; with a laugh, or a smile, or a sigh he is forced to admit that what seems absurd is sometimes, often, very often, almost always true.

The third section is based on a paradox which seems directly opposed to the first part: the folly of Christian fools throws them out of step with society at large. This sort of folly does not integrate men into their social surroundings; it separates them from the world and its values. Such folly may lead to ridiculous eccentricity, mental alienation, a kind of ecstatic madness in which even ordinary sense perceptions may be lost. Indeed, this folly seems to be oriented toward the final, perfect alienation of the beatific vision. Folly caps her

argument with a brilliant and daring pun: ecstasy, the alienation of a mind drawn out of itself into union with God, is
"Moriae pars," Folly's portion, "which shall not be taken from
her by the transformation of life, but shall be perfected."

Placed between these two contradictory paradoxes, the
middle section is essential to the impact of the whole work.
It agrees with the first part in that both find the establishment quite foolish and even the happier for its folly. Would
not grammarians and schoolteachers be among the most
miserable of men, tyrannizing futilely over a wretched and
filthy pack of cowed schoolboys, if they were not puffed up
by arrogant and foolish delusions of grandeur? The almost
incredible self-deception of quibbling theologians lets
them imagine that by their petty labors they support the
whole church, like Atlas holding the world on his shoul-
ders. If a king considered his responsibilities, would he not
be most miserable?

But these happy fools in the middle section also differ
from the fools in the first part. However beatific folly may be
for individual academic and social leaders, it has a disastrous effect on society as a whole. The fools in the first part
are not usually presented in responsible roles; they are alchemists, hunters, gamblers, fortune-hunters, lecherous old
men and women, thick-skulled soldiers. Even the gods indulge in folly in their off-duty hours, as it were, when they
have finished settling quarrels and hearing petitions. In the
first part the ineptness of wise men in public affairs might
be borne (we are told) if they were not such awkward and
cantankerous bores at parties, dances, plays. One important
reason why Folly is able to carry off the ironical paradox of
the first part is precisely that she does not sort out people according to their social functions but rather treats private
vices or depicts large, indiscriminate swarms of mankind.
The fabric of society is presented as essentially unreal, a
pageant or a play which can be maintained only by hiding
reality and accepting disguises. . . .

The medial survey not only leads us out of Folly's first
paradox, but also prepares us for the Christian paradox of
the third part. Here, the whole fabric of society is again dis-
solved. The world and all its ways are rejected by Christian
fools. They refuse to love even their country, parents, children, and friends except insofar as they reflect the goodness
of God. The survey agrees with this view in that it too rejects

the foolish establishment—the academics, politicians, and ecclesiastics who fail to fulfill their functions. Society as it has degenerated under their management is indeed the very world which is rejected by Christian fools. We can accept the final ironic paradox of the Christian who is absurd and foolish in the eyes of the world because that world has already been presented as vitiated by another less basic ironic contrast: the rulers of the world remain happy by ignoring their duty to regulate and purify the world.

The second part, whatever problems it may present about Erasmus' use of his persona, is clearly a necessary and integral part of the work. Even Folly could not have carried off a direct leap from the first part to the third, and no critical view of the *Folly* can be adequate if it does not take the medial survey into account. The reader's (or better, listener's) task is to remember all of Folly's speech, to consider it as a whole—a task in which Folly (not Erasmus) does her best to defeat him. Through vivid immediacy she tries to hide her shifting inconsistencies. For her prowess in the world she gives more credit to Self-love and Flattery than to her other handmaidens, but for her own sophistry the prime place must be given to Forgetfulness. At the end of her speech she claims—and we may be allowed to doubt her claim—that she cannot provide an epilogue because she does not remember what she has said. However much Folly may hate him for it, the reader must try to be a "listener with a memory." Only if he constructs the epilogue which Folly refuses to give can he hope to become not merely an initiate of Folly but an initiate of Erasmus' *Folly*.

Sir Thomas More and His *Utopia*

Burton A. Milligan

A towering figure of Renaissance humanism, Sir
Thomas More had a brilliant political career as well
as a literary career, according to scholar Burton A.
Milligan. More became Lord Chancellor of England in
1529 and served in that role until he was put to death
for treason by Henry VIII in 1535. His satire *Utopia*,
published in 1516, was a serious critique of kingship
and contemporary European society, written in the
guise of a fictitious travelogue. *Utopia* was written in
Latin, the common language of educated Europeans,
and it was first translated into English in 1557.

Sir Thomas More (1478–1535) stood in the front rank of the
English humanists at the very beginning of the English Renaissance. Educated at Oxford under Linacre and Grocyn,
brought up in the household of Cardinal Morton, who figures as a character in Book One of *Utopia*, More belonged,
along with Erasmus and Colet, to the group known as the
Oxford Reformers, who sought to apply humanistic principles to reforms in the Church and in education. From success in the practice of law, More passed to a brilliant career
in public life under Henry VIII, which culminated with his
becoming Lord Chancellor in 1529. His retirement from this
high office, in 1532, was followed in 1534 by his break with
Henry VIII over the King's claims to supremacy in the
Church and over the validity of the King's divorce from
Catherine of Aragon. Because More refused to compromise
with his conscience, he was accused of high treason and, in
1535, was executed. As even these bare details of his life
show, More wrote with authority about kings, government,
education, religion, and law, the subjects which most concern him in *Utopia*.

Reprinted with the permission of Scribner, a division of Simon & Schuster, from *Three
Renaissance Classics*, by Burton A. Milligan. Copyright © 1953 by Charles Scribner's
Sons; copyright renewed © 1981 by Burton A. Milligan.

Utopia, written in Latin, was first published at Louvain in 1516, and was reprinted in several other European cities within the next few years. The first English translation, by Ralphe Robynson, was published in 1551. It is the text used in the present volume. Sir Thomas More produced other works in Latin and in English, but they are of minor importance. His fame in literature rests upon *Utopia*.

AN INDICTMENT OF SOCIETY

The First Book of *Utopia* tells us what was wrong with the England, and for that matter the Europe generally, of More's time. The Second Book shows us an ideal commonwealth in which the social evils described in the First Book are corrected. Also, in a very important sense the Second Book is a continuation of the indictment of society in the First, because every wise and humane provision regulating government and society in More's Utopian state is a reminder of the foolish or inhumane conduct of affairs in the real world. No doubt More feared that the story of the Utopians would be regarded as an idle and pleasant fiction, and that his serious intention, his social satire, would be overlooked or only partly comprehended. At any rate, having written the Second Book, in 1515, he afterwards wrote the First. Its importance in providing verisimilitude is great, but its importance in providing explicit contrast between the real and the ideal is greater.

Although More was sufficiently politic to begin *Utopia* with a compliment to Henry VIII, a considerable part of the attack in Book One is directed against kings. The chief interests of most kings, according to More's spokesman, Hythloday, are war and conquest. Kings, he says, do not want the advice of philosophers, and they never will want it until they have followed Plato's advice and become philosophers themselves. Their greed for wealth is as insatiable as their lust for power.

Book One is also a penetrating study of the English penal system and of the basic economic and social evils underlying crime and poverty in More's England. In the conversations at Cardinal Morton's house, Hythloday sweeps aside the assumptions of some of the Cardinal's guests that people steal or beg because they are by nature dishonest or shiftless, and that the only preventive of crime is punishment. More's contentions are that the conditions that give rise to destitution and, consequently, to crime must be eliminated, and that punishment, however cruel, will not in itself prevent crime. The conditions in England leading to destitution and crime, Hythloday argues, are the unequal distribution of wealth and the denial to many people of an opportunity to make an honest living. Among these people are: the veterans maimed in war, unable to work at their old crafts or to learn new ones, and deserted by society; the serving men of the idle rich, untrained in useful work and left destitute at their masters' deaths; small farmers ejected from land enclosed for sheep-grazing, who, having no trade other than farming, can only wander through the countryside and become thieves or vagabonds. Most of these evils More blames upon "the unreasonable covetousnes of a few." The Church itself shares part of the guilt, through its own policy of land enclosure and through turning loose its hordes of begging

THE UTOPIANS EMBRACE THE ANCIENT GREEKS

In most of their radical and innovative practices, the Utopians point the way Thomas More believes Europeans should go, and their attitude toward the classical past of Europe is no exception. The narrator of the story relates how the Utopians were immediately attracted to the literature and learning of ancient Greece when it was revealed to them.

The people [of Utopia] in general are easygoing, cheerful, clever, and fond of leisure. When they must, they can stand heavy labor, but otherwise they are not much given to it. In intellectual pursuits, they are tireless. When they heard from us about the literature and learning of the Greeks (for we thought there was nothing in Latin except the historians and poets that they would enjoy), it was wonderful to behold how eagerly they sought to be instructed in Greek. We therefore began to study a little of it with them, at first more to avoid seeming lazy than out of any expectation that they would profit by it. But after a short trial, their diligence convinced us that our efforts would not be wasted. They picked up the forms of the letters so quickly, pronounced the language so aptly, memorized it so quickly, and began to recite so accurately that it seemed like a miracle. Most of our pupils were established scholars, of course, picked for their unusual ability and mature minds; and they studied with us, not just of their own free will, but at the command of the senate. Thus in less than three years they friars upon the country, idle and sometimes mischievous churchmen, who are regarded by More much as Chaucer regarded their earlier counterparts. Severe punishments, such as capital punishment for thievery, are, More argues, not only morally reprehensible, but also impracticable: "Neither ther is any punishment so horrible, that it can kepe them from stealynge, which have no other craft, wherby to get their living." And, says More, a thief facing capital punishment for his stealing has every practical motive for committing murder to cover up his theft.

For some of the social evils, however, More blames the people themselves. Joined to the miserable poverty not of their own making are "greate wantonnes, importunate superfluitie and excessive riote." The people are guilty of moral laxity, thriftlessness, and dissipation of their time and talents. They spend their time, says More, in "stewes, wyne-

---

had perfect control of the language, and could read the best Greek authors fluently, unless the text was corrupt. I suspect they picked up Greek more easily because it was somewhat related to their own tongue. Though their language resembles the Persian in most respects, I suspect them of deriving from Greece because their language retains quite a few vestiges of Greek in the names of cities and in official titles.

Before leaving on the fourth voyage, I placed on board, instead of merchandise, a good-sized packet of books; for I had resolved not to return at all, rather than to come home soon. Thus they received from me most of Plato's works and many of Aristotle's, as well as Theophrastus's book *On Plants,* though the latter, I'm sorry to say, was somewhat mutilated. During the voyage I left it lying around, a monkey got hold of it, and out of sheer mischief ripped a few pages here and there. Of the grammarians they have only Lascaris, for I did not take Theodorus with me, nor any dictionary except that of Hesychius; and they have Dioscorides. They are very fond of Plutarch's writings, and delighted with the witty persiflage of Lucian. Among the poets they have Aristophanes, Homer, and Euripides, together with Sophocles in the small Aldine edition. Of the historians they possess Thucydides and Herodotus, as well as Herodian.

Robert M. Adams, ed. and trans., *Utopia.* New York: W.W. Norton, 1992, pp. 57–58.

tavernes, ale houses and tiplinge houses," or in playing "noughtie, lewde and unlawfull games," among which he includes card playing, dice play, and bowling.

AN IDEAL REPUBLIC

In the Second Book, More is concerned not merely with correction of the evils examined in the First Book, but also with a larger consideration of what would be ideal in government, social organization, law, education, and religion.

In devising his Utopian government, More rejects kings, whose faults he has pointed out in Book One, and, like Plato, adopts a republic. Of the federal government all that More says is that there come yearly to Amaurote, the capital city of Utopia, from each of the cities three wise, experienced old men, "there to entreate and debate of the common matters of the land." In the chapter "Of the magistrates" More describes briefly the local governments, republican in form, carefully controlled by checks and balances, open to public scrutiny. The attitudes toward government that lie behind these meagre details are obvious, although not stated: distrust of great centralized power in a national government, fear of hasty or secret action by legislators, trust in the people acting through elected representatives.

More's position in regard to communism in Utopia is enigmatic, all the more so because, although Hythloday, usually his spokesman, praises it, More himself condemns it. Perhaps More held up the idea of common ownership as a warning to those who abused private wealth; perhaps he considered Utopian communism, whatever support he found for it in Plato's republic or in biblical teachings about wealth, to be an ideal, but not a practicable system. Whatever the fact, More makes every effort to make the Utopian system of communism seem practicable. It is no share-the-wealth plan for idlers. Every man may have his share, but only by working for it. Incidentally, More is greatly interested not only in the distribution of wealth, but also in the very nature of wealth, which he examines from the viewpoint of whether the scarcity of a thing, rather than its utility, should be the measure of its value.

Although More assumes that his communistic system will eliminate thievery, he does not assume that all crimes will be eliminated in his ideal state. He provides a legal and penal system of special interest when one recalls his criticisms of English law in Book One and remembers More's own unusual knowledge of law. In Utopia there are few laws, and they are so clearly stated that they are understandable to every man. There are no lawyers, for every man is able to plead his own cause. Capital punishment is employed as a last resort with only the most intractable criminals. Ordinarily the most severe punishment is bondage, itself inflicted upon only serious offenders. Bondmen are not shut uselessly in prisons, but are set to doing hard, useful work for the commonwealth. Thus, More gets the unpleasant work of his commonwealth done not by slaves, as in Plato's republic, but by convicted criminals. One of his most interesting conceptions is that the state should reward those who observe the laws as well as punish those who break them.

More's provisions regarding labor and agriculture offer reforms for the conditions exposed in the First Book. Not pointlessly, but recalling the plight of English workers deprived of their single trade or craft, More makes his Utopians learn both farming and a trade or craft. He provides for a six-hour working day, visionary indeed in the early sixteenth century, when the actual legal working day could extend to fourteen or fifteen hours; and he argues that it is feasible in a country where everyone—man and woman, priest and layman—works, and where no labor is wasted on the production of luxuries.

HUMANIST EDUCATION

It is More the humanist who dreams of this six-hour working day. The many hours freed from drudgery are to be used for education and self-improvement, not for vain or harmful recreations. In Utopia "there be neither winetavernes, nor ale houses, nor stewes, nor anye occasion of vice or wickednes." Games are intellectually or morally improving; the Utopians spend leisure time in hearing lectures, in listening to readings pertaining to good manners and virtue, in hearing music, or in conversing with the wise. But all this is aside from formal education, which resembles that in a somewhat idealized sixteenth-century England, in which medieval education had been enriched by the Renaissance. Before Hythloday brings the Renaissance to Utopia by bringing classical learning, the principal subjects studied there correspond closely to the seven liberal arts of the medieval trivium (grammar, logic, and rhetoric) and quadrivium (music, geometry, arithmetic, and astronomy). But the subject of most interest to the Utopians, since they are a virtuous people, is moral philosophy, which they esteem as much as they despise the subtleties and fruitlessness of scholastic philosophy. When Hythloday brings Latin and Greek learning to Utopia, the people respond to it as the humanists that they are would be expected to do.

In his concepts of the ideal in family life and in marriage, More exhibits a curious combination of unconventionality and of great conservativeness. His program of pre-marital physical inspections, his attempts to liberalize divorce while guarding against its abuse, and his provisions for euthanasia are often hailed as ideas far ahead of their time. On the other hand, the patriarchal family life is likely to repel or disappoint modern readers, even when they realize that More lived in a world in which women had not been emancipated, and even when they understand that to More age meant wisdom.

More's ideas concerning war and international relations are midway between idealism and cautious realism, even cynicism. He can conceive of an ideal state, but not of an ideal world; and the ideal state will always be threatened by the imperfect outsiders. He accepts wars as inevitable and merely tries to restrain them and to perfect the waging of them. Utopians fight wars only for what they regard as just purposes: defense of their country, liberation of friendly countries from invaders, destruction of tyrants, seizure of unused territory of neighboring countries when it is needed for their own expanding population and is denied to them. They prevent war when they can, by means of what we would call economic sanctions. They protect their own citizens as much as possible from the horrors of war by employing mercenaries except in extreme emergencies. They pride themselves upon using every device of bribery, propaganda, and deceit instead of fighting stupidly and brutally, like bears or dogs. They are, in short, More's humanists, in war as in everything else. Impelled by their distrust of other countries, they form no leagues or confederations. There is almost Swiftian satire in More's condemnation of the treaty-breaking habits of the benighted countries near Utopia and his ironical praise of the scrupulous adherence to treaties of the Christian countries of Europe.

Perhaps nothing in *Utopia* is more enlightened than More's

treatment of religion. Complete freedom of religious views prevails in his ideal commonwealth. Only atheism crosses the boundary of the Utopians' tolerance, and even it is not as severely condemned as bigotry, for the atheist is deprived of some of his civil rights, but the bigot is exiled. The priests, contrasting with those in the Christian countries of More's time, are few in number and exceedingly holy. The religion is a religion of good works and of cheerfulness, like More's own.

The Comic Vision of Rabelais

M.A. Screech

M.A. Screech, professor of French at University College London, concedes that it may be difficult for modern readers to access much of the humor of the French Renaissance writer François Rabelais. But the task is made easier by the recognition that his humor is based firmly on the Christian and classical values espoused by the humanists of the northern Renaissance. While making use of folk humor, Rabelais also derives much from the ancient satirists, especially the Greek writer Lucian. Rabelais's wide reading and use of classical sources helped shape his works *Gargantua* and *Pantagruel* into what Screech calls "philosophical comedy of lasting value."

The works of a comic writer of genius who lived four and a half centuries ago pose special difficulties of interpretation. These problems are more acute than those we face when we try to appreciate the tragedies of former ages. Tragedy, insofar as it is dealing with the fear of death, the destructive nature of much sexual passion, or the feeling of pity which the suffering of mankind evokes, is treating subjects which seem fairly constant preoccupations among civilised men and women. But the comedy, the laughter, the sense of humour of differing countries and differing ages, seem to arise out of circumstances and conventions which even a sympathetic reader cannot always recognise, let alone share spontaneously. Perhaps this is partly because comedy and humour are often linked with religious or philosophical beliefs, with ethical norms, with social morals and conventions, which are by their nature less stable and less permanent elements in human culture. There are, of course, actions, jests and plays on words, which do leap easily from country to country and across the centuries; but one only has to think of the puzzled or embarrassed silence with which an audience may greet some of Shakespeare's comics, and to compare that with the readier response the same audience may make to the anguish of Hamlet or the sufferings of King Lear, to realise that comedy is often circumscribed by time and place in a way that tragedy is not. . . .

It is best to come to Rabelais with the minimum of preconceptions, letting his text guide us to the books which the scholar must read, if he is to be of use to those who turn to him for help and elucidation, and if he is to make Rabelais's comedy come more fully back to life. Such sources range from Plato's *Philebus,* to Lucian, Plutarch, Homer and Virgil among the ancients, to dry works of legal, medical and linguistic erudition, dating from his own and earlier times.

To these classical sources must be added Christian ones, especially the Bible and the writings of admired contemporaries such as Erasmus. These classical and Christian authorities are not merely placed side by side: they are interwoven. Rabelais, like so many of his contemporaries, is a 'syncretist' making one complex whole out of his ancient learning and his dominant evangelical religion. Rabelais is a Christian for whom Plato, Plutarch, the sceptics, the cynics, the stoics, are not totally discredited rivals; they are, with Lucian, welcome allies in the laughing battle against ignorance, error, superstition, ugliness, and wickedness. Together, they enrich Rabelais's philosophy, without attacking the normative uniqueness of the Christian revelation. . . .

To recognise, to trace, and to study the books which Rabelais and his contemporaries knew requires time, trouble and patient industry. There is always a temptation to push aside the scholarship and leap in to explain what Rabelais must 'obviously' mean in the light of our temporally parochial prejudices. Such a method is disastrous: Rabelais moves in an intellectual world whose commonplace wisdom is now hard-won knowledge; almost all the terms of reference of ordinarily educated humanists have been abandoned by modern European culture, some very recently. To understand Rabelais's wisdom and to appreciate his comic vision means going back in time to a period whose doubts and whose certainties were not our doubts or our certainties: at least, they do not seem to be so at first. Yet within the dusty encyclopaedic erudition of the Renaissance can be found a system of comic wisdom and moral insight which cannot be lightly dismissed as being of only historical interest.

CHRISTIAN AND CLASSICAL VALUES

For Rabelais, the syncretistic learning of evangelical humanists is frequently normative. He seems to have often set himself the task of showing that departures from the norms of evangelical humanist Christianity are not merely wrong, but laughably so. The man who worships the wrong God; does not love his neighbour as himself; worships his belly or his backside; prefers ugliness to beauty; believes he can go against the wisdom of classical adage, proverb or apophthegm, is wrong, certainly, but more than wrong—stupid.

In this book I try to be as clear and precise as possible about these norms. Where they derive from the New Testament, they still partly linger on in general culture; but those deriving from classical times, from philosophical Christianity, from Renaissance legal precepts or Renaissance mythology, have ceased to do so. Not everybody can trot out in order the four cardinal virtues, the seven deadly sins, the three injunctions inscribed on the temple at Delphi . . . And the awe that Rabelais felt for Socrates, Plato, Plutarch or Virgil, has largely evaporated.

The ancient authors whom Rabelais cites are not simply 'sources'. In the ancient authors, sages, apophthegms and myths, Rabelais sought 'authorities'. For Rabelais, as for many of his contemporaries, authority was the key to knowledge. The hieroglyphs of Egypt, the philosophy of Plato, the myths of Greece and Rome, were not simply sources of stylistic ornament or of elaboration: they were examples of a partially veiled revelation of truth to mankind, needing only clarification, unveiling and slight adaptation, to bring them into line with Christianity, itself the greatest revealed authority of them all. . . .

Rabelais seems very odd indeed when read in isolation by a young man or woman battling backwards in time through the veil of the Silver Age of seventeenth-century French classicism. Rabelais is an author of balance, of harmony, of light-hearted laughter and joy, which is in easy harness with a contrasting seriousness and sobriety about humanity—which finds its expression in laughter of another stamp. The importance of this aspect of Renaissance culture in the works of Rabelais has only recently been widely appreciated outside English-speaking countries. It has tended to be both over-emphasised and over-codified. Yet it is a very necessary rectification of the balance, in cases where this basic truth had been lost sight of or underplayed. There is much in Rabelais to remind us of the juxtaposition of tragedy and comedy in Shakespeare, who delighted to make the dishonoured Falstaff play the fool and counterfeit death while the heroic Hotspur dies before our eyes; much to remind us that a chaste Romeo may be balanced by a bawdy Mercutio, to our considerable enrichment, just as there is much that is redolent of the Twelfth-night revel, the pre-Lenten Carnival, the undergraduate farce. . . . Many of Rabelais's jesting passages are balanced by passages of great seriousness. He knew how to laugh at what he loved and admired. . . .

SATIRE WITHOUT HATRED

Rabelais was a good hater, it seems, but this fact does not dominate his works as a whole. Hatred finds its outlets in scathing satire and diatribe more easily than in comedy. Rabelais has his diatribes, but his Chronicles are satirical in ways which subordinate satire to laughter and rarely divorce it from a sense of humour. The hatred, if hatred there be, is evaporated in the process and the mind left more open and purer, whereas hatred leaves it narrower and venomous.

Rabelais knew his Roman satirists and frequently draws upon them. Yet he has little enough in common with Juvenal, Horace or even Persius, where hatred is concerned. A satirist working in the Roman tradition of moral indignation and hatred of wickedness stirs up his reader to just such indignation and hatred, emphasising all that favours these unlovely passions. Where he does make us laugh, such a satirist (as Joachim du Bellay points out in his *Regrets)* exploits not true laughter but that 'bastard laughter' caused by pain and suffering: sardonic laughter. There are passages of that sort in Rabelais's writings, but they are rare. A comic satirist has both a more difficult and a more attractive task. His artistic challenge is to turn evil and error, even at their most frightful and terrible, into sources of amusement and laughter. This is Rabelais's special genius, one not to be found again in French literature until Molière.

Certain kinds of parody are not in the least unkind or destructive. Many examples of indulgent laughter are to be found in his pages. But when we laugh at an idea or a person in another way, we reject them far more satisfactorily than when we increase their stature by dignifying them, and diminishing ourselves, through our sharpened hatred. Rabelais can make his readers laugh at a bloodthirsty bishop who yearns to torture and to kill his enemies as a prologue to boiling them in Hell. And in the end, we do not find ourselves loathing the prelate; we find ourselves laughing his ideas out of court. Faced with a censuring Sorbonne [Parisian university], Rabelais writes pages of sheer delight, which not only make us laugh at the cruel old diehards of that citadel of anti-humanist, anti-evangelical reaction, but make us laugh in such a way that it is impossible to hate them, however totally we dismiss everything they stand for.

Rabelais knew how humane laughter can drive out fear at its most acute.

What makes his Chronicles sometimes difficult for us to disentangle, is that this kind of laughter which leads to mocking rejection is interwoven with the attractive indulgent laughter we reserve, in moments of relaxation, for our innermost beliefs or for objects of awe and veneration.

The sense of balance which Rabelais achieves in his Chronicles is one more at ease with the golden mean conceived as a resolution of Heraclitean tensions than as a wishy-washy compromise; more at ease with a religion that hates the sin and not the sinner, than with the hate-ridden political philosophies of other times or with the hate-ridden rival orthodoxies of his own.

This equilibrium can lead us to the core of Rabelais's comedy.

There is a sense in which *Gargantua* and *Pantagruel* show us a humanist at play. But the stakes Rabelais played for included truth herself and hope of eternal life. The risks he took in this desperate game included poverty, exile and precipitous flight—and might have included, had he not been lucky, torture and prolonged, painful death.

Without powerful and effective patronage these risks would have been certainties. So, naturally, his laughter is not all balance and harmony. The ideas he succeeds in laughing off the stage were not infrequently ones which his enemies held so dear that they would have killed him if they could. He knew from hard experience the risks he was taking. Sensible men do not take such risks lightly.

Rabelais combined wide erudition with acute comic

awareness: even his moments of laughing relaxation are likely to be unexpectedly profound. When he turns the light of his comic vision on to the darker or obscurer parts of the human condition, he finds a way to wisdom which leaves the mere theorists of comedy and laughter standing still in their traces. . . .

THE INFLUENCE OF LUCIAN

The importance of Rabelais's taste for Lucian can hardly be overemphasised. That his translation has been lost is a source of real regret. All four of Rabelais's definitely authentic Chronicles are evidently influenced by Lucian. The comparative easiness of Lucian's Greek made him one of the most accessible of classical writers; the lightness and happiness of his style was greatly appreciated by readers who were not over-supplied with lighter literature. Those who could not read him in Greek turned eagerly to the Latin translations, or else enjoyed him at second-hand, as transmuted into the pure gold of the *Colloquies,* in which Erasmus uses Lucianesque techniques of witty dialogue to deflate those errors in contemporary Christianity which seem to him to correspond to the pagan objects of Lucian's mockery. Lucian's influence on Rabelais's *forma mentis* [the shaping of his intellectual views] was so profound that one can postulate that there was a natural sympathy between the two authors, just as there was between Lucian and Erasmus. . . .

IMITATION OF ANCIENT AUTHORS

Great Renaissance authors who strove to emulate classical models did not do so slavishly. In choosing and emulating their models, authors of importance did not sacrifice their originality. Their approach to imitation is admirably summed up by Petrarch: 'An imitator,' he says, 'must take care to see that what he writes should be similar to his model, not identical with it'. He goes on to state that a successful imitator is not like a portrait painter, in whose case, the more a work resembles its model, the better it is. The similarity true artists should aim at is different, being that of a son's resemblance to his father. There will be many differences of detail. 'So too we should take care to see that, while something should be similar, many things should be dissimilar. Even the similarity should be so hidden as not to be detected except by silent investigation'. The best imitation is one where the similarity can be 'perceived rather than put into words'.

That even a writer of genius should be prepared to imitate classical models was one of the fundamental axioms of Renaissance aesthetics. Rabelais's striving to be the French Lucian is no different in kind from Ronsard's desire to be the French Pindar or Joachim du Bellay's aim of being the French Horace. Imitation of classical or Italian models was believed to be the way in which literature in the vulgar tongues could aspire to be placed beside those Greek and Latin works which were so universally admired. . . .

Rabelais sought his authority from a wide range of classical thinkers and from a multitude of contemporary writers. Whenever possible he seems to have selected his material from those aspects of his authors which had entered into the popularising compendia of the time: in this way he ensured that even moderately educated men could follow much of what he had to say. . . .

Since this is so, it follows that Rabelais's Chronicles are only 'popular' on the surface. They are the works of a highly-placed professional man considered unusually learned in a century outstanding for its scholarship and erudition. Behind the protection of powerful statesmen connected with his native Touraine and Anjou he turned his comic vision on to the follies and errors of his time, and addressed himself to readers of some real culture, while avoiding the error of only amusing the specialists. . . .

We do a disservice to Rabelais if we try and turn him into a popular author, especially if the overt or covert motivation for this is political. We do an equal disservice if we think of Rabelais primarily as a monk or as a doctor. He was never confined within the traditional horizons of such professions. At the times of writing his Chronicles his Christian humanism was widely based and growing wider still. Together with many of the best minds of his day in a score of European kingdoms and principalities he was convinced that the way to truth lay in a return to the sources. Vital truths, it was widely believed, could only be re-acquired by studying ancient texts in the original tongues. Where this concerns Rabelais, it includes a yearning to know one's New Testament in Greek—and if possible one's Old Testament in Hebrew, or at least in versions based on the *veritas Hebraica,* the true Hebrew text. *Mutatis mutandis* [all changes considered], in all areas of knowledge, the same applied. . . .

THE ATTACK ON SCHOLASTIC METHODS

Humanist Frenchmen of Rabelais's generation had received a thorough grounding in rhetoric and dialectic as codified by the scholastic philosophers. They mostly rebelled against it. Classical rhetoric aimed at enhancing the elegance of oratory; dialectic claimed to sharpen argumentative and logical skills. Ideally, both disciplines were concerned with truth: dialectic led towards a knowledge of the truth, sifting the true from the false; rhetoric made truth, once acquired, more readily understandable, more widely known, more persuasive in its force. But the codification of such skills by mediaeval scholastic theologians, lawyers, philosophers and preachers had led to barren battles of words. So the old scholastic methods were under attack, largely in the light of a renewed appreciation of classical rhetoricians such as Aphthonius and Quintilian. As for dialectic, Rabelais, like many others, was suspicious of chop-logic when divorced from the guidance of revered authorities and revealed truth. A word from Socrates or from Christ is worth volumes of *logomachia.* Rabelais achieves many of his comic effects by using rhetorical and dialectical techniques which his public was schooled to appreciate, having suffered an old-fashioned education themselves, and having also accepted new approaches to education, not least in these domains. When, in *Pantagruel* and *Gargantua,* Rabelais laughs at the gods of scholastic dialectic—at Peter of Spain, say, and his *Parva Logicalia*—his readers knew where he stood in the renewed controversies. When he bases the structure of part of the *Tiers Livre* on ideas drawn from Aphthonius and Quintilian, they were surer still.

Even without the technical knowledge which Rabelais took for granted, a modern reader sensitive to both elegant and comic oratory and to the use and abuse of argument will find his enjoyment of Rabelais greatly enhanced. But his enjoyment will lack an important dimension if it is not based upon a sensitive appreciation of what passed for authorities amongst the humanists.

With such knowledge, and such sensitivity, Rabelais's laughter can blossom into what at best it is: philosophical comedy of lasting value.

One final word. Rabelais's comic philosophy is firmly based on the twin pillars of classical and Christian verities. The student of Rabelais will find that even some of the best-known scholars are weak on theology—yet it was for theological *nuances* that people like Rabelais suffered, died, fled into exile, or inflicted the same anguish on others. As for the Bible, it is a major source of Rabelais's jests and wisdom. The effect of ignoring the theological dimension is to knock away one of the pillars on which Rabelais's intellectual achievement stands.

CHAPTER 3

The Forms of
Renaissance
Poetry

Renaissance
Literature

The Conventions of Petrarchan Poetry

Leonard Forster

The poetry of Francesco Petrarch, first published in the late 1300s, inspired a vogue for love poetry in the sonnet form that lasted over two hundred years, influencing poets in every European country. According to noted Renaissance scholar Leonard Forster, the essence of Petrarchan poetry is the melancholy longing of the poet for a beloved who is pure and essentially out of reach. The poet's powerful longing leads him to embrace a language of hyperbole and paradox, for normal language cannot possibly capture the beauty of the beloved or the depth of the lover's frustration. Petrarch's recurring paradoxes concerning love and death, freedom and servitude, pleasure and pain, and his similes concerning the beloved's beauty became the staples of Renaissance love poetry. In Forster's analysis, the stance of the poet involves self-pity and masochism, but it also involves self-reflection and vulnerability. The following essay is excerpted from Forster's seminal book on Petrarch, *The Icy Fire*.

In the fifteenth and early sixteenth centuries Petrarch's influence throughout Europe had been great; he was seen as a Christian humanist, whose concern was with the development of the human personality in accordance with the wisdom of the ancients and within the framework of the Christian religion. It was this side of Petrarch which found expression in Latin prose—in his letters and especially in the treatises *Secretum* [Secrets] (1343), *De vita solitaria* [*On the Solitary Life*] (1346), *De remediis utriusque fortunae* [*Remedies Against Fortune*] (1366), and *De ignorantia* [*On Ignorance*] (1367). The vogue for Petrarch as a vernacular poet came later. It is with this that the following pages are concerned; with petrarchism as a European phenomenon, with the conventions which developed out of Petrarch's poetry rather than with the *Canzoniere* [Songbook] (1347) or the *Trionfi* [Triumphs]. These conventions are concerned with love poetry; as [German scholar Hans W.] Pyritz and others have pointed out, they form the second great international system of conventional love, between the chivalric love of the middle ages and the romantic love of the eighteenth and nineteenth centuries. Some of them are not dead yet. They rest, like those of the troubadours, on one basic convention which sets the woman on a pedestal, and we are introduced to a world in which women dominate, seen through the eyes of men who languish and adore. This convention itself was a literary fiction to compensate for a real state of affairs in which it was a man's world and a violent one at that. But there are important differences between the chivalric and petrarchistic systems.

Troubadour and minnesang poetry does not exclude the treatment of final satisfaction in love, though the convention only permits it in certain circumstances: the very existence of the alba or song of lovers' parting at dawn indicates this clearly. Though the prevailing tone is one of lover's lament, what the lover is lamenting is the withholding of favours which *might* be granted. With the *dolce stil nuovo* [sweet new style poetry] in late thirteenth-century Italy the lady is assimilated to the divine, of which she becomes a sort of symbol. Love is equated with virtue, the pursuit of the good; sensual satisfaction is excluded almost by definition, and the lover's lament no longer maintains its central place since the beloved is unattainable *ex hypothesi* [by definition].

A POETRY OF MELANCHOLY

Petrarch takes up and assimilates both these traditions. Perhaps his original intention was to express genuine frustration in love through the inherited conventions of the *dolce stil nuovo*. He oscillates between restrained wooing and distant adoration. But the beloved Laura [the subject of his love poems] remains for him a real woman, whose beauty intoxicates him and whose physical presence excites him. Hence he can hymn her various physical attributes—eyes, hair, skin etc.—and do so with a better conscience in that she represents physical *and* spiritual perfection. Nonetheless, love is not a virtue in itself, for he realises that his love is a passion and that passion is sinful. But he wants both passion and purification, and cannot always balance the two. He longs to be free of his hopeless devotion and knows that he cannot escape. The fundamental note of his poetry is therefore melancholy and resignation, in which for more than thirty years he may fairly be said to wallow. He designates this state of affairs by a characteristic antithetical paradox: he speaks of 'dolendi voluptas' [voluptuous sadness].

This and similar conflicts find expression in a wide range of antitheses which run through his whole poetry and are characteristic of his work. In his finest poems they express the delicate balance of opposites, precarious and ever-endangered, which is Petrarch's own personal note. Later generations were less interested in the balance than in the antitheses, which they endlessly elaborated and exploited for their own purposes. This elaboration and exploitation is the essence of petrarchism. The point from which it starts can be seen, for instance, in two of the most influential sonnets in the *Canzoniere*—and the most petrarchistic, almost as though Petrarch were parodying himself. . . . They were so influential that it is worth considering one of them in some detail.

> Can it be love that fills my heart and brain?
> If love, dear God, what is its quality?
> If it is good, why does it torture me?
> If evil, why this sweetness in my pain?
> If I burn gladly, why do I complain?
> If I hate burning, why do I never flee?
> O life-in-death, O lovely agony,
> How can you rule me so, if I'm not fain?
>   And if I'm willing, why do I suffer so?—
> By such contrary winds I'm blown in terror
> In a frail and rudderless bark on open seas,
> Ballasted all with ignorance and error.
> Even my own desire I do not know;
> I burn in winter and in high summer freeze.

The octave consists of a series of rhetorical questions, each embodying a contrast. The formulation is intellectual, ratiocinative, but extremely simple; it is built to a pattern of 'if-why' for the first six lines, the impending monotony of which is then broken by the exclamation consisting of two paradoxical antithetical pairs, "O life-in-death, O lovely agony," which not only sum up in concentrated images the state of affairs described in discursive terms in the preceding lines but serve as a kind of invocation to Love itself, who is then addressed in a direct question. The first line of the sestet concludes the intellectual argument; the next lines deal in contrasting imagery—contrary winds, frail bark, rudderless on the high seas, light in wisdom, heavy with error. The last line but one breaks the series of images, before it too becomes monotonous, by the simple statement of confused desire (which, however, is itself an implied antithesis) and the sonnet culminates in two antithetical paradoxes. The first person appears in the very first line. . . . But this 'I' that speaks is not so individualised that it must be Petrarch and no one else.

THE PARADOX OF PETRARCHAN LOVE

Prodigal as Petrarch is with antitheses and oxymora in this poem, he never allows them to become wearisome; there is a nice balance of ratiocination and imagery, and the central seventh line of the sonnet forms an ecstatic cry, unlike any of the other lines, which at the same time sums up in four words, 'viva morte', 'dilettoso male' ('life-in-death' and 'lovely agony'), the paradox of Petrarchan love.

What later generations found interesting in Petrarch was precisely these antitheses and oxymora, of which Petrarch himself makes liberal but discreet use. Conceits of this kind could become the staple of 'wit' in the following centuries because, though they were the product of deep emotion, the formulation of them was intellectual and achieved in simple terms. They involved no technical terminology of the kind which makes troubadour or minnesang or *dolce stil nuovo* poetry difficult for us to understand or translate today without a good deal of specialised knowledge. . . . The only term in the sonnet discussed above which could perhaps fall into this category is the word *amor* [love] itself. Petrarch's conceits use simple concepts and concrete images: heat–cold, flame–ice; peace–war; the candle (the beloved) which attracts the moth (the lover); the salamander (the lover living amid the flames of his passion); the hooked fish (the lover); the sun (the beloved); so concrete in fact that they could later form the basis of love emblems, which exploited them pictorially. . . . Though Petrarch, like any great poet, is by definition impossible to translate, his imagery and his stylistic devices could be used in any language, more easily indeed than those of any poet of comparable stature known to me. They could be separated from Petrarch's personal ethos which had brought them into being, and then be used for a wide variety of purposes. Petrarch had forged for posterity a poetic idiom of great flexibility, which could be noncommittal or serious, as desired; which could be used to parade fictitious emotions or to conceal real ones; which permitted intense poetic concentration or endless elaboration. The drama and even the novel show that the petrarchistic idiom became the obligatory language of love.

PETRARCHAN CONCEITS

Before going any further it would be as well to classify some of these conceits. They may be set out under the following heads:

1 External: praise of the lady; the lady's accomplishments; objects belonging to the lady; celebration of the place of lovers' meeting; meeting the beloved in dreams.

2 Internal: the nature of love; relations between lovers; the effects of love; rejection of the beloved; death motifs.

3 Love as a cosmic phenomenon.

Praise of the lady, however indirect, is the basic subject matter of petrarchistic poetry, as it was for Petrarch himself. She is physical and spiritual perfection, which it is impossible to express adequately; hence any attempt must be in superlative, hyperbolical, terms, e.g. the lady's splendour makes the day brighter and puts the sun to shame. Her individual beauties can be added together to make an icon of perfection, as Petrarch himself does in a sonnet:

> Her head was of fine gold, her face of warm snow, her eyebrows ebony, her eyes were two stars, from which Love did not bend his bow in vain; pearls and red roses where sorrow received [in the heart] formed fair and burning words; her sighs were flame, her tears crystal.

Before the end of the fifteenth century in Italy the lady's beauties were codified—the golden hair, the fine white hands, the black eyes, the ebony eyebrows, the roses and lilies in her cheeks, her pearly teeth, her coral lips, her breasts like globes of alabaster. (The lady was traditionally blonde, so that Shakespeare was making a conscious and piquant departure from tradition in writing sonnets to a *dark* lady). The lady's beauties could be praised by metaphorical description (diamond-like countenance) or mythological association (lips sweeter than Venus' lips), or by expressing their effect on the lover (hair a snare that captures him). It

was common for individual poems, or even whole cycles of
poems, to be devoted to just one feature of the beloved;
Shakespeare's jest about sonnets on one's mistress's eye-
brow was well founded. Petrarch himself had written three
canzoni on Laura's eyes, and the theme constantly recurs,
e.g. in Janus Lernutius' Latin cycle *Ocelli* (1579). The lady's
eyes are like two suns, they put the sun to flight and illuminate the night. In the same way objects belonging to the lady
could be hymned: rings, necklaces, bracelets, furniture, pet
dogs and birds, even fleas; or things that had merely passed
through her hands (Ben Jonson's 'Drink to me only with
thine eyes'). This development appears to have its origin in
Petrarch's two sonnets on Laura's portrait. . . .

Her accomplishments were, of course, limitless, but the
most admired among them was her musical ability. . . . Almost all petrarchistic ladies can sing or play an instrument or
both. Places associated with the beloved may be treated; Petrarch usually speaks of scenery in which he wanders in order to meditate upon his love; or (in vain) to forget it. Petrarchists celebrate the place where the first meeting with the
lady occurred, the city or countryside where the lady lives or
which she has recently visited, or the garden, grove or grotto
which was the scene of the first embrace. Actual embraces,
though not by any means unknown, are comparatively rare;
fictional embraces, either imagined or spoken of as occur-
ring in a vision or in a dream, are very common. In Petrarch
dream-themes are of central importance. Whereas the troubadours created a genre in which the physical union of
lovers was deemed to have taken place, the Petrarchan convention could envisage it only in dreams. . . .

PLEASURE AND PAIN

Important as these external themes are, they are really subordinate to the internal ones, which are basically concerned
with the effect the beloved produces on the lover, Here we
may begin with commonplaces expressing the bitter-sweet
nature of love. The interpenetration of pleasure and pain,
and the satisfaction which could be derived from holding
these two opposites in an uneasy balance, is basic in Petrarch's work and becomes the fundamental theme of the
petrarchistic convention. It is in accordance with this dual-
ism that the lady should be seen as the 'sweet enemy' (Petrarch uses the phrase 'dolce nemica' more than once), that

love should be compared to war and be described in a wealth of military imagery. Allied to this is the freedom–servitude paradox—the service of the lady is the highest freedom—and cognate imagery of prisons, bondage, etc. The theme of the theft of the soul or, more often, the heart (Sidney's 'My

The Language of Desire

By the time the English poets of the Renaissance began to study Petrarch, his poetry had been imitated and analyzed for nearly 200 years. The long-lasting power of his poetry is largely attributable to its flexibility in describing the many psychological states involved in romantic desire. Scholar Gary Waller provides the following succinct summary of the essence of Petrarchism.

Let us first, then, look at Petrarchism as a flexible rhetoric of erotic desire. It rests on a series, even a system, of conventions about how love should be described. It sees love as a frustrating though inspiring experience, characterized by a melancholy yet obsessive balance between desire and hopelessness, possibility and frustration. Its fundamental characteristic is conflict, or—the key term in Petrarchism—'paradox', usually expressed as a balance of powerful opposites, forces in or outside the lover which simultaneously move him on and hold him back. . . .

Now to the particulars of the system. Petrarchan poetry is written predominantly in the subject position of a suffering male lover contemplating a beloved's, usually (though not exclusively) a woman's, effects on him. From thousands of poems, a composite beloved can be readily composed, her physical parts described or modestly alluded to. She might have, in the conventional conceits of Ralegh's 'Nature that washt her hands in milk', such features as 'eyes of light', 'violet breath', 'lips of jelly'; typically her hair would be likened to wires, 'crisped', in the words of another Ralegh poem, her breasts compared to young does, and so forth. Such charms would often be set forth, either rapturously or satirically, in a catalogue poem (or 'blazon') listing the ravishing physical characteristics of the Petrarchan mistress, with her 'fayre golden hayres', her doe-like breasts, rosy cheeks, and other physical charms. The most crucial characteristic is the contrast between her fair appearance and her icy or stony heart which inevitably causes the lover suffering.

Gary Waller, *English Poetry of the Sixteenth Century*, 2nd edition. New York: Longman, 1993, p. 75.

true love hath my heart and I have his') is sometimes combined with this; the lover's soul is sweetly imprisoned in the beloved's body. When the soul is stolen the lover is a mere walking corpse; this links up with death imagery, of which more below. Souls can also be exchanged—through a glance or through a kiss; this theme is widely exploited, e.g. by Johannes Secundus in his celebrated *Basia* (1539).

The hovering balance of opposites appears as total loss of self-possession; the senses are confused, the lover quite literally does not know whether he is coming or going, even the sense of individuality is lost. Michael Marullus can write:

> I am shaken, I am in despair, I am tortured and pulled this way and that; I do not even know who I am or where I am.

This state of affairs can be expressed in nautical imagery: the frail skiff adrift on the sea of passion.

It is thus not surprising that lovers sometimes decide to renounce love. Petrarch himself never gives up. He rails at love—though never at the beloved. Petrarchists, who are not necessarily tied to one woman, have a variety of motifs, e.g. scorn of women who keep their lovers dangling for ever; inner justification for rejection of the beloved (she is unworthy of his devotion); love is madness, illusory, mutable. Petrarchists often praise the 'golden freedom' which they regain on rejecting love, but of course they lose it again immediately; the renunciation of love can only be a temporary aberration.

HARDNESS OF HEART

Relations between lovers are in a constant state of delicious fluidity; if the lady is unkind, the poet is overcome with pain; if she is gracious, his delight knows no bounds. Only hyperbolic expression can do justice to this state of affairs. The classic petrarchistic situation is that the lady is hard-hearted; love has struck the poet alone but spared the lady, and he begs that love should strike her too. The lady is often shown as enjoying the lover's pain; she is crueller than a tiger. If there is something of the masochist about the petrarchistic lover, there is something of the sadist in his picture of his beloved. There ensues a whole repertoire of conceits about the lady's hardness of heart, usually expressed in comparative form—harder than stone, steel or diamond—and about her coldness. The various images for the whiteness of her body—alabaster, snow—can be aptly combined with these.

The physical effects of love offer a wide field for elaboration: the lover grows thin, cannot sleep, loses colour, acquires a death-like pallor; his tears make the river rise higher; his sighs can act as messengers of love; they become a tempest blowing upon the fire of love which is not put out by tears. Some petrarchists go in for continuous weeping and live on their tears. . . .

The commonplace of love as a fire is of course very ancient, and Petrarch used it extensively. The flames become a shorthand symbol for love itself, as in French classical tragedy, and the symbol still persists in our phrase 'an old flame'. Petrarch compares himself to a salamander living in the flames of love, and this image is widely used by his successors. The antithesis between the fire of love and the icy heart of the lady is endlessly worked out (even to the extent that the chilly lady induces a feverish cold in the lover).

LOVE AND DEATH

A convention working with hyperbole inevitably utilises imagery concerned with death. If the lover's longing is not fulfilled he dies. On the other hand the very presence of the beloved can, as we have seen, have an overwhelming physical effect, which itself may cause death. . . .

> When I am completely concentrated in the direction where the fair face of my lady shines, and that light, which burns me and little by little destroys me utterly within, still remains in my mind, I, fearing that my heart will leave me, and seeing the approaching end of my life, go away, like a blind man, deprived of the light [of reason], who goes he knows not where but goes nonetheless away. So it is that I flee before the blows of death; but not so quickly that desire cannot come with me, as it always does. I leave in silence, for my dead [i.e. unspoken] words would make people weep, and I prefer my tears to be shed alone.

Just as the masochism of the lover is complemented by the imputed sadism of the lady, so the necessity of death is complemented by a death-wish. Petrarch says that if he thought that death would end his sorrows he would kill himself. But of course the church forbids suicide, so he would escape from love's frying-pan only to fall into hell fire; later petrarchists, for whom the idea of death has largely lost concrete meaning in this context, are not troubled by this particular scruple. For them death and life appear as states of mind, into which the lover can fall according to circumstances—if the lady is cruel he is dead, but she can revive him at once by kindness; 'life' and 'death' are dispensed by her. In this way the lady can be equated with the life and the death of the lover, a paradox which is widely used in the seventeenth century—lovers are dead alive. . . .

It is not difficult to systematise the totality of commonplaces of this kind, and critics often speak of a 'petrarchistic system'. It is doubtful whether petrarchists themselves were conscious of the existence of such a thing. The convention was coherent and pervasive, it was invaluable, it was part of the air they breathed, and many of them probably thought very little about it. What we see as a system was for them a natural mode of conventional utterance and conventional behaviour in certain circumstances. The concept of a petrarchistic system is, however, a useful critical tool, as long as this proviso is borne in mind. It is perhaps better to speak of a flexible convention which expresses itself in an arsenal of commonplaces, images or *topoi*, which poets could use in ever-varying combinations for whatever purpose they liked. As they worked within a well defined tradition, there were certain natural bounds to the use they made of them. Nonetheless, these commonplaces were the ready-made bricks with which accomplished artists could fashion structures of great originality and beauty.

Edmund Spenser's *The Faerie Queene:* Educating the Reader

Russell J. Meyer

Understanding Edmund Spenser's *The Faerie Queene* requires some familiarity with the culture of Renaissance England, according to Russell J. Meyer, professor of English at the University of Houston. Spenser's long epic-romantic poem is deeply informed by the educational ideals and values of Renaissance humanism, and it is shaped by both classical and Italian models of epic poetry. Further, the poem reflects important moments of English history in an allegorical way, especially England's religious controversies, and it contains unabashed praise of Queen Elizabeth and the Protestant settlement in England. But Spenser's deeper purpose, according to Meyer, is to educate his readers about the challenges faced by true Christians in a world of hypocrisy and self-deception.

It is virtually impossible to understand *The Faerie Queene* without understanding something of the age that produced it: the English Renaissance. Every era may, perhaps, be characterized as "an era of change," but that appellation seems especially appropriate for the Renaissance, that vast period which stretches (in England at least) from the ascension of the first Tudor monarch, Henry VII, in 1485, through the restoration of the monarchy in 1660. This period saw momentous discoveries—the New World not being the least of those; the rise of new sciences and technologies, including the advent of movable print and the inexpensive books this technology permitted; a new cosmology, promulgated by the new astronomy that began to take seriously the notion of a heliocentric universe, one in which all the known world did not necessarily reflect God's grand plan for order and harmony; greatly revised forms of government leading to a renewed emphasis on education; and new (or at least significantly revised) forms of accepted religion. All of these factors are examined in greater detail elsewhere, but let us at least give three of them more than just a passing glance: the new monarchies, the Reformation, and the role of Tudor humanism.

THE HOUSE OF TUDOR AND THE REFORMATION

In 1485, Henry VII came to the throne, uniting the warring factions of Lancaster and York and establishing the Tudor dynasty, which was to last until the death of his granddaughter and Spenser's queen, Elizabeth I, in 1603. Henry brought with him to the throne not only peace, but also the English version of what has come to be known as the "New Monarchies." Much earlier, in the Middle Ages, centralized and powerful monarchies had existed throughout Europe, but they had given way to loose conglomerations of powerful and less powerful nobles who allowed the king to rule, either for the sake of convenience or for the sake of form. Now, however, powerful central monarchies were being renewed as the kings of Europe asserted their dominance over their nobles and the common people. Henry was the first English king to do just that, consolidating power in his own hands and turning the monarchy from symbol to reality.

But he also brought something entirely new to English rule: recognizing that government can best operate under the guidance of able bureaucrats, he stressed the importance of ability rather than mere birth as an instrument of advancement in the court and government. This policy played a large role in establishing the importance of education among the English, for if ability and not birth is a prime requisite for political success, if commoner and noble must compete equally for advancement, then education takes on an immensely more important role than it could ever have had in a society in which governing was limited to those of privileged birth.

The change in the role of education had barely gotten underway when it was supplemented by vast changes in religion as well, changes that had far-reaching effects on both politics and education. In 1517, Martin Luther posted his 95 Theses on the doors of the cathedral in Wittenberg, effectively beginning his attempts to reform the established church. In 1521 Henry VIII, second of the Tudor kings, wrote a tract denouncing Luther and arguing for the supremacy of the Roman Church. Thirteen years later, having earned the honorific title "Defender of the Faith" for his literary efforts, Henry broke with Rome over his right to divorce Catherine of Aragon and marry the English Anne Boleyn, who, he hoped, would prove able to produce for him a son and heir. Religion, always an important issue in the Middle Ages, was now even more crucial for practical and nationalistic rather than just theological reasons.

By the time Spenser began work on *The Faerie Queene,* England had undergone vast changes in its religious orientation: from Catholic to Protestant under Henry VIII, violently back to Catholicism in the reign of his elder daughter, Mary, and then back once more just as violently to Protestantism under Elizabeth. It is little wonder religious and theological issues play such a large role in *The Faerie Queene* and other literature of the day.

HUMANISM AND EDUCATION

But religion was not the only subject of change. By the middle of the second decade of the sixteenth century, classical texts were widely available in Europe, thanks largely to the efforts of Aldius Mantuis, founder of the Aldine Press, which, beginning in 1511, had used the relatively new technology of movable print to issue inexpensive editions of virtually the entire corpus of classical literature as we know it today. And, thanks to the movement of learning from the East, there were scholars available in Europe who could teach Greek, so the new texts were not wasted on ignorant readers. By the time Henry VIII died in 1547, the classics were the mainstay of English education. St. Paul's School had been founded in 1509, and it was soon followed by many institutions devoted to the new education. By the time Elizabeth came to the throne in 1558, such educators as Roger Ascham and Spenser's schoolmaster, Richard Mulcaster, had established the new education as the norm.

Education flourished in the sixteenth century for three reasons: the availability of books; the need for educated courtiers in the government of the Tudors; and the new interests in the classics and in scholarship, thanks to those whom we have since called the "humanists."

A popular misconception about the Renaissance is that

these humanists, placing their interests in humanity and an anthropocentric universe, abandoned religion, preferring the secular life. Nothing, in fact, could be less correct. True, the humanists were more likely to concern themselves with

Edmund Spenser

things of this world, to perceive the world in less theological terms than their medieval ancestors. They were more likely to concentrate on the present life on earth rather than on the afterlife in Paradise, and they were likely to hold Greek and Roman—pagan—authors in far higher regard than their medieval forebears. But they were nonetheless profoundly religious, and their religion pervaded their everyday life. One need look no further than Book I of *The Faerie Queene*, "The Legend of Holinesse," with its familiar allusions to religious and theological concerns, to see the extent to which religion was held dear by the humanists and their students.

But the knights Spenser uses as his examples "to fashion a gentleman or noble person" are politically and socially involved, not merely contemplative. Their role is in the world of action, not the world of prayer, although prayer always forms an important part of their lives. In the newly rediscovered classical literature the Renaissance humanists found precisely the examples for behavior that best suited their needs. The educated man (and it was virtually always men who received formal education) was trained to play important roles in governing the nation, an ideal expressed in such classical authors as Cicero and Quintilian. This classical concept did not fit well with the medieval ideal of the contemplative life, but, in this new era, it added the respectability of tradition to the necessity of practice. . . .

AN EPIC-ROMANCE

Strictly speaking, *The Faerie Queene* is not an epic. After all, it does not reach the requisite 12 books, nor is it, like the *Iliad* or the *Odyssey*, an account of the exploits of a single hero, unless we pervert its narrative to claim such a primary role for Prince Arthur. Nonetheless, it does have what film publicists like to call "epic sweep," and it certainly concerns itself with the origins and worth of the English nation as well as Faerie Land. It is closer, though, to a form popular in contemporary Italy, the epic-romance (or romance-epic). It is influenced not only by classical models, but also by two great Italian poems of the sixteenth century, Torquato Tasso's *Gerusalemme Liberata* and Lodovico Ariosto's *Orlando Furioso*. The influence of these two works is so pervasive, in fact, that even to list specific episodes and shorter passages for which Spenser was indebted to Tasso and Ariosto would take several pages. But a mere list of passages would still not do justice to the influence particularly of Ariosto on Spenser's plans and methods for *The Faerie Queene.* The difficulties many readers have perceived with the episodic, disjointed nature of Books III and IV, for example, become far less problematic when the Ariostan methods are taken into account. In general, an understanding of Italian Renaissance literature is central to a fuller appreciation of not just *The Faerie Queene,* but other sixteenth-century English literature as well. . . .

The Letter to Ralegh

Dated 1589 and appearing with the first published version of *The Faerie Queene,* Spenser's letter to his friend Sir Walter Ralegh may reflect his early thoughts on the poem. The letter is dated 23 January 1589 but may in fact have been written earlier, perhaps originally, in fact, even to some other recipient. There are inconsistencies in the letter, deviations from the poem it purports to describe, that make the 1589 date suspect. But there are also comments that promote a better understanding of Spenser's view of his own poem. In particular, as he expresses it in the letter, Spenser sees a specific educational purpose for *The Faerie Queene:* "to fashion a gentleman or noble person in vertuous and gentle discipline." That purpose colors not only the events Spenser presents to us in the poem, but his method of presentation as well, for he continually seems to be attempting to ensure that his reader will indeed be "fashioned"—that is, educated—in the virtues he presents in his heroes.

We should also note in the letter Spenser's specific praises of Queen Elizabeth, for portraying her and her nation never seems to have been far from his mind. Furthermore, his remarks about Gloriana and Prince Arthur help us better understand their allegorical significances. In Gloriana, he says, "I meane glory in my generall intention, but in my particular I conceiue the most excellent and glorious person of our soueraine the Queene, and her kingdome in Faery land." And with Arthur he means to "sette forth magnificence."

Such remarks also help make clear that Spenser intended his poem to be read allegorically: there are, he says, those who would prefer their lessons in a more straightforward manner, but he has preferred to present them "thus clowdily enwrapped in Allegoricall deuices." . . .

READING THE ALLEGORY OF *THE FAERIE QUEENE*

Most modern readers find the general surface of *The Faerie Queene* relatively difficult to follow. After all, the language is archaic, even by Elizabethan standards, and the values and events Spenser portrays are not always the most compatible with our own experiences. Even those who overcome the linguistic and intellectual barriers often find themselves faced with a still more difficult impasse: the allegory.

Spenser makes clear in his letter to Ralegh that he considers his poem "a continued Allegory, or darke conceit." Allegory should be relatively easy to define. We might say that allegory occurs "when the events of a narrative obviously and continuously refer to another simultaneous structure of events or ideas, whether historical events, moral or philosophical ideas, or natural phenomena." One need not read very far into *The Faerie Queene,* however, to realize that such a definition is inadequate for this poem, for at times the allegory is neither obvious nor continuous, although we have no doubt that it is there. Let us, though, for the moment, be content that there are correspondences between the narrative of *The Faerie Queene* and "historical events, moral or philosophical ideas, or natural phenomena" of concern to Spenser and his contemporary readers. It is in the relationship of the narrative to these events, ideas, and phenomena that we will find the allegory, if like Spenser's contemporaries, we can read the poem allegorically. . . .

We must, then, come face to face with the allegory, no matter how daunting the prospect. But how are we to read the allegory, to confront the difficulty not just of reading on a literal level a poem that is often frustratingly complex, but also of simultaneously recognizing that the poem has several layers or shades of meaning, some of which are not necessarily compatible with others?

In many ways, reading *The Faerie Queene* is unlike reading any other work of art, for it demands more than just a willing suspension of disbelief, but also a recognition that normal interpretations of texts do not necessarily hold here. We must be willing to recognize and appreciate not only the literal level of the story, the narrative, as it were, but also that each character, each action, has a meaning beyond the literal. In addition, there may be more than one such meaning and the meanings may shift, Proteus-like. A lion may represent Henry VIII, the Defender of the Faith, in one canto, and something horrid in another. It looks like the same lion, sounds like the same lion—but has become a very different allegorical figure.

The tendency among some modern readers is to dismiss such inconsistencies or to criticize Spenser for being something his contemporaries never would have expected him to be: consistent within the entire work, or at least within its individual books. If we are to read this poem well, however, we must dismiss our own demands for allegorical and narrative consistency, settling instead for the rich textures Spenser achieves through his infinite variety. We must be willing to set aside our preconceptions of how narratives, even allegories, should work, and we must be willing to allow the shifts Spenser demands; without such an attitude, we cannot successfully read *The Faerie Queene*.

Perhaps the easiest way of considering the allegory and narrative in *The Faerie Queene* is to follow A.C. Hamilton's advice in his edition of the poem and think of it as analogous to a dream. In a dream, events are connected in only the most tenuous ways, yet the dreamer doesn't question those connections. The same can be said for the poem; if we look for logical connections among its parts, we may be both confused and disconcerted. If, on the other hand, we are willing to accept that at one moment a lion may represent Henry VIII and all that is good in British history and at another the Roman Catholic Church and all that a loyal Renaissance Englishman might see as horrid, then we can get along with the poem. If we demand consistency of the surface narrative, then we are almost bound to be disappointed, just as we would be disappointed by our dreams if we really demanded such consistency of them.

There is a kind of consistency throughout the narrative of *The Faerie Queene,* but it is not the same kind of consistency we would expect from a nineteenth-century novel: Spenser is not writing a Renaissance *David Copperfield,* and to expect the same sorts of narrative techniques from him that we find in a nineteenth-century novelist would almost surely lead us to disappointment if not disgust. The trick, in short, to reading *The Faerie Queene* is to meet the poem on its own terms, to allow it its multiplicity of meanings and allow ourselves the freedom of interpretation that Spenser demands. Approaching the poem with a complex of preconceptions can result in our being misled into expecting something quite different from what is there.

Reading *The Faerie Queene* also requires that one be aware of multiple narrative voices throughout the poem. There is not, as in most other works of literature, a single narrator who is "reliable" or "unreliable," "omniscient" or "objective." At times the narrator who serves as our guide in *The Faerie Queene* is wholly objective, at times fully omniscient, at times naive. In fact, there are many portions of the poem where one senses more than a single narrator at work, as if there is a second voice, one we might call "the poet" (or even "Spenser") rather than just the "narrator." This is the voice that tells us that the "haven is nigh at hand" or that he intends to "delay until another canto" finishing an event or that he is "exhausted." This narrator serves as our guide, in effect, not presenting the chronology of events, but rather guiding our responses to what goes on in the poem. Spenser often uses this second (or "secondary") narrator to color our responses by giving us some generalizations at the opening of a canto that will determine how we are to react as that canto progresses. At the same time, however, he never stops playing games with us, giving us one reaction when in fact he wants us to have quite another. At the opening of the canto dealing with Timias and Belphoebe in Book III, for example, he discusses how various types of people are affected by love, spending a few lines on the responses of those of the "baser sort." Timias, hardly the baser sort, responds just as the baser people do—and thus reminds us that, regardless of social position and training, we all have the potential to be base.

Perhaps the most interesting experience in reading *The Faerie Queene,* however, has to do neither with the allegory per se nor with the multiple narrators, but rather with the constant challenges Spenser presents, essentially daring us to fall prey to the sins his various heroes are trying to overcome—and if we are not careful, we will indeed join the heroes in falling prey to those sins. If, for example, we believe that the Redcrosse Knight has actually overcome error by defeating the dragonlike monster Error and her offspring in canto i of Book I, then we are likely to fail to recognize that Redcrosse almost immediately falls into another form of error in believing Archimago just a few stanzas later. In defeating the monster Error, Redcrosse gains a certain confidence in his own abilities—a confidence that we soon learn is entirely unwarranted, for he falls prey to the very worst type of error, accepting hypocrisy as truth. But we can fall prey to precisely the same flaw if we fail to recognize Archimago for what he is. In effect, if we are to learn from the poem, we must recognize very early on what so few of the heroes learn until near the end of their adventures: overcoming the obvious manifestation of a vice does not mean that one has actually overcome that vice; rather, it merely means that one is capable of recognizing it in its most blatant forms. Recognizing the more subtle manifestations is the real test of virtue and the quality Spenser wants his readers to develop. This, in fact, seems to me to be Spenser's main aim in *The Faerie Queene.* Spenser is continually tempting us to fall by portraying sin not as just acceptable, but as almost overwhelmingly attractive. At the same time, we learn how to avoid falling prey to even the most attractive and appealing of vices, so that by the end of the poem, the reader is fully fashioned into that "vertuous and gentle discipline" Spenser sets as his goal.

John Donne and the Metaphysical Poets

Richard Willmott

While John Donne, George Herbert, and Andrew
Marvell are frequently called "metaphysical" poets,
they produced such a wide variety of poetry that
defining the term "metaphysical" becomes very difficult. As scholar Richard Willmott comments in the
following essay, their poetry shares a common striving to capture human "experience" and emotion. Yet
these poets often tried to convey the essence of these
emotions and experiences through unusual images
and analogies, and through the kind of logic that led
critics to first call their poetry "metaphysical."

A study of their careers will show how deeply involved in
the affairs of their time Donne, Herbert and Marvell were.
They were all of them men of wide education and interests
and of considerable ambition and they were all, incidentally,
Members of Parliament; not that that was particularly a path
to power. It is also interesting to note that none of the three
published volumes of poetry, as opposed to individual poems, during his life time. Herbert might well have done so if
he had lived longer, but they did not think of themselves primarily as poets. This also explains the difficulty of some of
the poetry, which was written for a circle of friends rather
than for the public at large. . . .

Donne (1572–1631) was brought up in a Roman Catholic
family that was very much involved in religious and political
struggles, but in time he broke away from the faith of his
youth and later still became an Anglican. . . . He was educated
at Oxford, but unable to take a degree as he was still a
Catholic. He may have then gone to Cambridge and possibly
travelled in Europe before going first to Thavies Inn and then,
in 1592, to Lincoln's Inn. It was necessary to belong to one of

the Inns of Court to become a lawyer, but the Inns also served as a kind of third English university, one situated furthermore in the capital. Donne read widely while he was there and was, according to a contemporary, Sir Richard Baker, 'a great visitor of ladies, a great frequenter of plays, a great writer of conceited verses'. He also met influential people such as the sons of his future employer, Sir Thomas Egerton.

It was after taking part in the naval expeditions to Cadiz and the Azores that he was employed by Sir Thomas, who as Lord Keeper of the Great Seal was a man of considerable influence. However a secret marriage to Ann More, his employer's wife's niece, led to his dismissal in 1602. There followed a long period of frustration, but finally he overcame hopes of secular advancement and a genuine sense of unworthiness, and was ordained in 1615. It is quite probable that Donne wrote most of the *Divine Meditations* during this interim period. In 1616 he was appointed Divinity Reader at Lincoln's Inn and the following year his wife died. In 1621 he was appointed Dean of St Paul's, a position he held until his death in 1631.

One of Donne's patrons was Magdalen Herbert, mother of George Herbert (1593–1633), and well-known for her intellectual and literary interests. Herbert's own learning and his influential family connections led him to expect a successful public career like that of his brother, who was ambassador to Paris and later became Lord Herbert of Cherbury. Although his poetry smacks little of worldly matters his disappointment that this career failed to materialise is clear enough in a poem such as 'Affliction'. . . . In 1626 he was ordained deacon and finally in 1630 he was ordained priest and accepted the living at Bemerton near Salisbury. He led a life of outstanding piety there and in this final period wrote over half the poems in *The Temple* as well as revising the earlier ones. Taken together they can be seen as forming a spiritual autobiography revealing his struggles and disappointments and his final confidence in God's grace. In Donne's religious poetry the struggle still rages, but in Herbert's it has been resolved and there is a note of joyful praise in poems such as 'Easter' that is never heard in Donne.

In one sense the career of Marvell (1621–78) is the reverse of Herbert's, for he moved from a period of quiet retirement in his early thirties to public life. At that point he probably ceased to write poetry apart from a few occasional poems

and political satires. . . . It is to the four years prior to [1653]
that his best-known poems probably belong. They reveal the
tension between the desire for a retired, private life and the
sense that the demands of public life should not be resisted.
The ironic detachment of Marvell's poetry makes it rash to
treat the poems autobiographically, but in 1650 Marvell
could write:

'Tis time to leave the books in dust,
And oil the unusèd armour's rust.

('An Horatian Ode', 5–6)

Nevertheless by the end of the year Marvell had joined Lord
Fairfax, who had retired as commander of the New Model
Army rather than invade Scotland, to act as tutor to his
daughter. 'The Garden' makes clear how strongly Marvell
felt the attractions of seclusion. In 1657, however, he became
Milton's assistant as Latin Secretary to the Council of State
and in 1659 he was elected MP [Member of Parliament] for
Hull, a position which he held for the rest of his life. . . .

LOVE POETRY AND RELIGIOUS POETRY

There is, I suppose, a danger that too much background material will merely seem to emphasise the differences between our own times and those of the metaphysical poets. It
needs to be stressed, therefore, that the poems under consideration are alive and not fossils. Background knowledge
may deepen our understanding and quicken our responses,
but the poems can stand by themselves. The sceptical new-
comer may object that the oldest of these poets was born
over four hundred years ago and that his concerns cannot be
ours, but Donne's uncomfortably honest treatment of death
is typical of his willingness to treat fundamental facts with
the very honesty that we like to pride ourselves is particularly modern. In 'Satire 3' Donne's discussion of the different
churches may seem remote to us, but we can sympathise
with his contempt for those who unthinkingly accept others'
ideas, and with his insistence that we should 'doubt wisely'
but not passively. . . .

The same rejection of received ideas is seen in his treatment of love. The Petrarchan convention of the sighing lover
prostrate at the feet of his cruel mistress is never accepted at
face value. If Donne is the unhappy lover he mocks himself
for saying so in 'whining poetry' or comically exaggerates
his feelings as in 'The Computation'. Where he does hark

back to an earlier tradition it is to the sexually frank one of Ovid's elegies, viewing love with cynicism or imagining himself in bed with his mistress. His treatment of such themes remains, however, strikingly original as in 'The Dream' or 'The Sun Rising'. Marvell too can argue the case for love with vigour and humour in 'To His Coy Mistress' or write of it with subtly ambiguous detachment:

> But sure as oft as women weep,
> It is to be supposed they grieve.

('Mourning', 35–6)

The variety is considerable and includes occasionally in Donne's verse a tender simplicity which speaks directly to us:

> Sweetest love, I do not go,
>   For weariness of thee.

('Song', 1–2)

A number of the love poems also attempt an analysis of love's nature. Marvell's 'The Definition of Love' is more ingenious than convincing, . . . and Donne offers a view of love which approaches the ideal when the platonic and sexual are combined:

> But since my soul, whose child love is,
> Takes limbs of flesh, and else could nothing do,
>   More subtle than the parent is
> Love must not be, but take a body too.

('Air and Angels', 7–10)

It is easy enough to see the continuing appeal of love poetry, but the religious poetry does offer more of a problem, especially to the non-Christian reader. It would be a mistake, however, to view these poems in a historical light as no more than evidence of a series of outmoded theological viewpoints. They are, above all, an account of *human* experience. Donne's fear that God does not love him enough to save him is not so very different from his fear that his mistress may leave him; indeed the imagery overlaps startlingly when he addresses God in these terms:

> for I
> Except you enthrall me, never shall be free,
> Nor ever chaste, except you ravish me.

(*Divine Meditations* 14, 12–14)

A number of Herbert's poems also give us a picture of struggle and doubts, even at times of bitter impatience:

> As good go any where, they say,
>   As to benumb
> Both knees and heart, in crying night and day,
>   *Come, come, my God, O come,*
>   But no hearing.

('Denial', 11–15)

Against these emotions can be set the rueful admission of self-interest in Marvell's 'The Coronet', the calm acceptance of death and hope of salvation at the end of Donne's 'Hymn to God my God in my Sickness' and the sheer elation of Herbert's 'Easter':

> Rise heart; thy Lord is risen. Sing his praise
>   Without delays.

('Easter', 1–2)

There is also an interest in what makes man fully human. The interplay of mind and body that interests Donne in love poems like 'Air and Angels' and 'The Ecstasy' also concerns Marvell in 'A Dialogue between the Soul and Body'. Another topic which is common to both groups of poems is that of sincerity. Marvell recognises the danger of writing for the wrong motive in 'The Coronet', and just as Donne mocks the unconvincing language of love by exaggerating it, so Herbert sees the danger of being too ingenious:

> My thoughts began to burnish, sprout, and swell,
> Curling with metaphors a plain intention,
> Decking the sense, as if it were to sell.

('Jordan' (2), 4–6)

A POETRY OF LOGIC AND EMOTION

. . . These emotions are common to us all, but the question that must now be answered is what makes these poems *uncommon*, metaphysical in fact. The word 'metaphysical' has become a useful label, but it is not in itself particularly helpful. Dryden once criticised Donne for 'affecting the metaphysics' in his love poetry, in other words 'perplexing the minds of the fair sex with nice [pedantic] speculations of philosophy'. Dr Johnson writing his *Life of Cowley* took up this accusation that Donne and a number of his successors were unduly philosophical, or metaphysical, and proceeded to coin the expression 'metaphysical poets' even while he pointed out that he did not consider them to be genuinely metaphysical!

There is in fact no single word or definition that can adequately sum up the range of poetry described as metaphysical. Donne was the great innovator, but those who followed had personalities, as well as minds, of their own and each poet's verse has its own distinctive quality. Personality, indeed, is a major factor, for much of the poetry expresses personal feelings as can be seen from the survey of its subject matter above. This is especially true of Donne and Herbert, although in the case of the latter the tone is calmer since the conflicts are seen in retrospect and the poet has their resolution in mind. (The conclusion of a poem like 'The Collar' may indeed seem too simple, but we come to realise that Herbert's calm is something that he has had to fight for.) The quieter, more meditative poems of Herbert . . . also give the impression of a personal response to a specific situation or place. . . .

We are aware, then, in most of this poetry of the individuality of the poet, but it is not this in itself that makes the poetry metaphysical. It is rather the way in which feeling is related to thought that is the hallmark of the style. The personal feeling gives an urgency to arguments which are often developed by means of striking and extended analogies to a wide range of things, sometimes learned, sometimes homely and often contemporary. . . . The imagery is, in fact, used more for its logical than its emotional impact. Very often the analogy or conceit seems improbable, but as the poet works his idea out the reader is forced to accept its validity and as he struggles to follow the reasoning (this is not poetry for the passive reader) he gains new insight. It is frequently the logical (or apparently logical) argument that gives shape and structure to the whole poem.

Neither thought nor feeling could be adequately expressed, however, if it were not for the remarkable adaptability and variety of metaphysical versification. The harshness of 'Satire 3' and the music of 'Virtue', the apparent disorder of 'The Collar' and the suave smoothness of the couplets in 'To His Coy Mistress' all have this in common: they are carefully calculated to convey both logic and emotion.

Some poems are dominated by a single argument. 'To His Coy Mistress', for example, is divided into three clear sections: if the poet had time he would devote it to praising his mistress; but life is short; and so he reaches the conclusion: 'let us sport us while we may'. Each of the three sections is expanded and decorated with wit, but the structure stands

THE WIT OF THE METAPHYSICAL POETS

Metaphysical poetry was radical and somewhat "difficult" to understand even in its own day. The playwright Ben Jonson, for example, was a big fan of John Donne's poetry, but he doubted that it would be read at all by posterity. In the following excerpt, scholar Louis Martz summarizes the essential features unifying the metaphysical poets, especially their use of "wit."

The term "metaphysical poetry," as used by literary critics over the past fifty or sixty years, has come to include poetry, notably that of Herbert or Donne, which possesses the following characteristics. First, abrupt and dramatic openings, often with a vivid image or exclamation: "For Godsake hold your tongue, and let me love." Secondly, a colloquial, familiar manner of speech, used in the most adored and sanctified presences, whether it be the presence of a Lady, or the presence of the Lord. Thirdly, a firm argumentative construction, which makes the last line of the poem implicit in the first and gives to the whole poem a peculiar tautness and concentration. Fourthly, an introspective quality, an element of self-analysis, particularly when the poet is dealing with the nature of love, whether sacred or profane. And finally, most distinctively, the quality that Samuel Johnson described when he found in this poetry "a combination of dissimilar images, or discovery of occult resemblances in things apparently unlike." "The most heterogeneous ideas are yoked by violence together; nature and art are ransacked for illustrations, comparisons, and allusions; their learning instructs, and their subtilty surprises; but the reader commonly thinks his improvement dearly bought, and, though he sometimes admires, is seldom pleased." Modern readers, more often pleased by this daring use of metaphor, have come to accept the "metaphysical conceit" as a valid and significant mode of poetical action.

Metaphysical poems tend to begin in the midst of an occasion; and the meaning of the occasion is explored and grasped through this peculiar use of metaphor. The old Renaissance conceit, the ingenious comparison, is developed into a device by which the extremes of abstraction and concreteness, the extremes of unlikeness, may be woven together into a fabric of argument unified by the prevailing force of "wit." *Wit*, in all the rich and varied senses that the word held in this era: intellect, reason, powerful mental capacity, cleverness, ingenuity, intellectual quickness, inventive and constructive ability, a talent for uttering brilliant things, the power of amusing surprise.

English Seventeenth-Century Verse, edited with an Introduction by Louis L. Martz. New York: W.W. Norton, 1963, pp. 1–2.

out. Donne in 'The Flea' also presents a single argument to the same purpose, but the structure here is much denser, moving from the idea that the lovers are already united since their blood is mingled in the flea to the idea that the flea is their 'marriage bed' and 'temple'. Then when his mistress kills the flea to disprove his argument by implying that the blood the flea had sucked from her was of no importance, he switches the argument to suggest that she would lose no more honour than she had blood, if she complied with his wishes.

The image of the flea as the marriage temple is far fetched and comic, but other poems make more serious use of a single image in an extended conceit that again shapes the entire poem. Marvell's 'On a Drop of Dew' is devoted to the analogy between the drop of dew that has come from heaven and yearns to be drawn up to heaven again by the sun and the human soul which also yearns for heaven. . . .

One aspect of metaphysical wit is the sheer range of imagery used. Donne may compare himself on his sick-bed to a map and Marvell describe ideal lovers as parallel lines; at the same time such ordinary things as the taper and the fly are brought in. Herbert in a fit of depression can claim that he is no more use than 'a blunted knife'. In some cases it is not the image that is original, but the use that is made of it. This is true in particular of a significant number of images in the religious poems which are already heavily laden with associations both from the Bible and from centuries of Christian usage. . . .

THE SPOKEN VOICE

The poetry of Marvell is not as ruggedly dramatic as that of Donne. Nevertheless the tone of the spoken voice can still be heard in his poetry. At times it is suavely ironic and best expressed in the smoothness of a polished couplet:

> The grave's a fine and private place,
> But none, I think, do there embrace.

('To His Coy Mistress', 31–2)

At other times a sudden sense of urgency breaks into the rhythm:

> But at my back I always hear
> Time's winged chariot hurrying near.

(21–2)

In 'A Dialogue between the Soul and Body' the somewhat abstract subject is brought to life in an acrimonious debate in which the Soul sneers at the Body, stressing its inadequacies with a series of paradoxes ('fettered stands/In feet; and manacled in hands') and complaining of both the Body's sickness and its health:

> Constrained not only to endure
> Diseases, but, what's worse, the cure.

(27–8)

The Body gives as good as it gets and interestingly is left with the last word. Not only is the tone wittily contemptuous with its rhetorical question, but also the Body is given one of Marvell's strongest images; the natural innocence of the Body before it is corrupted by the Soul's sin is compared to the greenness of Nature before it is harmed by man:

> What but a soul could have the wit
> To build me up for sin so fit?
> So architects do square and hew
> Green trees that in the forest grew.

(41–4)

Here indeed is a poem which is literally metaphysical in its subject matter. In the satirical tone of its rhyming couplets it might be thought to look forward to the Augustan satire that was to follow and yet it is also metaphysical in the poetic sense. Some of Donne's earliest poetry in the 1590s had been satirical and that too had been typically metaphysical in its dramatic style, blending wit and feeling, and using complexity of expression to mirror complexity of thought.

It is finally to Donne, the originator, that we must return. In the words of Thomas Carew's elegy he 'opened us a mine/Of rich and pregnant fancy' and drew 'a line/Of masculine expression':

> The Muses' garden with pedantic weeds
> O'erspread, was purged by thee; the lazy seeds
> Of servile imitation thrown away,
> And fresh invention planted, thou didst pay
> The debts of our penurious bankrupt age . . .
> Here lies a King, that ruled as he thought fit
> The universal monarchy of wit.

(25–9, 95–6)

The Epic Sensibility of Milton's *Paradise Lost*

Merritt Y. Hughes

Although John Milton's *Paradise Lost* was not published until 1667, nearly fifty years after the glory
years of the English Renaissance, it is still very much
a Renaissance work. It takes the form of an epic
poem along the lines of Homer and Virgil, and it
bears the imprint throughout of the author's wide
reading in ancient and Christian sources. As noted
Milton scholar Merritt Y. Hughes observes, the poem
reads at times like drama, but it is rooted firmly in
the tradition of epic poetry. As an epic poem, it puts
forward Satan in the beginning as its potential epic
hero. But, as Hughes contends, Milton insistently undercuts the heroism of Satan through his use of irony.

A reader coming to *Paradise Lost* for the first time, and going rapidly through it to the end of Book X, is likely to get the
impression that he is reading drama. It is a heightened kind
of drama which is too big for the stage and too rich for it in
poetic perspectives around the conversations and debates
that take up more room than the narrative does. If he reads
on through the unfolding of the never-ending but finally defeated waylaying of good by evil in human history as
Michael unfolds it to Adam in a quiet dialogue in the last two
books of the poem, he will miss the clash of characters and
ideas in the earlier books, but he may find satisfaction in the
sombre but not tragic resolution of the plot as the final step
in the development of Adam's character. Looking back, he
will see a series of dramas composing the epic plot: the
council of the devils in Book II, with Moloch, Belial, and
Mammon making bids for leadership which wonderfully reveal their characters but fail to shake Satan's leadership; the
council in heaven in Book III, where the Son of God discov-

From *John Milton: Complete Poems and Major Prose*, edited by Merritt Y. Hughes
(Indianapolis: Odyssey Press, 1957). Copyright © 2000. Reprinted by permission of
Prentice-Hall, Inc., Upper Saddle River, N.J.

ers his character by making himself responsible for mankind's redemption; Satan's first attempt to seduce Eve, by a dream, in Book IV; the revolt of Satan's followers against God as Raphael reports it to Adam in Books V and VI; pausing to tell him of the refusal of a single seraph in the throng, Abdiel, to be swept into the crime; the dialogue about creation and nature in Books VII and VIII, which should have made Adam proof against the temptation to betray his own nature by disobedience to God's order in Book IX; the great temptation scenes in that book; and the hardly less psychologically interesting scenes of reconciliation between Adam and Eve, in which she takes the initiative and becomes almost, if not quite, the stronger character in Book X.

AN EPIC BUILT OUT OF DRAMAS

But *Paradise Lost* is not a drama; it is an epic built out of dramas. Its plan is epic. It begins as the *Iliad* and the *Aeneid* begin, with a plunge into the action at a point where it has reached its third crisis, the time when the devils after the decision to revolt in Heaven and their defeat in battle there, debate their policy against God and man in Hell. The first two crises wait for narration by Raphael to Adam in Book V. The fourth crisis in the order of events is the scene in Heaven in Book III. Here we find a new kind of drama—the drama of contrast between situations. What has just happened in Hell is a parody of what happens in Heaven. As Satan has established his right to rule the devils by monopolizing the glory of undertaking man's destruction, so the Son of God proves his right to reign in heaven by undertaking man's redemption. There is direct narrative in Book II of Satan's flight through Chaos and in later books more of it about his travels in our universe. But the high peaks in his later story are dramatic—his soliloquies on the theme of "Myself am hell," his seduction of Eve, his encounter with his daughter Sin and grandson Death on their bridge across Chaos, and the grand opera scene in Pandaemonium where his final disappearance in serpent form begins with the rising orchestral roar of recognition by his followers and ends in their involuntary hisses—hisses that Dr. Edith Sitwell thinks are the finest sibilant music in all English poetry. We seldom see Satan except at moments of high drama, but his career is epic.

Just how epic Satan's career is we can see only in the light of the whole poem. His revolt in Heaven depopulates it by drawing off perhaps a third of the angels. Out of that evil good comes immediately in the creation of the universe and of man, who is intended to sire a race which—as Raphael explains to Adam—can ultimately achieve a virtually an-

This engraving shows John Milton in 1670 at the age of sixty-two. His epic poem Paradise Lost *was published three years earlier.*

gelic nature and live at will on earth or in Heaven. When Satan wrecks that plan in Book IX the result is the epic struggle for man's redemption in the three following books. For Milton's contemporaries that story had the fascination simply as a theory of history which historical writing like [historian Arnold] Toynbee's has for us today, but with the difference that its redemptive hope for both humanity in general and for individual men was absolutely assured by the scriptural texts that stud Milton's lines. And in creation Milton had the great epic theme of his century, the theme of the *Divine Weeks* of the French Calvinist poet Guillaume Salluste Sieur du Bartas, which was more popular in the English translation of Joshua Sylvester that Milton knew as a child than the original ever was in France. Creation was the theme of Torquato Tasso's *The Creation of the World* and—to some extent—of pagan poems like Hesiod's *Theogony*, Ovid's *Metamorphoses*, and Lucretius' *On the Nature of Things*. Milton's cosmic passages bear the occasional print of all these poems as plainly as his first two books occasionally reflect facets of the hells of Homer and Virgil, Dante and Spenser. Such poems were not Milton's models but they were a part of the sinews of his strength as he pursued

Things unattempted yet in Prose or Rhyme.

SATAN AS HERO?

. . . It is only in the first two books of *Paradise Lost* that Satan seems heroic. There is grandeur but no heroism in his later soliloquies and after the seduction of Eve he departs to Hell, leaving the world to his vice-gerents Sin and Death. There is no doubt of Milton's intent to degrade him, step by step, down to the scene of his second and involuntary appearance in serpent form in Book X. The first shock to any admiration for him in a reader's mind comes when he meets his allegorical daughter Sin and his incestuously begotten grandson Death at Hell's gates (II, 648–883). For over two centuries critics agreed that the step into pure allegory in Sin and Death was a blemish on the poem and an external incrustation. Recently they have been wondering whether it is not a part of the structural irony of the whole design. Satan, Sin, and Death are now seen to be a parody of the Trinity of Heaven. Satan's "daughter and . . . darling without end" is the antitype of the Son of God's bosom who is his "word, wisdom, and effectual might" (III, 170). Sin makes only one further appearance, but again it seems—as Ernest Schanzer observes—that the purpose is to extend the over-arching dramatic irony that ties the poem together. When she meets Satan in Chaos she tells him that she has been drawn to him from Hell by "a secret harmony" that moves her heart with his, "joined in connexion sweet," and that the distance of worlds between them has not broken the "fatal consequence" that will forever unite them. Her words can hardly be an accidental parallel to Adam's protestation to Eve at the moment of decision in Eden:

> So forcibly within my heart I feel
> The bond of Nature draw me to my own;
> My own in thee; for what thou art is mine.

Everything in the poem, of course, depends on the way in which this speech of Adam's is read. [Scholar A.J.A.] Waldock has read it as both the most dramatic and the noblest utterance in the entire poem—a brave and beautiful expression of human love at its heroic best. He will not even consider it as an honest effort by Milton to accept the hardest element in the biblical account of the Fall—the deception of Adam by Eve. And Mr. Waldock had nothing but contempt for the critics who variously condemn or palliate Adam's act as "uxoriousness" (Milton's term for it in the *Christian Doctrine*), "gregariousness," "passion," or "sentimentality." For Mr. Waldock then Adam becomes the hero of the poem though he behaves rather badly with Eve later on and is in danger of losing his laurels as a human being to her.

By the same token Mr. Waldock saw Satan as a dramatic failure and a hopelessly inconsistent personality in the course of his whole story. He constantly misses his opportunities for tragedy. His character does not degenerate; it is degraded. In the later books he becomes essentially an allegory and a kind of emblem of evil. This criticism seems wide of the mark when we think of Satan's intelligently and shrewdly consistent play on Eve's vanity in the two temptation scenes and compare his flattery of her half-formed wish for "godhead" with his flattery of the same craving in his followers in Books V (772–802) and I (94–124). But in general Mr. Waldock's objection to Satan as a dramatic character is sound, and it is a searching criticism of the poem itself. In substance, it comes close to Mr. Rajan's view of Satan as a great opportunist, putty to be molded by the changing situation, constant only to his resolve in Book I (165) "out of good still to find means of evil." But Mr. Rajan's view of Satan is less critical than it is historical. For Milton's contemporaries Satan was simply the Adversary whom John Calvin described as "an enemie that is in courage most hardie, in strength most mightie, in policies most subtle, in diligence and celeritie unweariable, with all sorts of engins plenteously furnishd, in skill of warre most readie." The Satan of the seventeenth century was a figure to hate and fear. In poetry and in life alike, he was the father of lies, "with all sorts of engins plenteously furnishd." And that was his main character.

THE COSMIC IRONY OF *PARADISE LOST*

But he was also courageous and "in skill of warre most readie"—a fact that we overlook even though we see him fighting in spite of his wounds, like Turnus or Hector, through the three days of battle in Heaven, and proving his skill by inventing artillery on the eve of the second day. As a field marshal in Heaven, the critics agree to find Satan disgusting and to say as little as possible about him except to deplore his jibes and Belial's at the angels whom their first salvo topples over. But the jeers at God are a part of Satan's nature. We hear them in his first speeches to his followers in Book V, and we hear them still echoing in Book X (625–27) when God speaks of

> my scornful Enemies
> That laugh, as if transported with some fit
> Of Passion.

The contrast of Satan's jeers with the laughter of Him "that sitteth in the heavens," is a part of the cosmic irony of *Paradise Lost*. In the battle in heaven Satan is a much more comic than tragic figure, and he is constantly skirting comedy all the way through the poem. In the allegory of his defeat by the Son of God on the third day of that battle Satan ceases to be comic only because the situation is too serious. All the faith in Truth's power to crush Falsehood in any open encounter that Milton poured into *Areopagitica* is symbolized in the all-seeing eyes of the victorious Son's chariot.

Probably Milton regarded the war in Heaven as both allegorical and historical. For centuries various commentators had regarded the drawing off of a "third part of the angels" by Lucifer, in Revelation xii, 4–11, and his battle there with Michael, as a record of angelic war before the creation of Adam. Others regarded it as a prophecy of a battle to be fought at the end of the world, or an allegory of some moral crisis in Heaven. In *Lucifer* the poet Vondel treated it as allegory with the resonance of history behind it. In the moment of Lucifer's defeat he and his rebel angels are all suddenly transformed into monsters more terrible than the serpents into which Satan and his followers are changed when we see them for the last time in *Paradise Lost.* Here no grim comedy is intended—as it may be intended in Milton's scene. . . .

But Milton was too much a humanist and at the same time too much interested in the historical truth to be found in the Bible to be content to treat the battle in heaven as sheer allegory. The biblical warrant for it as history might be small, but in the traditions of battles between the Olympian gods and the Titans which Hesiod tells, and which left their marks widely in classical literature and sculpture, Milton—like most of his contemporaries—saw a survival of sacred history in the legends of the pagans. This belief was part of a larger one that is mentioned below. It is cryptically involved in the allusion to Eurynome in *Paradise Lost* X, 581. Once more the rebels, the Titans, or at least many of them, were traditionally described as taking serpent or other monstrous forms. The forms might be allegory, but for Milton the legends about the Titans' war with the gods of light on Olympus were proof of a core of some kind of historical truth in the revolt of the angels.

As the battle in heaven was in one of its aspects actual for Milton, so was Satan himself. He believed in the existence of the historical Author of Evil at least in the Augustinian sense that evil is deprivation or negation of good and is produced by pride. The only way to portray Satan then was as a voice confessing and vaunting the proud will and the discovery that in his assault on heaven the speaker has himself created a hell within him. In achieving that kind of a Satan, Milton earned the praise of William Hazlitt and the Romantics generally for having got away from the medieval devil of Tasso and of all the poets up to his time, Italian and English, too, who had drawn portraits of the fiends. But pride is self-deception, and Milton's Satan deceives himself so well that he deceived Shelley into thinking him a Promethean apostle of human regeneration, and Byron into thinking him an inspiring symbol of revolt against political tyranny. For Milton Satan was the archetypal tyrant. His reign in hell is the express antitype of the reign of the Son of God by merit in Heaven.

And at the moment of commitment to the attack on Eve in Book IV, 393–94, it is "with necessity, The Tyrant's plea," that he justifies his act. It is not the courage of Satan's revolt against God that counts; it is the ambition which betrays him into what Arnold Stein calls "the trap of leadership.". . .

It should be clear that in drawing his portrait of Satan Milton was objective. Its weakness is its greatness—its power to fool readers into its own delusion of power and make them say that Milton's Satan is a noble anticipation of the Nietzschean superman. If, to give the devil his due, we must say that in the first two books of *Paradise Lost* he is drawn with too many virtues, the answer is perhaps in Socrates' words in the *Republic* [by Plato] when he says that the finer virtues—"courage, temperance, and the rest"—belong to the most evil men: "Or do you fancy that great crimes and unmixed wickedness come from a feeble nature and not rather from a noble nature that has been ruined?"

CHAPTER 4

Renaissance Prose

Renaissance
Literature

Renaissance Women Writers

Katharina M. Wilson

The many women writers of the Renaissance period
owe a great debt to the humanist educational
agenda, according to noted scholar Katharina M.
Wilson, of the University of Georgia. Humanist leaders such as Erasmus and Thomas More pressed for
expanded education as a means of moral improvement, and they included girls in their program. This
inclusive attitude only came to fruition in the elevated classes of European society, however, which
produced learned ladies who became rulers, patrons
of arts and writing, translators, and poets. As Wilson
notes, these women were frequently "discouraged
from composing original texts," yet they made important contributions to Renaissance culture in spite
of the restrictions placed on them.

Generally acclaimed as an age of growth and expansion, the
Renaissance was a period marked by various changes, social, religious, and moral: by the rise of national states in the
wake of the Black Death; by the Reformist movement; and
by the recovery of and reemphasis on the classical past. It
was a period gloriously replete with new opportunities of
which Renaissance men and women were joyfully aware.
How did women writers of the fifteenth and sixteenth centuries avail themselves of these new opportunities? Did they
have a distinctive voice? How did their contemporaries view
them? It is quite clear that women, predominantly from the
upper or well-to-do classes but also from other levels of society, contributed importantly and prodigiously to Renaissance letters and that many of them enjoyed contemporary
literary success. However, while many women profited
greatly from the availability of the new learning, it is also ev-

From *Women Writers of the Renaissance and Reformation*, edited by Katharina M. Wilson. Copyright © 1987 by the University of Georgia Press. Reprinted by permission of
the University of Georgia Press.

ident that, regardless of their talents or accomplishments, the full range of opportunities opened by the humanist movement were not available to them in the same manner or to the same extent as to men and that the vocational and moral goals of education enunciated by the humanists were almost invariably different for men and women. Clearly, the social (and economic) mobility made possible for male humanists through the pursuit of professional careers was not an available option to women.

Literary endeavors of men and women alike are not the results of poetic genius alone: education, some financial independence—either in the form of personal wealth, individual or institutional patronage—a modicum of leisure, access to source materials and books, some form of encouragement, and/or religious, political, or emotional zeal are also of significant import. Perhaps the most seminally important contribution of Renaissance humanism to the burgeoning of female literary activity was the availability, on a large scale, of a diversified education to laywomen fortunate enough to have had access to books and teachers. Indeed, the education of women was one of the most persuasively argued topoi in the famous Renaissance debate on woman's worth, the *querelle des femmes* [the quarrel about women].

EDUCATION AND UPPER-CLASS WOMEN

A prodigious appetite for learning and an eager delight in the fruits of philological endeavors created a large class of men and women that mastered the rudiments of humanist learning: proficiency in Latin, competency in Greek, knowledge of ancient and patristic literature, history, moral philosophy, as well as the conventions of Petrarchism and Ficinian Neoplatonism.[1] In particular, ladies of the upper classes and women relatives of the humanists profited from the humanist curriculum. In Italy, Isotta Nogarola, Laura Cereta, and Cassandra Fidele, among others, were esteemed for their learning. The reputation of Cassandra Fidele spread far and wide, prompting Queen Isabella of Spain to invite her to her court and the Venetian senate, in turn, to proscribe her departure because she was deemed "too valuable" to lose. In Spain, Isabella's Latin tutor, Beatriz Galindo,

---

1. Petrarchism refers to the conventions of love poetry derived from the influential Italian poet and scholar, Francesco Petrarch. Ficinian Neoplatonism is the idealistic philosophy derived from Plato's thought and espoused by the Italian scholar Marsilio Ficino.

famed for her learning, founded schools and may have written a commentary on Aristotle, while the Portuguese court also boasted a woman Latin tutor, Luisa Sigea, who penned a letter to Pope Paul III in five languages. In France the literary salons of Catherine de Medicis and Marguerite of Navarre attracted leading poets and scholars; Marguerite of Navarre, educated with her brother Francis, the future king of France, was herself polyglot and wrote in many genres; the Dames des Roches consciously dedicated their lives to the pursuit of learning, and the Lyonnese school boasted such learned women as Louise Labé and Pernette Du Guillet. In England, Queen Elizabeth's philological training and knowledge of the classics dazzled the ambassadors at her court, and the erudition of Lady Jane Gray, Mary Sidney, and Margaret More Roper, to mention only a few, was eulogized by their contemporaries. Margaret Roper's philological expertise, for example, enabled her to offer an emendation to a passage in Saint Cyprian. Katerina Jagellonica, queen of Sweden, demonstrated perhaps the widest linguistic range among Europe's rulers by corresponding with facility in seven languages. Margaret of Austria and Louise of Savoy, both avid readers of the classics, ruled their realms with political and administrative acumen and their literary salons with erudition and wit. . . .

How did education for women of the Renaissance differ from that for men and from medieval teaching? With slight variations, Renaissance curricula were the same for men and women (Latin, Greek, some Hebrew, some of the more useful vernaculars, a study of the classics, the Church Fathers, history, moral philosophy, poetry, grammar, music, some math, and some astrology) but differed in goal, application, and emphasis. For men, the goals of education were almost invariably public; for women, private. . . .

THE HUMANIST AGENDA

Education was of central interest to the Renaissance humanists, and their great contribution of making learning available to women cannot be overestimated. Theoretically, equal education was advocated for both sexes and for all social classes, but practically, formal education was restricted to the daughters, wives, and sisters of learned men, and to women of the nobility and the upper bourgeoise. Moreover, the emphasis on learning not for its own sake but as a means of moral improvement (or even for Castiglione's "pleasing affability") is almost omnipresent in the educational treatises written by men for women, underscoring, thus, a continuity of purpose with the medieval tradition. Erasmus stresses the importance of education for moral goals because "study busies the entire soul—it is not only a weapon against idleness but also a means of impressing the best precepts upon the girl's mind and of leading her to virtue." Thomas More, similarly, joins moral probity with woman's learning:

> Since erudition in women is a new thing and a reproach to the sloth of men, many will gladly assail it. . . . If a woman (and this I desire and hope with you as their teacher for all my daughters) of eminent virtue of mind should add even moderate skill in learning, I think she will gain more real good than if she obtain the riches of Croesus and the beauty of Helen. Not because that learning will be a glory to her, though learning will accompany virtue as a shadow does a body, but because the reward of wisdom is too solid to be lost with riches or perish with beauty since it depends on the inner knowledge of what is right. (Letter 105)

In addition, both emphasize the importance of woman's education as an aid in rearing and instructing children competently at an early age. As Ruth Kelso observes, "The training of the well-born girl was directed in every respect . . . toward fitting her to become a wife. . . . Marriage alone was held the proper vocation for women mainly because she was fitted only to learn the duties that belonged to her as a sort of junior partner to her husband. . . .

Education for women of less elevated status was little changed from that of the Middle Ages. As a fifteenth-century Florentine bookseller observes, there were two rules for the behavior of women: "One: to bring up her children piously, and two: to be quiet in church, to which I myself would like to add: to be quiet everywhere else also."

This strong "functional" distinction between the educational opportunities of royal and aristocratic ladies on the one hand and those of the rest of womankind on the other not only reflects the power-dynamics of historic reality but also addresses itself to the question of whether or not women indeed had a Renaissance. Never before (and seldom thereafter) was Europe ruled by so many learned ladies: Elizabeth of England, Mary of Scotland, Marguerite of Navarre, Catherine de Medicis and Louise of Savoy in

France, Margaret of Austria, Mary of Hungary and Margaret of Parma in the Netherlands, Elizabeth of Hungary, Catherina Cornaro, queen of Cyprus, Eleanor of Aragon and Isabella of Spain. Some of the Italian principalities, too, were sometimes governed by ladies, among them, Veronica Gambara, Isabella d'Este, and Catherine Sforza. All these female rulers were exemplars of the new humanistic learning—stateswomen, patrons of the arts and writers, translators, writers, builders, educators, administrators, and peacemakers: Elizabeth of England and Margaret of Austria, for example, counted the maintenance (or conclusion) of peace in their territories as their greatest triumphs. Indeed, the negotiation of the peace of Cambrai, also known as the Ladies Peace (since it was concluded by Margaret of Austria, Louise of Savoy, and Marguerite of Navarre), reminds one of Christine de Pizan's observation that queens and female regents are better suited than kings for making peace.

A LACK OF OPPORTUNITIES

Education, however, did not make these women queens or princesses. Study and formal training enabled them to develop their intellectual potential, but the future of that potential was predicated at and by birth. Women of the "middling rank" or of the lower estates, on the other hand, lacked such opportunities, and neither group was free to pursue unidirectionally learning and scholarship. The meteoric rise of some men's careers, such as Sir Thomas More's through learning, from lawyer's son to royal chancellor, or Shakespeare's, through poetic talent from glover's son to court dramatist, is unparalleled when compared to the lives of Renaissance women scholars and writers. Very little, if any, opportunity existed in the power structure of Renaissance courts, principalities, universities, or professional organizations for the woman scholar to rise above her born position through education and intellectual accomplishments. Normality for her was tied to her sexual and social roles rather than to her mental abilities. Faced with these restrictions, fifteenth- and sixteenth-century women writers were nevertheless able to stretch their roles so as to encompass some of their talents. Mary Sidney, for example, used her role as translator and patron to foster the Reformist cause and to establish the cult of her brother as a Protestant martyr. Marguerite of Navarre extended her protection toward reformers

and expressed some "subversive" ideas in her *Miroir*, much
to the dismay of the doctors at the Sorbonne. . . .

THE CATEGORIES OF WOMEN WRITERS

Education, talent, experience, religious and political zeal,
and emotional need largely determine the scope and nature
of the artist's work. Social and/or functional identity, however, is also a determining factor. The women writers [of the
Renaissance] . . . fall accordingly into six categories: the
grande dame, the woman scholar, the nun, the religious or
political activist, the *cortigiana onesta*, and the patrician. By
and large, *grande dames* wrote secular and even public
works, with lyric poetry, letters, translations, orations, and
novelistic texts predominating, though some, notably Marguerite of Navarre and Vittoria Colonna, did compose devotional poems and Elizabeth I penned several homilies. By
and large, they wrote in the vernacular, and almost invariably they were held in high literary esteem by their contem-

THE FREEDOM TO STUDY

*One of the best French poets of the Renaissance, Louise
Labé was very much influenced in her love poems and sonnets by the Petrarchan tradition from Italy. In the following excerpt from her "Dedication," which she also calls "preface, to a
friend," she laments the restrictions women have suffered; yet
she also exhorts other women to take advantage of the new opportunities opened up by the New Learning.*

Since a time has come, Mademoiselle, when the severe laws of
men no longer prevent women from applying themselves to
the sciences and other disciplines, it seems to me that those of
us who can should use this long-craved freedom to study and
to let men see how greatly they wronged us when depriving
us of its honor and advantages. And if any woman becomes so
proficient as to be able to write down her thoughts, let her do
so and not despise the honor but rather flaunt it instead of fine
clothes, necklaces, and rings. For these may be considered
ours only by use, whereas the honor of being educated is ours
entirely. . . . If the heavens had endowed me with sufficient wit
to understand all I would have liked, I would serve in this as
an example rather than an admonishment. But having devoted
part of my youth to musical exercises, and finding the time left
too short for the crudeness of my understanding, I am unable,
in my own case, to achieve what I want for our sex, which is

poraries. Second, the woman scholar, occupying perhaps the most Renaissance of the six categories, was almost invariably related to a literary man and was frequently of well-to-do but not necessarily aristocratic descent. Renaissance women scholars devoted themselves to philological pursuits: translations, essays, letters, dialogues, and even invectives, both in Latin and the vernacular. It is this group, together with the writers of the urban patriciate (that is, women for whom humanist education was not a matter of self-evident necessity) that seems most concerned with educational opportunities for women and with the obligations women have to take advantage of these new opportunities. Women scholars were occasionally attacked and ridiculed, and they were the most vociferous advocates that women should learn for learning's sake. Third, the nun, the major representative of medieval women writers, no longer occupied that preeminent position in Renaissance letters. Writing in Latin and the vernacular, she came from all social classes

to see it outstrip men not only in beauty but in learning and virtue. All I can do is to beg our virtuous ladies to raise their minds somewhat above their distaffs and spindles and try to prove to the world that if we were not made to command, still we should not be disdained as companions in domestic and public matters by those who govern and command obedience. Apart from the good name that our sex will acquire thereby, we shall have caused men to devote more time and effort in the public good to virtuous studies for fear of seeing themselves left behind by those over whom they have always claimed superiority in practically everything. . . .

If there is anything to be recommended after honor and glory, anything to incite us to study, it is the pleasure which study affords. Study differs in this from other recreations, of which all one can say, after enjoying them, is that one has passed the time. But study gives a more enduring sense of satisfaction. For the past delights us and serves more than the present. . . . When we write down our thoughts, no matter how much our mind runs on infinities of other matters . . . long afterward, on looking back at what we wrote, we return to the same point and humor as we were in before. Then our joy is doubled, for we revive the pleasure experienced in the past. . . .

Louise Labé, "Dedication," in *The Renaissance Reader.* Ed. Kenneth J. Atchity. New York: HarperCollins, 1997, pp. 193–94.

and her compositions include not only visions, revelations, and *vitae*, as in the Middle Ages, but also translations, biographies, and autobiographies. Fourth, the *cortigiana onesta*, the Italian Renaissance brand of the Greek hetaira, exemplifies the single woman's other alternative. Cultured, though rarely if ever of aristocratic descent, she most often wrote vernacular lyric poetry. Fifth, the religious political activist, militant descendant of the medieval Margery Kempe, often belonged to the urban poor, invariably wrote in the vernacular, and was seldom rewarded for her activism and pamphleteering. Finally, the gentlewoman writer: usually a member of the provincial urban patriciate, she was a Renaissance novelty. She is ordinarily learned as well as cultivated, she could be either single or married, she was rarely related to a literary man, and she composed almost always in the vernacular and in a variety of devotional or fictional forms. Conspicuously absent from this catalog of Renaissance women and their writings are the learned commentary or treatise and the original epic or secular drama.

In addition to their awareness of their social and functional identity, women writers, especially those not of the upper aristocracy, were also quite conscious of the relationship of their sex to their work. This concern lends their works a distinctive voice that must be seen in the context of the splintering, doubling effects of the mirror phenomenon, that is, as an incorporation of, as well as reaction to, male aesthetics. Most wrote of themselves as women; they explored their emotions, desires, frustrations, and aspirations in their texts; they advocated learning and even ecclesiastical ministry for women; they wrote defenses of women and elaborate catalogs of famous ladies and of female accomplishments of the past and the present. Even those women who eschewed direct and ostensible literary interest in women exhibited awareness of this relationship; they knew what they could or could not write. Margaret Tyler, translator of popular Spanish Catholic works, for example, protested the view that "women were intellectually unfit for anything but translation," and Anne Locke, translating Taffins's *Markes of the Children of God*, introduced her text by saying, "But because great things by reason of my sexe, I may not doe, and that which I may, I ought to doe, I have according to my duety, brought my poore basket of stones to the strengthening of the wals of that

Jerusalem, wherof (by Grace) we are both Citizens and members." Women were particular citizens and members of the Renaissance world, and their literary aspirations, albeit inherently ambiguous and restricted by the limited number of opportunities and modes of expression available to them, do leave us fascinating glimpses of the world of the fifteenth and sixteenth centuries.

THE RANGE OF RENAISSANCE LETTERS

Before addressing the contribution women writers made to Renaissance literature, perhaps we should remind ourselves of the changing criteria of literary canonization. Much of what was considered the best of Renaissance letters was derivative in some sense. The sweeping prestige of classical antiquity, of the conventions of Petrarch, Boccaccio, and of Ficinian Neoplatonism fostered adaptations and reworkings of these sources. Classical erudition was deemed the fundamental prerequisite for literary endeavors; education and philological training, therefore, were necessarily the cornerstones of the canonized writer's literary path. By extension, editions, abridgements, collections, and adaptations were considered crowning achievements of humanist learning and literary skill, and translations and paraphrases were deemed useful and important endeavors. The many women translators, most well born, who wrote during the Renaissance, were profusely praised by their contemporaries. Translation, by and large, was considered a "feminine" (because nonoriginal) endeavor, best suited for women. But Renaissance women translators, while discouraged from composing original texts, did often authenticate their works—if perhaps only marginally—by adding or shifting emphasis, coining new terms, extending metaphors, omitting phrases, and successfully adapting the source language into their native idiom. They played seminally important roles in creating the literary vernaculars. Mary Sidney, the countess of Pembroke, and Lady Ann Bacon, for example, were recognized for helping to forge the English literary vernacular in their translations, and Ann Bacon's translations continued to be used by the Anglican Church as standard texts well into the twentieth century. . . .

A RENAISSANCE FOR WOMEN?

Did women writers have a Renaissance during the Renaissance? Judged by the traditional definition of the availability of education, the secularization of instruction, the study of the classical past, the manifold opportunities of expression, and the emphasis on individuality, the answer to this question depends more on the woman's social position and familial circumstances than on her sex. The question, phrased in this conventional mold, however, does not address one of the most important aspects of education: its goals and the opportunities it provides. For those women who had a living of five hundred a year and "book-lined" cells of their own, Renaissance education provided a stupendous opportunity for personal and intellectual growth, a means for the realization of their potential; their decisions to write and to publish were their own and went beyond the expectations placed upon them. For those women, on the other hand, whose intellectual aspirations were generously fostered by the humanist learning but who were not born to public positions, scholarly endeavors frequently came to an abrupt halt when adulthood set in. No institutional and seldom personal patronage were available to single secular women, nor were the customary paths of administrative or advisory careers open to them. Ecclesiastical sponsorship of predominantly devotional literature by women was, as in the Middle Ages, a viable alternative for women, but the Renaissance shift from the educational protectorate of monastic institutions to royal and seignorial courts or enlightened home tutoring did not necessarily carry over into subsequent secular career opportunities. The learned Cassandra Fidele wrote as she reached her twenties:

> As for the utility of letters, enough said. Not only is this divine field, abundant and noble, amply useful, but it offers its copious, delightful, and perpetual fruits profusely. Of these fruits I myself have tasted a little and have esteemed myself in that enterprise more than abject and hopeless; and, armed with distaff and needle—women's weapons—I march forth to defend that belief that even though the study of letters promises and offers no reward for women and no dignity, every woman ought to seek and embrace these studies for that pleasure and delight alone that comes from them.

In addition to the private pleasure derived from learning that, even if it afforded no professional rewards, could be the source of private satisfaction, those women in comfortable circumstances or those whose militant reformist or anti-reformist zeal could be employed in religious polemics who aspired to write, could do so and, in doing so, were often able to burst the confines placed upon their art.

Participation—any participation—in the shaping of language is social power. The written word as a signifier of status and power, is capable of bestowing parity to male and female in that privileged space. The literary labor of Renaissance women writers thus articulates a desire, however subliminal, for the status and power which that equity implies. Assuming the voice of the poet, engaging in the shaping, defining and ordering of experience, participating in constructing and creating, women of the fifteenth and sixteenth centuries could temporarily offset the hierarchies of gender and become the equals of men in the act of creation.

Montaigne and His Readers

Richard L. Regosin

After an active career in courtly politics, the French-man Michel de Montaigne retired to a life of reading, contemplation, and writing in his library. In this essay, Professor Richard L. Regosin of the University of California-Irvine describes how Montaigne's quest to know himself resulted in the collection of writings called the *Essais,* or *Essays* in English. Montaigne addresses a wide range of subjects in his *Essays,* all of which reveal the influence of the ancient Greek and Roman writers from whom he continually borrows and with whom he constantly converses. The *Essays* may also be described as Montaigne's written attempts to understand himself; as Regosin puts it, they reveal "the unfolding of a mind of genius in dialogue with itself and the world."

In 1571, after thirteen years as a counselor in the Chambre des Enquêtes (Chamber of Hearings) of the Bordeaux parlement, Michel de Montaigne, having resigned his position, returned home to care full time for his estate. On the wall of the study next to his library he had inscribed in Latin the official statement of his retirement:

> In the year of Christ 1571, at the age of thirty-eight, on the last day of February, his birthday, Michel de Montaigne, long weary of the servitude of the court and of public employments, while still entire, retired to the bosom of the learned virgins [the literary muses], where in calm and freedom from all cares he will spend what little remains of his life, now more than half run out. If the fates permit, he will complete this abode, this sweet ancestral retreat; and he has consecrated it to his freedom, tranquillity, and leisure. *(Complete Essays)*

But Montaigne's years of retirement until his death in 1592 were not spent entirely in domestic quiet and leisure.

Reprinted by permission of the publisher from "Montaigne and His Readers," by Richard L. Regosin, pp. 248–53 in *A New History of French Literature,* edited by Denis Hollier (Cambridge, MA: Harvard University Press). Copyright © 1989 by the President and Fellows of Harvard College.

During those two decades he received the Order of Saint Michel, was made a gentleman-in-ordinary of the king's chamber by three kings of France, traveled through Italy, was twice elected mayor of Bordeaux, and on numerous occasions played a role in national political affairs on behalf of Henri de Navarre, the future King Henri IV. And in the bosom of the muses, which we might think of as his library in the tower where he worked surrounded by his books, Montaigne wrote and rewrote what he called the trials or tests of his judgment, his *Essais* (from *essayer*, to test, try out). . . .

COMPASSIONATE INSIGHTS

Although [French theorist Blaise] Pascal objected to Montaigne's secular perspective and to what he called the essayist's nonchalance about salvation, and although [French philosopher Jean Jacques] Rousseau criticized Montaigne's modesty as self-serving, generations of readers have venerated Montaigne for the generous and compassionate wisdom of his insights into the human condition, the understanding and moderation of his comments on social and political affairs, and the gentle and sympathetic irony with which he viewed the world and himself. In the personal, conversational essays of the learned humanist, readers have identified a voice whose naturalness, sincerity, and spontaneity guarantee the truth and validity of its words. The text's frequent humble proclamations of its own vanity, and the writer's insistence on his own ignorance—the writer who took as his model Socrates and as his motto the words "What do I know?"—notwithstanding, a figure of towering authority, an imposing authorial presence has dominated the traditional reading of the *Essais*. Though not a chronological life history, the text has been treated as autobiographical writing, as the unfolding of a mind of genius in dialogue with itself and with the world, a Renaissance humanist speaking to all humanity.

Montaigne himself fosters this view that he and his work are one. In the prefatory note "To the Reader," he offers his writings as a faithful and sincere portrait of his natural self and claims that he himself is the matter of his book. The diverse subjects on which Montaigne writes—on sadness, liars, education, friendship, cannibals, names, practice, presumption, repentance, vanity, and experience, to name just a few—appear to provide him the opportunity to try out his judgment and to measure the quality of his mind. The essay "On Democritus and Heraclitus" explicitly makes this "trial" the essential subject of the writing:

> Judgment is a tool to use on all subjects, and comes in everywhere. Therefore in the tests that I make of it here, I use every sort of occasion. If it is a subject I do not understand at all, even on that I essay my judgment, sounding the ford from a good distance; and then, finding it too deep for my height, I stick to the bank . . . Sometimes in a vain and nonexistent subject I try to see if it will find the wherewithal to give it body . . . Sometimes I lead it to a noble and well-worn subject in which it has nothing original to discover . . . There it plays its part by choosing the way that seems best to it . . . I take the first subject that chance offers. They are all equally good to me. *(Complete Essays)*

IMMERSED IN THE CLASSICS

. . . Montaigne's education and his reading habits reflected the 16th-century French reverence for Greek and Roman letters and its interest in the intellectual and artistic expression of Renaissance Italy. According to his own testimony, his library contained over 1,000 volumes of classical, Italian, and French literature, philosophy, and history. Those who have treated the *Essais* as autobiography have used this reading to explain the evolution of the essays in two ways: they have imagined a movement in Montaigne's writing from stoic to skeptic to a broadly humanistic posture and from less personal, derivative essays to more personal ones as the essayist discovered successively the writers representing these attitudes (such as Seneca the Stoic, Sextus Empiricus the Skeptic, and the personal and intimate Plutarch). But the relation between Montaigne's reading and his writing is more complex than this clear-cut schema allows. Recent scholarship has demonstrated convincingly that the early essays, though on the whole not as richly developed as the later ones, express the personal voice of their author and his pursuit of self-knowledge and that, rather than simply mirroring his reading in some evolutionary way, Montaigne's writing at all periods of his intellectual life engages in dialogue with a spectrum of thinkers and ideas. Accordingly, scholarly concern has turned from the "man" to inquire about the textual function of this reading, both in terms of how an individual "self" might be formed through interaction with reading as the embodiment of tradition, of the past, and of culture itself, and in terms of how its specific presence as quotation operates in Montaigne's writing.

The sheer volume of borrowed ideas and borrowed writing in Montaigne's text reflects the authority of tradition and might imply as well that a "self" can indeed be conceived out of that which was originally foreign to it. Renaissance culture—and Montaigne himself—used the metaphor of the bee gathering pollen to make its own honey as a commonplace to suggest that this process was in fact an aspect of the organic nature of things. But Montaigne's text does not only claim that it appropriates the past through the workings of judgment; it also turns in a self-reflexive gesture to question its own basic assumption. More than once Montaigne denounces the practice of quotation, challenges and contests tradition, belittles his quotations as pilferings, and claims that his book is little more than borrowed flowers. In the interest of coherence, past readers tended to underplay this inclination. More recent readers have directly confronted this tendency of the text to undermine its own project, interpreting it as a sign of the unavoidable tension between the writer's desire to constitute an integral, personal self and his realization that the self is always constituted out of what is borrowed. The status of quotation, like that of language generally in the 16th century, emerges as relative and unstable, like the status of the subject itself.

Montaigne writes about himself and his experience in the world, giving opinions, discussing moral themes, citing examples, seeking to have his text mirror himself, be "consubstantial" with him, as he puts it in the essay "On Giving the Lie." But as was clear as early as 1571 in the inscription of his retirement, Montaigne also projects himself self-consciously *through* his writing as "Michel de Montaigne," and in the self-performance of the *Essais* this textual figure emerges as a metaphor of self, a function of the language—its vocabulary, syntax, topoi—in which it articulates itself. The risks of conceiving of one's "self" in language and its figures are real, but there is no other way to give birth to oneself. The metaphor always risks taking the place of the "living" author, because he is absent when the text speaks for him; but, just as significantly, it risks revealing itself in all its factitiousness. Alongside his claims of being present in his text, Montaigne affirms the vanity and emptiness of the self and of the discourse into which it casts itself. The unresolved dualities of Montaigne's *Essais* admit neither of unitary resolution nor of simple opposition, but in dynamic relationship compose a figure built up—like the endless digressions and parentheses that characterize the text—of supplements and deferments of wholeness and closure. "Who does not see," Montaigne writes in "On Vanity," near the end of his *Essais,* "that I have taken a road along which I shall go, without stopping and without effort, as long as there is ink and paper in the world?"

The Educational Writings of Sir Francis Bacon

Brian Vickers

While his standing in the canon of English literature is secure, Sir Francis Bacon never produced what may be called a piece of "pure" literature in the conventional genres, according to Professor Brian Vickers of the University of Zurich in Switzerland. All of Bacon's writings were designed to educate rather than to entertain in a narrow sense. Even in his *Essays*, perhaps his most "literary" effort, his goal was to improve the state of knowledge for whatever subject he addressed. Yet as Professor Vickers concludes in the following essay, Bacon's employment of a wide range of literary devices, strategies, and figures qualifies all of his writings as literature.

Bacon's writings have long enjoyed a firm place in English literature. The qualities that continue to attract readers—a powerful intellectual grasp, analytical penetration, a mastery of the expressive resources of language, the ability to adapt style to subject-matter and purpose—have been celebrated by many distinguished writers, from Ben Jonson and Abraham Cowley to Dr Johnson and [Alexander] Pope, [Samuel Taylor] Coleridge and [William] Hazlitt, [Thomas] De Quincey, [Percy Bysshe] Shelley, and [John] Ruskin. Bacon's high standing in the English literary canon seems assured, yet it rests on a strange paradox, namely that he never wrote a single piece of 'pure' literature. Everything that he ever produced was dedicated to his lifelong goal of improving the amount and quality of knowledge available to mankind, so as to alleviate the miseries of human existence. As he wrote in his programmatic letter to Burghley in

From the Introduction, by Brian Vickers, to *Francis Bacon*, edited by Brian Vickers. Copyright © 1996 by Oxford University Press. Reprinted by permission of Oxford University Press.

1592 (echoing Cicero's prescription for the perfect orator), 'I have taken all knowledge to be my province; and if I could purge it of two sorts of rovers [distracting influences] . . . I hope I should bring in industrious observations, grounded conclusions, and profitable inventions and discoveries'. They would be 'profitable' not in the sense of financial gain but in terms of his distinctive conception of the true goal of intellectual pursuits, to be applied for 'the benefit and use of men', knowledge itself being 'a rich storehouse, for the glory of the Creator and the relief of man's estate'. All Bacon's writings are dedicated to this functional, charitable goal, whatever categories editors subsequently assign them to—and the categories are many: natural philosophy, or what we would call the physical sciences (embracing the logic of scientific discovery, the forms of matter, physics, astronomy), the life sciences (studies of life and its prolongation, human and animal biology), psychology, sociology, the communication sciences (logic, rhetoric, ciphers, emblems), and much else.

The *Essays* have been traditionally valued as a literary work, but, as R.S. Crane first showed, they should also be seen as a contribution to the study of human life from what we would describe as a psychological and sociological viewpoint. In the *Advancement of Learning* (1605) Bacon called for more research into 'the several characters and tempers of men's natures and dispositions', in particular the differences between people caused by 'those impressions of nature which are imposed on the mind by the sex, by the age, by the region, by health and sickness, by beauty and deformity, and the like, which are inherent and not extern; and again those which are caused by extern fortune, as sovereignty, nobility . . . riches . . . prosperity, adversity . . . and the like'. Also, he suggested, we need studies of 'those points which are within our own command, and have force and operation upon the mind to affect the will and appetite and to alter manners', such as 'custom, habit . . . friends . . . fame . . . laws . . . studies'. For each of these topics Bacon wrote an essay, to collect his own observations from life and reading into just such a 'storehouse', not arranged systematically but in the form of aphorisms, disconnected utterances which illuminate different, sometimes opposed aspects of the topic studied. If the 1597 *Essays* present this aim in embryo, glimpsed but not fully articulated, those of 1625 are its fulfilment, and can be linked at every point to Bacon's wider project for a science of man.

The writings of Sir Francis Bacon were dedicated to improving the quality of knowledge available to mankind.

Use of Literary Genres

But even while we make this point, that none of his works is purely literary, we have to add its corollary, that throughout his life Bacon constantly used literary genres to embody and disseminate his ideas. If we review his career, for once in reverse order, we may be surprised at the range of genres he drew on. The posthumously published *Sylva Sylvarum, or a Natural History* (1627), was divided into ten books, each of ten centuries, a mode of organization common in meditational literature, such as Joseph Hall's *Meditations and Vows, Divine and Morall, III Centuries* (1605, 1606). At the end of that volume appeared *New Atlantis,* a hybrid work combining the genres of voyage literature, utopian fable, and secular apocalypse (a revelation handed down orally, from teacher to pupil or initiate). In 1624 Bacon published his *Translation of Certain Psalms into English Verse,* and made at least one other verse translation (from the classics); also in that year he released his collection of *Apophthegms New and Old,* pithy sayings, usually by famous historical personages. The psalms were celebrated throughout the Christian Church as the supreme example of divine poetry, also as an example of sacred epideictic rhetoric, praising God, while the apophthegm was one of several rhetorical storehouses that Bacon recommended all writers to have in readiness. In 1624 he drafted *Considerations Touching a War with Spain,* the last of his many treatises of advice to the Sovereign, a central genre in Renaissance political literature. As for historiography, his *History of the Reign of King Henry the Seventh* (1622) was a major work, the only one of the several histories that he drafted (from 1602 onwards) to be actually completed. In 1622 he began his only work in the dialogue genre, the *Advertisement Touching a Holy War,* a fragment first published in 1629, in which, true to one of the conventions of Renaissance dialogue, each of the speakers represents a different philosophy or religious creed, so that their discussion comes to resemble a debate in which personalities clash, as well as ideas.

These experiments with different genres were all products of the frantically busy period after he was driven out of office. In the preceding twenty-five years Bacon's written output derived mainly from his two main careers, politics and law. Many of his speeches in both Houses of Parliament survive, and after the enormous developments of parliamentary history over the last thirty years the time may soon be ripe for a full study of his contribution to both the substance and the form of parliamentary debate. The literary genre that Bacon used most frequently of all was the oration, as could be expected from his choice of the *vita activa*. His political and legal speeches largely fall into the two dominant forms of the classical oration, the deliberative, giving advice to a constituted authority on matters of public policy, and the judicial, arguing for the guilt or innocence of a person on trial. But Bacon also left distinguished examples of the epideictic (or demonstrative) oration, which praised virtuous behaviour and censured evil. Such is his tribute to Queen Elizabeth I, . . . a composition which he valued so highly that he gave express instructions in his will for it to be published. . . .

This continuity of interest in intellectual matters across a period of more than thirty years of public life testifies to Bacon's tenacity, but also to the limited amount of time that he could expend on the projects so majestically announced in his 1592 letter to Burghley. The *De Augmentis* is in effect a vast repository of fragmentary treatises in many genres. One of them is an 'Example of a Treatise on Universal Justice or the Fountains of Equity, by Aphorisms; one Title of it', highlighting another genre important throughout Bacon's career, the aphorism. Bacon first used the aphorism in two works dating back to 1597, the *Essays*, which he published, and the *Maxims of the Law* which he did not. There he first outlined a coherent and original theory of the aphorism, further developed in the *Advancement of Learning*, and used as the basic form in most of his mature scientific works. The main value of the aphorism for Bacon was not so much its brevity as the fact that it could contain original observations of nature or human life in separate, uncoordinated units. This meant that they could not be prematurely forced into a system, which would then close down further development. 'Knowledge, while it is in aphorisms, is in growth', as he put it. . . .

INVOLVEMENT WITH THE MASQUE

The most striking example of Bacon's involvement with a literary genre over and above its rhetorical usefulness as a vehicle for his ideas is his lifelong flirtation with the masque. The masque, a popular court entertainment between 1590 and 1642, was a proto-dramatic form which united theatrical spectacle, dancing, singing, and instrumental music around a stylized literary theme, often an encounter or temptation fable (where virtue regularly defeats pleasure), or a debate between exponents of varying forms of life, good and bad. The performers were partly professional (the musicians, painters, and choreographers), and partly amateur,

OF STUDIES

Sir Francis Bacon wore many hats in his day: politician, philosopher, scientist, and essayist, among others. But whenever he put pen to paper, his eloquent literary style was clear. This quality is quite evident in the following excerpt from his brief essay on reading and scholarship titled "Of Studies."

To spend too much time in studies is sloth; to use them too much for ornament is affectation; to make judgment wholly by their rules is the humour of a scholar. They perfect nature, and are perfected by experience, for natural abilities are like natural plants, that need proyning [pruning] by study; and studies themselves do give forth directions too much at large, except they be bounded in by experience. Crafty men contemn studies; simple men admire them; and wise men use them, for they teach not their own use, but that is a wisdom without them and above them, won by observation. Read not to contradict and confute, nor to believe and take for granted, nor to find talk and discourse, but to weigh and consider. Some books are to be tasted, others to be swallowed, and some few to be chewed and digested; that is, some books are to be read only in parts; others to be read, but not curiously; and some few to be read wholly and with diligence and attention. Some books also may be read by deputy, and extracts made of them by others, but that would be only in the less important arguments and the meaner sort of books; else distilled books are like common distilled waters, flashy things. Reading maketh a full man, conference a ready man, and writing an exact man. And therefore, if a man write little, he had need have a great memory; if he confer little, he had need have a present wit; and if he read little, he had need have much cunning, to seem to know that he doth not. Histories make men wise, poets witty, the mathematics subtile, natural philosophy deep, moral grave, logic and rhetoric able to contend. *Abeunt studia in mores.* ["Studies become ways of life" (Ovid)].

Francis Bacon, "Of Studies," in *The Literature of Renaissance England.* Eds. John Hollander and Frank Kermode. New York: Oxford University Press, 1973, pp. 943–44.

but all saw their activity as directed to the Sovereign or high-ranking courtier being honoured by this single performance. Taking them in reverse order again, Bacon's essay 'Of Masques and Triumphs' in the 1625 volume simultaneously deprecates the genre and justifies it, as a legitimate form of entertainment for princes and rulers to indulge in during their leisure intervals from the serious activities, 'Civil and Moral', to which the rest of the volume is dedicated: 'These things are but toys, to come amongst such serious observations. But yet, since princes will have such things, it is better they should be graced with elegancy than daubed with cost'. The page that follows displays a detailed, first-hand knowledge of the genre, giving a quite individual evaluation of its various ingredients. . . .

While the ephemeral splendours of the court masques and shows evaporated during their single performance, the words remain, and Bacon's texts show his already considerable skills in argument. He first establishes each speaker with all his topics fluently organized, then allows every subsequent speaker to damage or even disqualify the preceding arguments, giving the concluding decision to the Prince or moderator. These devices remain both intellectually stimulating and eloquent, with many memorable passages. The speaker praising Fortitude in 1592 gives a penetrating account of one completely lacking that virtue, 'the timorous man', who when confronted with 'his pleasures and desires' is afraid to hope, and even more afraid to enjoy, for

> he ever imagineth some ill is hid in every good: so as his pleasure is as solid as the sands, being interrupted with continual fears and doubts. And when the pleasure is passed, then he thinketh it a dream, a surfeit of desire, a false joy. He is ungrateful to nature, for still the sense of grief printeth so deep, and the sense of delight so lightly, as the one seemeth unto him a truth, the other a deceit.

The psychological penetration there is but one of several impressive elements in that speech. But its speaker, having stated his case so vigorously, is instantly routed by his successor, who argues that while fortitude may free us 'from the tyrannies of fortune, yet doth it not in such perfection as doth love. For Fortitude indeed strengtheneth the mind, but it giveth no filling. It leaveth it empty': only love can give it a worthwhile content. To intellectual and psychological penetration these devices add more emotional appeals, as in the speech by the 'Hermit' (contemplative philosopher) in *Of Love and Self-Love*, urging Erophilus to abandon earthly love and become, rather, a Philosophus, for

> The gardens of love wherein he now playeth himself are fresh to-day and fading to-morrow, as the sun comforts them or is turned from them. But the gardens of the Muses keep the privilege of the golden age; they ever flourish and are in league with time. The monuments of wit survive the monuments of power. . . .

That eloquent argument is given still more resonance when it reappears in the conclusion to Book One of the *Advancement of Learning*.

EXPERIMENTATION AND EXCELLENCE

Bacon's place in English imaginative literature, we can argue, has been earned by his unceasing experimentation with so many different genres, from aphorisms and apophthegms to dialogues and speeches, essays and treatises, fables and masques. But it also derives from his excellence as a writer within these often hybrid works. From his own times to the present day he has been praised for his power with metaphor, that ability to see resemblances between things which Aristotle defined as a mark of genius. For Bacon, as for all writers within the Renaissance rhetorical tradition, the use of metaphor was not some optional literary grace but an organic part of intentional utterance. According to theorists in rhetoric and poetics, from the Greeks to the seventeenth century, metaphors properly used could both illuminate an argument and give it more force, appealing simultaneously to the intellect and to the affections (passions, feelings). Aristotle, followed by the author of *Rhetorica ad Herennium*, among many others, said that metaphor could be used to raise or lower the value of our subject-matter; Quintilian wrote that 'metaphor is designed to move the feelings, give special distinction to things, and place them vividly before the eye'; many Renaissance rhetoricians agreed that metaphors and similes can produce greater 'vehemency' than other verbal resources, that they 'confirm our understanding and fastest cleave unto the memory', and do 'not onely bewtifie our tale, but also very much inforce & inlarge it'.

Metaphor is particularly important in epideictic rhetoric, juxtaposing praise and blame. This can be seen most vividly from Book One of the *Advancement of Learning*, which is in effect an extended epideictic oration, defending the pursuit of knowledge from its enemies, attacking those movements and fashions (medieval scholasticism, Renaissance Ciceronianism) which pervert true knowledge, and ending with a still inspiring celebration of the power of knowledge to survive the vicissitudes of time and chance. . . .

The first Book of the *Advancement* is one of the most carefully composed pieces of writing in Bacon's whole output, as if he sensed that the accession of King James offered a decisive chance to realize the reforms of knowledge to which he hoped to devote his life. Bacon uses these rhetorical structures creating syntactical symmetry completely effectively in the celebratory mode, as in discriminating the proper ends for which learning should be pursued, but in the *Advancement of Learning* they appear most brilliantly for two extended sequences of *vituperatio.* One attacks the scholastics, the other that peculiar group of writers who perverted knowledge in the early Renaissance. These were the overzealous imitators of Cicero, who devoted so much energy to the form of language that they neglected its content. . . .

Bacon used the resources of rhetorical figures as a way of organizing argument throughout his writing career, disproving claims that he practised a 'baroque', 'asymmetrical', or 'Senecan' prose style. They are just as effective in the early device 'Of Tribute' as in the *Essays*, indeed a comparison of the double revision of that collection, in 1612 and 1625, will show that Bacon made previous symmetries more pointed, and introduced new ones. Such are the parallels and contrasts in 'Of Regiment of Health', 'Of Studies' or 'Of Goodness and Goodness of Nature', where Bacon recurs, as so often, to the fall of man:

> The desire of power in excess
>   caused the angels to fall;
> the desire of knowledge in excess
>   caused man to fall;
> but in charity there is no excess;
>   neither can angel or man come in danger by it.

Set out visually such symmetries seem more obvious; in the experience of reading they are unpredictable, regularities which make any deviations from them more striking, as in this little sequence from 'Of Friendship':

> For a crowd is not company;
> and faces are but a gallery of pictures;

and talk but a tinkling cymbal,
where there is no love.

These and other literary resources, adapted so often and so effectively to context and intention—whether readers absorb
them unconsciously or become aware of their operation—
help account for Bacon's power as a writer over the last
three and a half centuries.

CHAPTER 5

English Renaissance Drama

Renaissance
Literature

Shakespeare's Predecessors: Lyly, Greene, Kyd, and Marlowe

David Bevington

In the years just before Shakespeare's greatest achievements, four Elizabethan dramatists—John Lyly, Robert Greene, Thomas Kyd, and Christopher Marlowe—helped establish the power and appeal of the Elizabethan popular theater. While Lyly and Greene contributed to the vogue for light romantic comedies, Kyd established the pathway for revenge tragedy that eventually led to Shakespeare's *Hamlet.* Marlowe provided a new sense of dignity and power to English tragedy through his use of language and his conception of the tragic hero. According to David Bevington, professor of humanities at the University of Chicago, Shakespeare learned and borrowed from all four of these playwrights, though it is to Marlowe, perhaps, that he owes his greatest debt.

In facing the problem of understanding just what Elizabethan drama was and how it became what it was, we must recognize that the classification of drama into comedy and tragedy by the ancients does not tell the whole story. Even when we add the history or chronicle play to these two divisions of drama, we have, at best, a rough classification that leaves out a great deal and implies that these three forms were sharply discriminated. In fact, Elizabethan drama is, generally speaking, a blend of many elements. Nearly all Elizabethan tragedies have in them comic scenes and by-plots; most comedies have in them serious issues that might conceivably result in disaster; and history plays are often capable of being classified as comedies or as tragedies. To appreciate further this protean quality of genre in early Elizabethan drama, we might consider the varied works of a number of dramatists whose practice was successful on the stage and who influenced Shakespeare and his immediate contemporaries. Of these, John Lyly is one of the most important.

John Lyly (1554?–1606), grandson of the grammarian William Lyly or Lilly, educated at Oxford and Cambridge, first acquired fame not as a dramatist, but as a writer of prose. His *Euphues, The Anatomy of Wit,* published in 1578, and its sequel, *Euphues and His England* (1580), stand as the most sensational and brilliant effort in the struggle of English Renaissance prose to acquire a conscious artistic manner. The style is, to a remarkable extent, composed of rhetorical devices: antithesis, personification, rhetorical question, metaphor, simile, and, above all, balance reinforced by alliteration. Recondite tidbits and fanciful legends about natural history are garnered from Plutarch, Pliny, and many other writers. The overall result is a kind of handbook for the courtier, the lover, the traveler, and the statesman. Lyly's deliberately outrageous style was imitated by dozens of other writers, including Robert Greene and Thomas Lodge, and seems to have set a new fashion of smart speech in the court of Queen Elizabeth. "Euphuism" itself had a vast influence on the style of the drama and other literature, both in poetry and in prose. Shakespeare is one of those who imitated and also ridiculed euphuistic speech. (For amusing examples of Shakespeare's parodying of the euphuistic style, see Falstaff's speech in *1 Henry IV,* 2.4.397 ff., beginning "for though the camomile, the more it is trodden on the faster it grows, yet youth, the more it is wasted the sooner it wears," or Don Armado's love letter in *Love's Labor's Lost,* 4.1.61 ff.: "Shall I command thy love? I may. Shall I enforce thy love? I could. Shall I entreat thy love? I will," and so on.)

Lyly was also the author of at least eight comedies, written to suit the taste of the court and possibly all acted before the Queen by the children of the Chapel Royal or of St. Paul's School. The plays are often courtly debates in the tradition of Medwall's *Fulgens and Lucrece,* with much combat of wits and philosophical argument. These comedies are also sufficiently modeled on Plautus or Terence to indicate that the characteristic features of Latin comedy by this time (1580–1590) had become naturalized on the English stage.

Mother Bombie, for example, is an adaptation of Latin comedy, containing such stock figures as the pedant, the rascally servant, the duped parent, the parasite, and the aged lover, although, as usual, in Lyly the clownery has an English flavor as well.

Indeed, however much Lyly may recall classical Latin comedy, he is most important as the inventor of a gay and fanciful type of love comedy to which Shakespeare was significantly indebted in several of his plays. Lyly's *Sappho and Phao*, *Endymion*, and *Midas* have romantic plots derived from Ovidian mythology. *Gallathea* uses a pastoral setting for its love story and male disguises for the heroines, as in *As You Like It. Love's Metamorphosis* and *The Woman in the Moon* are also pastoral comedies. *Campaspe*, like *The Merchant of Venice*, portrays conflicts of love and friendship. Lyly's flattery of Queen Elizabeth through topical allegory and his appeal to a courtly clientele are, to be sure, modes that Shakespeare does not generally adopt. On the other hand, Shakespeare learned a good deal from Lyly's sensitive portrayal of the psychology of love. The depiction is often wryly comic: Lyly's men abase themselves before women, vacillate between idealization and misogyny, and not infrequently fail as wooers—much as the young lords do in Shakespeare's most Lylyan play, *Love's Labor's Lost*. Shakespeare's lovers generally work toward a more successful and realistic completion of romantic expectations, but Shakespeare's interest in love comedy began, in part, with what Lyly had achieved. . . .

ROBERT GREENE

Robert Greene (1558–1592), more than any other dramatist, opened up for Shakespeare the world of Greek romance—the kind of fiction ultimately derived from Heliodorus, Achilles Tatius, and other protonovelists of the Mediterranean world in the second through fourth centuries. The Greeks of that era were the merchants, traders, sailors, and schoolmasters of the Roman Empire, and the early form of prose romance they created was a reflection of the adventurous life they lived. This romantic fiction reveled in strange and improbable encounters, piracies, the exposure of infant children to the elements and their eventual restoration as grown-ups to their aging parents, the separation and reunion of indistinguishable twins, and many other plot devices rendered familiar to us in the writings of

Renaissance authors for whom this kind of sensationalism was every bit as interesting and worthy of imitation as the classics of Virgil and Ovid. Stories of the Greek kind, translated into various languages and ultimately into English, were to serve as models for a number of Shakespeare's late romances, especially *Pericles, The Winter's Tale,* and *Cymbeline.* Indeed, the plot of *The Winter's Tale* came to Shakespeare by way of Greene's prose romance, *Pandosto.*

From Greek romantic fiction, and also, no doubt, from his own experience in life, Greene devised a type of plucky romantic heroine for his plays and novels that Shakespeare was to develop further in his comedies. The society depicted by Greek romance gave women great liberty, and, like them, Greene's heroines are independent, witty, and resourceful, though at the same time feminine. Greene's dramas are almost the first modern productions in which woman is in any degree represented as assuming a relatively dignified station in a mutually supportive love relationship with a man.

Greene also borrowed from Greek romantic fiction, and from other sources, an important element of pastoral. His plays, particularly *James IV* and *Friar Bacon and Friar Bungay* (c. 1589–1592), give us that blend of the pastoral and the romantic which the world has enjoyed in *As You Like It* and *Love's Labor's Lost. Friar Bacon* is particularly noteworthy for its multiple plot, its resourceful heroine, and its embracing of serious issues in a comic world. Greene must be regarded as the first great master of plot in English comedy. . . .

THOMAS KYD

While romantic comedy was being shaped and developed in the hands of Lyly, Peele, and Greene, the Senecan tradition was also finding its proponents on the English stage. The greatest genius in adapting Senecan action to the English theater was Thomas Kyd (1558–1594). His influence on his contemporaries and on later dramatists was immense; *The Spanish Tragedy* (c. 1583–1587) was probably acted more times during the sixteenth century than any other English play and became a pattern for subsequent revenge drama. Although Senecan tradition by no means accounts for all of the play's successful qualities, it remains a central part. Kyd catches the unabashed brutality and horror of the Senecan story and reveals it openly. Instead of having the action reported as taking place off the stage, as in Seneca and in most classical tragedy, he presents it directly. For tales of Greek mythology, he substitutes a modern story of love, conspiracy, murder, and political intrigue. He retains the Senecan ghost, the revenge motive, the spirit of stoicism, and a modified form of the chorus. The play deals both seriously and sensationally with the conflicting codes of revenge and Christian faith in God's providence. The protagonist Hieronimo, confronted with his son's murder and seemingly unable to obtain justice through the state, finds his pleas to the heavens unanswered and turns instead to a revenge that hardens his spirit and requires his own violent death as payment. The action is presided over by the spirit of Revenge, a choruslike figure whose aims share nothing in common with Christian views of justice and mercy. *The Spanish Tragedy* is also noteworthy for a style that is a tour de force of rhetorical figures, such as climax and oxymoron—an achievement both imitated and mocked by later dramatists. Probably Kyd is also the author of the first dramatic version of the story of Hamlet.

Kyd's work gave rise to a series of revenge plays, not only in his own time, but also later, in 1600 and the years following, when the revenge tragedy again became fashionable. Moreover, Kyd seems to have had a shaping influence on Greene and on Marlowe. For example, Marlowe's *The Jew of Malta* (c. 1589), in its extravagance and sensational intrigue, seems particularly indebted to *The Spanish Tragedy.*

CHRISTOPHER MARLOWE

Nevertheless, however much Kyd may have contributed in matters of style and form, Marlowe remains the leader in the great English type of Elizabethan tragedy. He shaped the genre that subsequently was perfected by Shakespeare. His achievement is all the more remarkable when we consider that he was born in the same year as Shakespeare (1564) and died in 1593, when Shakespeare had written no more than six or seven of his earliest plays. Marlowe's great contribution to English drama was a type of protagonist expressing something of the aspiration of the very Renaissance itself. Tamburlaine thirsts for world conquest; Dr. Faustus would go to the utmost bounds of knowledge and the power which knowledge gives; and Barabas in *The Jew of Malta* sets no limit to his longing for wealth.

Structurally, *Tamburlaine* (1587–1588) is a good deal

closer to the English popular morality play than to classical drama. Each of the play's two parts consists of a linear sequence of conquests by the humbly born but seemingly invincible Tamburlaine, until at last death ends his glory. Because many characters appear in one episode only, the cast is large and yet within the capacities of an Elizabethan acting company. Doubling of parts, as in Shakespeare's early history plays, is both common and necessary. Structural unity is achieved through thematic repetition rather than through a narrowing of the narrative focus. At the same time, the language of *Tamburlaine* is rich and new in its vibrant appeal to limitless human aspiration. The Elizabethan playgoer is invited to forget moral considerations in evaluating the play's ruthless hero and to revel instead in the intoxicating spectacle of a baseborn shepherd "threat'ning the world with high astounding terms."

A profound ambivalence permeates all of Marlowe's plays and gives them a restless, brilliant energy that is characteristic of the times for which they were written. Tamburlaine is both a remorseless butcher of his enemies and a superhuman quester. He is fierce, mysterious, oriental, exotic, unknowable; as the projection of a universal human dream of aspiration, he is to be both admired and feared. Barabas in *The Jew of Malta* is at once colossally rich and colossally evil. Similarly, the protagonist of *Doctor Faustus* (c. 1588) is both a sinner who falls from grace and a noble but doomed Overreacher (as Harry Levin describes him), daring like Icarus to fly toward the sun. In medieval and Christian orthodox terms, Faustus is guilty of pride, the deadliest of the Deadly Sins; but in Renaissance terms he at least fleetingly resembles Prometheus, challenging the hierarchy of an oppressive and outmoded universe. In its free mixture of comedy and tragedy and its wholesale disregard of the classical unities, *Doctor Faustus* brilliantly demonstrates what the native and homiletic tradition of tragedy had to offer Shakespeare.

Edward II, perhaps Marlowe's last play (1591–1593), is ambivalent toward its paired central figures, Edward and Mortimer Junior. At first, the effeminate King seems chiefly in the wrong, while his baronial opponents lament England's decline. Toward the end of the play, however, the King becomes the sympathetic victim of a power-mad and Machiavellian Mortimer. Queen Isabella also changes radically from a long-suffering, neglected wife into a scheming adulteress. This shift in sympathy from the barons to King Edward is structurally much like that of Shakespeare's *Richard II*, and, unquestionably, Marlowe's history play had a profound effect on Shakespeare. Yet Marlowe's tone, as in his other plays, remains one of naturalistic amorality. He wryly regards England's political struggles as one more manifestation of the restlessness and ambition afflicting all mortal endeavors. His world is one of constant turmoil in which persons of insatiable will must assert themselves and rise to the top, at whatever cost to themselves and to society. Shakespeare's world is basically different, even though he learned a great deal from Marlowe's tragic vision.

Marlowe first gave to English tragedy its realization of character and, still more, its dignity and seriousness. He endowed English drama with a spirit of aspiration. His enthusiasm for beauty of language, shared by Spenser, Greene, Peele, and others, provided a rich heritage for the young Shakespeare. Not the least among Marlowe's gifts to English drama was a new and more flexible blank-verse style. In the following prologue to *Tamburlaine the Great*, Part I, Marlowe does not treat each blank-verse line as a separate unit but runs the sense on from line to line in order to produce what might be described as a blank-verse paragraph, a thing most necessary to drama if it is to represent widely varying emotions, thoughts, and characters:

> From jigging veins of rhyming mother wits,
> And such conceits as clownage keeps in pay,
> We'll lead you to the stately tent of war,
> Where you shall hear the Scythian Tamburlaine
> Threat'ning the world with high astounding terms,
> And scourging kingdoms with his conquering sword.
> View but his picture in this tragic glass,
> And then applaud his fortunes as you please.

This is not only a manifesto of tragic seriousness; it is also, in spite of its elevated style, one of the first examples in English tragedy of vigorous, natural, straightforward expression. Tamburlaine in his utterances is a typical Renaissance poet on the themes of both love and war, as can be seen in the following evocation of the aspiring mind:

> If all the pens that ever poets held
> Had fed the feeling of their masters' thoughts,
> And every sweetness that inspired their hearts,
> Their minds, and muses on admired themes;
> If all the heavenly quintessence they still
> From their immortal flowers of poesy,

Wherein, as in a mirror, we perceive
The highest reaches of a human wit;
If these had made one poem's period,
And all combined in beauty's worthiness,
Yet should there hover in their restless heads
One thought, one grace, one wonder, at the least,
Which into words no virtue can digest.
                                   —*Tamburlaine*, Pt. I, 5.2.98–110

SHAKESPEARE'S DRAMATIC HERITAGE

Shakespearean tragedy began, roughly speaking, with marked indebtedness to the tragic writing of Marlowe and Kyd: poetry, character, and style from Marlowe; motive, plot, and tragic intensity from Kyd. No evidence suggests that Shakespeare was ever particularly aware of, or influenced by, Aristotelian theories of tragedy. His wish was to hold "the mirror up to nature" and show "virtue her feature, scorn her own image, and the very age and body of the time his form and pressure" (*Hamlet*, 3.2.22–24). Sometimes he approximated Aristotelian ideals in his plays (most nearly, perhaps, in *Othello*, *Macbeth*, and *Coriolanus*), but not by conscious design. Nor was he a slavish borrower from Marlowe and Kyd, even in his early tragedies, such as *Titus Andronicus*. Greene and many others sought to imitate Marlowe in tragedy, with but indifferent success. Shakespeare, Marlowe's only successful imitator, soon outdistanced Marlowe in those very qualities for which he was indebted to him.

Similarly, the elements of Shakespearean comedy are, in part, derived from Lyly, Peele, and Greene. The contributions of Lyly and Peele were those of style, setting, and movement. Greene, primarily a writer of romance, an adapter of Greek romantic fiction, furnished the element of love and adventure which makes so many Elizabethan plays delightful merely as stories. He also put upon the stage the witty, independent-minded woman, usually in boy's clothes, who gives point and naturalness to love intrigue whether in serious drama or in comedy. Not only did Shakespeare, who was a far greater genius than any of them, combine the elements of the comedies of these men and better the instruction, but, as his career went on, he realized on a broad scale the possibilities of the comic point of view in the representation of human life and character.

In the English history play, though he may have learned much from Marlowe, Peele, and others, Shakespeare was clearly an innovator as well. His early history plays on the reigns of Henry VI and Richard III were among the earliest such plays seen in London and were (at least some of them) enormous stage successes. Even here, however, we can see how much Shakespeare learned from such earlier plays as *Gorboduc* and *The Troublesome Reign of King John.*

Marlowe's *Dr. Faustus* and Renaissance Aspiration

Roma Gill

Christopher Marlowe and his tragedy *Dr. Faustus* embody many of the paradoxes and tensions of the Renaissance. Marlowe held a masters degree in theology but was widely known as an atheist. The heroes of his plays were grandiose and larger than life, but Marlowe himself died in a tavern fight over the bar bill. In a time exploding with the new learning, *Dr. Faustus* explores the paradox of Renaissance aspiration. Roma Gill, of the University of Sheffield in England, argues that the play examines "the dangers inherent in the pursuit of knowledge." The play also exposes contradictions and tensions between classical values and Christian values in the Renaissance.

At the age of twenty-nine Marlowe was murdered. His death was welcomed by Her Majesty's Privy Council, which later pardoned the murderer, and by certain popular moralists who hailed it as 'a manifest sign of God's judgement' on a life of impiety and debauchery.

Marlowe was born into a turbulent Canterbury family. His father was a shoemaker of modest means and excessive pugnacity, while two of his sisters, Dorothy and Ann, were notorious in the town—the former for various trade and matrimonial intrigues, the latter a noted 'scold, common swearer and blasphemer of the name of God'. Marlowe escaped from the family environment with the aid of those charitable Elizabethans who had endowed scholarships for the encouragement of learning in poor boys. The first scholarship, of £4 a year, took him to the King's School, Canterbury, from where he proceeded to Cambridge as a Matthew

Parker scholar at Corpus Christi College. The Parker scholarship was awarded for three years in the first instance, and
might be extended for a further three on evidence that the
holder intended to take Holy Orders. Marlowe held his for
the full six years. The College's Buttery Book shows him as
an undergraduate whose expenditure easily exceeded his
income but who from time to time spent nothing at all.
There were, evidently, frequent and prolonged absences
from Cambridge, and these gave the University cause to
question his activities and to threaten, in 1587, to withhold
his final degree. But Marlowe had strings to pull. A letter
from the Privy Council, with the overruling authority of,
among others, Archbishop Whitgift, Sir Christopher Hatton,
and Lord Burghley, explained in veiled hints the reason for
these absences: Marlowe 'had done Her Majestie good service, and deserved to be rewarded for his faithfull dealinge'.
He probably went abroad—perhaps to visit the English
Catholics at Rheims [in Holland]. Amidst much speculation
one thing is clear: this 'good service' was not of the kind that
is officially recorded and recognised.

A RECKLESS LIFE

A secret agent with an M.A. degree, Marlowe left Cambridge
for London. There he consorted with playwrights, at one
time sharing a room with Thomas Kyd, author of *The Spanish Tragedy;* quite possibly he associated also with the group
of young intellectuals led by Sir Walter Raleigh. Although the
facts of his life are largely unknown, its tenor is certain. Arrested once on a charge of homicide, bound over at another
time to keep the peace, Marlowe emerges from contemporary legal documents as a rash and fearless quarreller.
Mario Praz calls him a *libertin,* using the word to mean both
'free-thinker' and, with its accumulated secondary meaning,
'man of loose morals'. For the free-thinking there is ample
evidence of surprising consistency. Richard Baines libelled
Marlowe only a few days after the murder. The now famous
libel accuses the dramatist of blaspheming the Bible and
mocking the state, reporting him as having said:

> That the first beginning of Religion was only to keep men
> in awe . . .
> That Christ was a bastard and his mother dishonest . . .
> That all the new testament is filthily written . . .

To the Elizabethans, fearing for the sanctity of their church and the security of their state, these were 'monstruous opin-ions', menacing heresies. A warrant was issued for Marlowe's arrest, on evidence supplied perhaps by his former friend Kyd. Kyd himself had been arrested, accused of inciting mob vio-lence and race riots against the Flemish protestants who were then settling in England. Under torture he broke down, and in two letters to Sir John Puckering, the Lord Keeper, he charged Marlowe with heresy and blasphemy.

Before the warrant could be executed Marlowe was killed. The inquest report tells of a squalid encounter in a Deptford tavern on 30 May 1593. Marlowe spent the day there with three 'gentlemen', talking and walking in the garden. But in the evening a quarrel was struck up over who should pay the bill, *'le recknynge'*, and in the scuffle that followed Marlowe drew his dagger and wounded one of his companions. The man, Ingram Frizar, snatched the weapon and

> in defence of his life, with the dagger aforesaid of the value of 12d. gave the said Christopher then & there a mortal wound over his right eye of the depth of two inches & of the width of one inch; of which mortal wound the aforesaid Christopher Morley then & there instantly died.

The coroner's account puts a good face on the matter. Yet Ingram Frizar and one, if not both, of his accomplices had connections in some uncertain way with the secret service. Their past histories, and the speed with which, one month later, Frizar was granted a free pardon for the murder, sug-gest that the 'recknynge' settled in the Deptford tavern was an old score, and probably connected with Marlowe's secret service career.

Marlowe's contemporaries accepted the story of the brawl, but only one seems to have known its ostensible cause. Shakespeare's reference to Marlowe's death serves as an epitaph of his life, the brief life of his most brilliant col-league whose achievement, in five years, is second only to Shakespeare's own:

> A great reckoning in a little room
>
> > *As You Like It*, III, *iii*, 11

THE TRAGEDY OF DR FAUSTUS

... Boundless in its aspirations, unceasing in its compulsions, the Renaissance mind is the theme of all Marlowe's plays:

> Our souls, whose faculties can comprehend
> The wondrous architecture of the world,
> And measure every wand'ring planet's course,

Still climbing after knowledge infinite,
And always moving as the restless spheres,
Wills us to wear ourselves and never rest . . .
1 Tamburlaine, II, vii, 21–6

Dr Faustus, the first figure on the English stage who deserves to be called a character, is the epitome of Renaissance aspiration. He has all the divine discontent, the unwearied and unsatisfied striving after knowledge that marked the age in which Marlowe wrote. An age of exploration, its adventurers were not only the merchants and seamen who sailed round the world, but also the scientists, astronomers who surveyed the heavens with their 'optic glass', and those scholars who travelled in the realms of gold to bring back tales of a mighty race of gods and heroes in ancient Greece and Rome. The first soliloquy is [according to critic Harry Levin] 'no mere reckoning of accounts but an inventory of the Renaissance mind'. Faustus is one of the new men. For him, as for Marlowe, lowly birth was no bar to a university education; and as he sits alone in his study reading from the Latin textbooks, he is linked in a common language with scholars from Oxford, Cambridge, and all over the civilized world. Rhetoric, jurisprudence, and medicine have trained a mind apt for questioning, eager for learning, and reluctant to take on trust even the most elementary facts, let alone those hypotheses incapable of empirical proof. The Faustus who refuses to accept from Mephastophilis the evidence for hell's existence is true to himself. His pitiful shortsightedness is all too evident, but there is also a determination to believe only what he himself can prove. This has made him the distinguished scholar he is, the man whose triumphant cry '*sic probo*' has echoed his fame through the German universities. Men of Faustus' calibre were not unknown to Marlowe's age. They were valuable, and they were dangerous. Representative were Sir Walter Raleigh and his friends, meeting together to discuss philosophy, to debate religion, and to gaze at the stars through Thomas Heriot's new telescope. They attracted much unwanted attention, with accusations of witchcraft and devil-worship. . . .

The more man discovered about the universe and his place in it, the more imperative it became for Authority to stress the dangers inherent in the pursuit of knowledge. The wrath of the Almighty and the threat of eternal damnation were powerful deterrents.

THE DANGERS OF ASPIRATION

The soliloquy with which the play opens should not be read as the random notions of a single idle moment; rather, it is the utterance of thoughts that have been formulating for years in Faustus' mind. He stands at the frontiers of knowledge. The whole of Renaissance learning is within his grasp, but on closer scrutiny of the parts the whole crumbles away and he is left with nothing but a handful of dust. Nothing in the great university curriculum can overcome the melancholy fact—'Yet art thou still but Faustus, and a man' (Scene 1, line 23). Faustus shares with Hamlet, equally a product of Wittenberg scepticism, this perception of man's paradoxical nature:

> What a piece of work is a man! how noble in reason! how in-finite in faculties! . . . the beauty of the world, the paragon of animals! And yet, to me, what is this quintessence of dust?
>
> *Hamlet*, II, ii, 293–7

It is this that gives rise to the irony that is the characteristic mode of the play: Faustus begins by longing to be more than human; he ends by imploring metamorphosis into the sub-human. Incidental ironies have a sharp impact within this structure—as when Faustus seals his deed of blood with the last words of Christ on the cross: *'Consummatum est'* (Scene 5, line 74). The impassioned appeal

> Ah Christ my Saviour, seek to save
> Distressed Faustus' soul
>
> Scene 5, lines 257–8

is answered by the emergence of the infernal trinity looking, as J.B. Steane comments, like 'the party bosses in a totalitar-ian state before one guilty of thought-crime. . . .

Faustus envisages a world of power and delight which 'Stretcheth as far as doth the mind of man' (Scene 1, line 61). Human potential is set against human limitation in a single word. It is to redeem himself, by his own efforts, from this paradox that Faustus turns longing eyes on the magic books that will make him 'a mighty god'—and ultimately damn him for ever.

THE DETERIORATION OF FAUSTUS

Dr Faustus is a tragedy of damnation. In his source Marlowe found the story of a scholar who gave his soul to the devil in return for twenty-four years of knowledge and pleasure. The rewards were miserably inadequate, and are shown as such in the play, where Faustus is seen as a spectator at a conventional masque of the Seven Deadly Sins; as an astronaut circling the world; as a common illusionist entertaining at a Royal Command performance; and as a mystical greengrocer contenting a pregnant duchess with out-of-season grapes. Some critics, like Warren D. Smith, claim that the trivialities of the middle parts of the play show Marlowe intent on 'establishing evil, though terrible in consequence, as actually petty in nature'. On such a reading one can trace a gradual deterioration in the character of the protagonist. [In the words of critic Helen Gardner]:

> From a proud philosopher, master of all human knowledge, to a trickster, to a slave of phantoms, to a cowering wretch: that is a brief sketch of the progress of Dr Faustus.

Robert Ornstein, however, sees no such deterioration in Dr Faustus, arguing that the scholar 'grows more gracious' as he approaches his catastrophe; and Clifford Leech finds that

> Faustus's moment of highest authority, the moment when he is nearest to freedom, is not when he signs the bond but when he addresses the shape of Helen and puts himself into hell.

Perhaps every critic creates his *own* Faustus, interpreting 'Dr Faustus'—both the play and its eponymous hero—according to his personal experience and philosophy! ...

Faustus takes his first step along the primrose path when he sets material benefits before spiritual blessings. Contemplating magic, anticipating its rewards with Valdes and Cornelius, he promises himself all the glory and riches of the Renaissance world. From Mephastophilis he demands to 'live in all voluptuousness' (Scene 3, line 93). Even before he succumbs to the lure of magic, his mind has been tempted by thoughts of wealth: 'Be a physician, Faustus, heap up gold' (Scene 1, line 14). Yet although this obsession with luxury is a flaw in the nature of one dedicated to the search for knowledge, its seriousness must not be magnified until it obscures the real issues. In the first soliloquy Faustus rejects the study of law, leaving it to the 'mercenary drudge Who aims at nothing but external trash' (Scene 1, lines 34–5); all the gold that the doctor can heap up will not reconcile him to the limitations of medical skill, through whose aid he can restore only health, not life. And when, in an early agony of indecision, he weighs the profit and the loss, it is not riches that he puts into the opposite scale:

> Have not I made blind Homer sing to me

> Of Alexander's love, and Oenon's death?
> And hath not he that built the walls of Thebes
> With ravishing sound of his melodious harp,
> Made music with my Mephastophilis?
>
> > Scene 5, lines 202–6

With the help of magic he has gained entry into another world, later to be represented in the form of Helen of Troy, whose value far exceeds the riches of all the Venetian argosies, Indian gold, and Orient pearl.

The process of damnation begins with the signing of the pact. . . . By signing the bond with its ominous first clause Faustus is not cut off from forgiveness; but the effects of his sin, in turning away from God, make it virtually impossible for him to accept the offered mercy. Repentance is all that is needed, yet to his dismay he finds 'My heart's so hardened I cannot repent' (Scene 5, line 194).

THE DAMNATION OF FAUSTUS

The devils are adept at pricking the bubble of human self-glorification, and Faustus' pride is punctured in his first encounter with Mephastophilis. Soaring, as he thinks, to the height of his powers as 'conjuror laureate', he is jolted sharply back to earth by the fiend's casual admission that the conjuring was of no real import: 'I came now hither of mine own accord' (Scene 3, line 45). Hell's rewards are as the Dead Sea apples to Milton's fallen angels: mere ashes in his mouth. Repeated questioning of Mephastophilis brings no satisfaction; the devil can tell him only what he already knows and, forbidden to speak the praise of God, cannot give him the answer he wants to hear:

> FAUSTUS   Tell me who made the world?
> MEPHASTOPHILIS   I will not.
>
> > Scene 5, lines 241–2

His pride dashed, Faustus becomes increasingly aware of the emptiness of his bargain and the reality of damnation. The pride with which this Renaissance superman scorned his human nature and aspired to become 'a mighty god' leads him inevitably to its opposite, despair; and from this there is no salvation. . . .

Helen of Troy, twice passing over the stage, pausing for one brief moment yet speaking nothing, is the key figure in *Dr Faustus*. For this, Faustus has sold his soul. All the glory that was Greece was embodied, for the Renaissance, in this woman; her story was the story in brief of another world, superhuman and immortal. . . . Helen is the 'only paragon of excellence' in the eyes of these sober men, and their ordinary understanding is 'Too simple . . . to tell her praise'. The second appearance, attended by two Cupids and heralded, we must assume, by the music directed for the earlier entrance, has a ritual solemnity. This, and the formal ordering of Faustus' speech, mark the episode as what T.S. Eliot would have called 'a moment in and out of time'. Faustus breaks the silence with the awed amazement of some of Marlowe's finest lines:

> Was this the face that launched a thousand ships,
> And burnt the topless towers of Ilium?
>
> Scene 12, lines 81–2

Declaring his devotion, he is exalted to heroic stature and promises vigorous action in verse of soaring energy which comes to rest at last on Helen's lips:

> And then return to Helen for a kiss.
>
> Scene 12, line 93

The speech is a rapture of applause—for Helen herself, for the eternal beauty of form, for all the glory that defies and withstands the canker of Time. But it is more than this. As the delighted verse surges forward to praise what is lovely and enduring, an undertow drags back to remind us that this beauty brought destruction: a city was burnt, topless towers laid in the dust. In the stillness of a single couplet the two movements are balanced:

> Brighter art thou than flaming Jupiter
> When he appeared to hapless Semele.
>
> Scene 12, lines 96–7

Semele, despite repeated warnings, persisted in her demands to see her lover in all his splendour. But the sight of Jupiter's divine majesty was greater than mortal eyes could bear to look upon, and the 'hapless Semele' was consumed by the glory. Helen has all of Jupiter's terrible burning beauty—and Faustus is damned by the vision. This is no mere fancy of Marlowe's, powerful though such a fancy would be. That which appears as Helen is no more the woman herself than the apparition which so pleased the German emperor was indeed Alexander. Faustus sees a spirit, a devil, in the form of Helen and, forgetful of his admonitions to the emperor, he speaks to it and touches it. Helen's lips 'suck forth' his soul in more than metaphor. The

kiss signals the ultimate sin, demoniality, the bodily inter-
course with spirits. Now the Old Man gives up hope of sav-
ing Faustus. After such knowledge there is no forgiveness.

SYMPATHY FOR A REBEL

The last soliloquy reverses the first. The proud scholar who
had fretted at the restrictions imposed by the human condition and longed for the immortality of a god now seeks to
avoid an eternity of damnation. Like a trapped animal he
lashes out against the mesh he has woven for himself, and
becomes more entangled. To be physically absorbed, to be 'a
creature wanting soul', 'some brutish beast', even, at the last,
to be no more than 'little water drops'—this is the final hope
of the pride of Wittenberg. Time is the dominant in this
speech. The measured regularity of the opening gives way to
a frantic tugging in two directions as Faustus suffers the op-
posing forces of Christ and Lucifer:

> O I'll leap up to my God! Who pulls me down?
>
> Scene 13, line 71

The pace and the passion increase as the clock strikes relent-
lessly, and the second half-hour passes more quickly than the
first. We are agonizingly aware of the last minutes of Faustus'
life, trickling through the hour-glass with what seems like
ever-increasing speed. But as each grain falls, bringing Faustus closer to his terrible end, we become more and more conscious of the deserts of vast eternity and damnation that open
up beyond death. When Macbeth or Lear dies the tragedy is
ended with a final harmonious chord, but the discords of
Faustus' last lines cannot be easily resolved.

    Dr Faustus has much in common with the late medieval
Morality Plays; but there is much that is different. The
eponymous heroes of *Mankind* and *Everyman* are, like
Faustus, tempted to sin; and they fall. But, counselled by the
representations of Mercy and Knowledge, they recognize the
error of their ways, repent, and are redeemed. Faustus, however, finding his heart 'so hardened [he] cannot repent', is in
a worse dilemma than his predecessors—perhaps because
he is more intelligent and individual than them. John
Donne's Sonnet IV articulates the problem:

> Yet grace, if thou repent, thou canst not lack;
> But who shall give thee that grace, to begin?

Marlowe's sympathies (if the energy of the verse means anything at all) are for the rebel, who is impeded in his pursuit

of science and frustrated in his efforts to assert his individuality. But he also feels deeply for the bleakly unhappy Mephastophilis, who is possessed of all the knowledge that Faustus desires, and who is 'tormented with ten thousand hells' because he has forfeited the 'everlasting bliss' that the doctor is so ready to part with.

Shakespeare's Earlier Plays: History and Romantic Comedy

Derek Traversi

According to noted Shakespeare scholar Derek Traversi, Shakespeare's early plays constitute a set of "creative experiments" in which the playwright frequently
made up his own rules. Taken together, Shakespeare's
early English history plays provide a sustained study
of the nature of kingship, and they bring both tragic elements to the history, as in *Richard II*, and comic elements, as in the plays with the humorous Falstaff. To
illustrate Shakespeare's early comic genius, Traversi
analyzes two plays, *A Midsummer Night's Dream* and
Twelfth Night, for their presentation of the trials and
tribulations—and undeniable power—of romantic
love. Traversi, Professor Emeritus of English Literature
at Swarthmore College, is author of several seminal
books on Shakespeare.

A contemporary observer, viewing the state of the English
stage in 1593, the year of Marlowe's early death, and comparing him with the emerging figure of William Shakespeare, might well have concluded that Marlowe was the
more impressive and powerful figure. He would, however,
have been mistaken in his estimate of the final stature of
these two great writers. Shakespeare, whose earliest work
might well have seemed less striking in its individuality than
the products of Marlowe's meteoric genius, developed more
slowly but, as time would show, on a wider front and with
more varied possibilities for development. Showing from the
first a consistent and, for his time, unique interest in the implications of the dramatic illusion, he began by experimenting in various styles and different varieties of play, largely

creating his own forms in the process of writing. From first to last every play of Shakespeare's represents, not only a development from what has gone before, but a new beginning, a fresh attack on problems involved in the very decision to write a particular kind of play. These creative experiments were carried out on a variety of material, and developed with a refusal to be confined by limiting conceptions of genre, which answer to his uniquely self-conscious conception of his art.

PLAYS ABOUT HISTORY

The plays with which Shakespeare embarked upon his career show him variously concerned with perfecting the mastery of his craft. Almost the earliest works attributed to him, the three plays on the reign of Henry VI (1591–92?), can be seen as attempts to discover what a "history play," built upon certain coherent and dramatically viable ideas as distinct from an episodic pageant, might be. The three plays show, indeed, by the end if not at the beginning, a remarkable continuity of purpose in weaving together two contrasted ideas. (The date of *Henry VI* Part I, and the extent to which Shakespeare's hand is to be detected in it, have been the subject of much discussion. Most scholars are now inclined to recognize Shakespeare's authorship and to propose a date which may be as early as 1591. In this case the play is likely to have preceded Marlowe's *Edward II,* and Shakespeare can be thought of as the *creator* of the history play as a serious dramatic form.) The first is the notion, derived from a great body of medieval thought, that sin is eventually repaid in the form of retribution upon the sinner; the second, more "modern" in its implications and supremely reflected in the writings of Machiavelli, relates the existence of disorder in the body politic to elements of weakness in the ruler. Both elements are developed consistently and side by side. The first finds expression in the unhappy fate of nearly all the principal contendants as they become involved in the consequences of their blood-thirsty and short-sighted appetite for power; and the unhappy figure of Henry VI serves to join the two, in so far as he is at once a good man against whom sin is almost continually committed, and a feeble ruler who is at times disposed to admit that his claim to the throne is in some respects uncertain.

By the end of the series, in the more accomplished play of *Richard III* (1592?) to which it led, the implications of the drive for power are revealed in their related intensity and limitation. The villainous royal hunchback whose presence dominates the action (it is, after Hamlet, the most extended role in all Shakespeare's work) is a character so far without precedent in English drama. He is presented as a man constrained by his awareness of being excluded from the forms and fictions of polite society and indeed from the sources of "love" itself to make the pursuit of power his exclusive and obsessive aim. In following it he shows a combination of intense passion and ironic clear-sightedness which causes

him to stand out against the world of shallow, time-serving politicians and helpless moralists in which he moves; but in the very act of attaining the golden crown which is his goal, the cost of success is also revealed as he reflects, before his final overthrow, upon the inevitability of his isolated doom. "Richard loves Richard; that is, I am I." The result of a lifelong dedication to the egoist's drive for power is seen to be the impossibility of self-evasion, escape from what at the last emerges, with dreadful clarity, as the limits of the isolated self. The realization will be taken up, in various and infinitely more complex forms, in the great tragedies to come.

William Shakespeare

These early experiments in the chronicle play bore fruit, a few years later, in a second and greater series of historical dramas, running from *Richard II* (1595–96?) to the Two Parts of *Henry IV* (1596–98?) and *Henry V* (1599). The broad conception underlying these plays answers to the current political notions, intensely nationalistic and monarchical, of the age. All four plays are conceived as successive stages of a study in kingship. The power of the king is assumed to be conferred upon him by God as a guarantee of order and of that hierarchical structure of society which cannot be rejected, according to this line of thought, without plunging society itself into anarchy and chaos.

STUDIES IN KINGSHIP

The interest of these plays lies, however, less in these traditional conceptions than in their implications in terms of human behaviour. Already in *Richard II* the pattern of feudal loyalty has been broken by an act of murder; the play turns upon the contrast between a king, lawfully enthroned but personally irresponsible, and a born politician, Bolingbroke, who achieves his ends through what is, in the traditional terms to which his victim appeals, an act of sacrilegious rebellion. In the next two plays the new king calls his followers to unite in a Crusade which is intended to provide a focus for the national unity which he now sincerely desires, but finds that his original crime fatally engenders the strife which he aims at ending. The political success which eludes him is finally achieved, in the last play of the series, by his son. In describing the achievement, and in the process of giving it full value, Shakespeare brings out what has become for him a chief meaning of the whole story: a conviction, tragic in some of its implications, that political capacity and moral sensibility tend necessarily to diverge. The public vocation, upon the exercise of which depends order in the kingdom and success in its foreign wars, demands from the monarch an impersonality that borders on the inhuman. The king, as one of his soldiers says to him in a scene particularly searching in its implications, "is but a man as I am"; and just because he is so like them, and can share their thoughts and feelings at moments of stress, there is something precarious in the iron self-control which his vocation imposes upon him and in the absolute claim he is required to make on the allegiance of his subjects.

COMEDY MEETS HISTORY

It is as a reaction against this precariousness that Shakespeare's greatest comic creation, Falstaff, appears in these plays as both the embodiment of all that the king must repudiate and as a reminder of the human loss which this necessary repudiation implies. In Part I of *Henry IV*, where the comic aspect prevails, Falstaff is a connecting link between two realities, the tavern world of broad if corrupt humanity in which he is at home and that of political rhetoric and intrigue to which he also has access. Thus situated in two worlds, and not entirely limited by either, he is used by Shakespeare to throw a detached light on the heroic sentiments to which the more respectable characters are given in their weaker moments and to comment, bitingly if irresponsibly, on the "honour" which they so freely invoke on the battlefield, often to urge others to die in their cause.

The Falstaff of *Henry IV*, Part II, is in many ways a different person in a very different kind of play. Age has replaced youth in the main action, fear and calculation assert themselves openly, and success is sought without illusion and without disguise. Falstaff himself, no longer engaged in an exuberant attempt to ignore the reality of time, is subdued to this changed spirit. Finding his companions among aging dotards, and himself haunted by disease and the premonitory thought of death, he strips them of their pitiful pretensions. The repudiation of verbal "honour" in the preceding play is reinforced by a more sombre evaluation of the human condition. Whereas in Part I his attitude on the battlefield at Shrewsbury had implied an affirmation of life beyond the selfish calculations of politicians, the Falstaff of Part II is content to allow those of his enforced soldiers who have the means to buy release from service and to accept the resignation of the helpless to their fate: for such, and no other, is the nature of things. The "young dace is a bait for the old pike," and "necessity," the law of nature, justifies all.

This growing conviction that the moral and political orders are barely to be reconciled finds its final expression in the scene in which Prince Henry, newly crowned, rejects the dissolute companion of his younger days. Here, as so often in Shakespeare, we must not simplify the issues. Henry, with the responsibilities he has just shouldered and which, as he has said in his first soliloquy, he "never promised," never asked to assume, *must* abandon Falstaff; but there is a sense that his judgments, just and inevitable as they are in a king, strike us as impositions, rigidly and almost violently asserted, upon his normal humanity. It is significant that in *Henry V* Falstaff is only remembered in the account of his death which is by general consent the most moving moment in the play. In an action where the touchstone of conduct has become success, and in which humanity has to accommodate itself to expediency, there is no place for him. Shakespeare has prepared us for the necessary change in the later stages of *Henry IV*, and now his death affects us as the last glimpse of a more human if flawed world. No doubt the dramatist drew his Henry V with a sense of necessary public vocation in mind. One aim does not, in Shakespeare, exclude another, and the fact is that, as we follow the uncompromising study of achieved success which rounds off the trilogy, a certain coldness takes possession of our feelings as it took possession, step by step, of the limbs of the dying Falstaff; and we too find ourselves, like him, in our own way disposed to "babble of green fields."

EXPERIMENTS IN COMEDY

Side by side with his early experiments in the chronicle play, we find Shakespeare in the early 1590's engaged in exploring the possibilities of the comic convention, shaping it by a process which initially resembled trial and error into an instrument for expressing the finished statements about life—and more especially about love and the human need to live imaginatively—that he was already, beneath the obvious desire to entertain, concerned to make. The early stages of this exploration from the early *Comedy of Errors* (1593?) to *Love's Labour's Lost* (1594?), involving in each play a new approach, a fresh beginning, are too various to describe in the space available; but a brief consideration of two assured successes from different periods may give some idea of what Shakespeare was able to achieve through what turned out to be a life-long interest in the comic form.

The earlier of the two plays, *A Midsummer Night's Dream* (1595), can be thought of as a comic counterpoise to the "romantic" tragedy of *Romeo and Juliet* which equally engaged Shakespeare's attention at this time. Within the frame-work of a rational and social attitude to marriage, expressed in the opening scene through the preparations for the union of Theseus and Hippolyta, the action transports two pairs of young lovers—Lysander and Hermia, Demetrius and Helena, who feel that they cannot achieve their largely wilful purposes in the "real" daylight world—from civilized life in Athens to nocturnal wandering in the mysterious woods. There the irrational but potent impulses which "love" normally covers are released and the capacity of the young lovers to master them tested. The woods, in fact, are the scene of jealous rivalry between Oberon and Titania, respectively king and queen of the fairies; and the spell which Oberon, acting through his elusive servant Puck, casts upon Titania, obliging her to dote on the "translated" figure of Bottom the weaver with his ass's head, is evidently a central symbol of the irrationality and potential destructiveness which form part of the reality of love. . . .

In the conclusion the various elements of the action are drawn together under the renewed control of Theseus in a social and civilizing vision of love. The marriage union is presented as life-giving, joining body and soul, reason and feeling, imagination and fancy in its assertion, qualified indeed but none the less humanly potent, of essential "truth." It is this "truth" which Hippolyta, hinting at the limitation of her husband's rational distrust of poetry and the imagination—the domain, as he somewhat sceptically dismisses it, of "the lunatic, the lover, and the poet"—celebrates in her comment on the outcome of the action just witnessed:

> . . . all the story of the night told over,
> And all their minds transfigured so together,
> More witnesseth than fancy's images
> And grows to something of great constancy,
> But howsoever, strange and admirable.

Against this assertion of imaginative truth Theseus, as he looks forward to the entry of Bottom and his "mechanicals" with their Pyramus play, can still speak feelingly of "the anguish of a torturing hour." In easement of this "anguish" the lovers, whom we have watched in the woods following their absurd impulses of passion to "preposterous" conclusions, are to witness an action in which romantic love is exposed to ridicule. Their reactions to what they see—their charity or lack of it—will throw light upon what kind of men and women they are. To accept this "lesson," balancing truth against the ever-present possibility of illusion, is to affirm the faith in life and its ongoing processes which comes readily to the simple-hearted and which the arrogant and the sophisticated ignore at their mortal peril.

More Serious Comedy

Some six years after *A Midsummer Night's Dream,* Shakespeare wrote *Twelfth Night,* a play which replaces the "framework" structure of the earlier work by one which turns upon the interplay and contrast between two plots conceived on different levels and significantly interrelated. The play, written at a time when a dramatist's mind was already turning to tragedy, seems to have been intended to mark the festivity which the title recalls. It adds to many of the qualities of an aristocratic entertainment those of a children's merry-making, an occasion for dressing-up to mock the absurdities committed in all seriousness by their elders. In so doing it gives comic recognition to that sense of the incongruous, and to the need for providing it with a salutary outlet in the interests of continued social and personal harmony, which is one of the most persistent aspects of the comic impulse. Very roughly, one could say that the element of "masque" prevails in the "poetic" part of the action, and that the sentiments and situations developed in this are given a comic reflection in the prose underplot which is interwoven with it. The result is a comedy notably different in kind from *As You Like It*, which must have been written not long before and which also represents a high point in Shakespeare's comic achievement, and one perhaps even more closely knit in its interplay of contrasted levels of meaning.

The "serious" part of *Twelfth Night* deals principally with conventions of romantic love derived from the literary taste, aristocratic and sophisticated, of the day. Orsino's passion for the unresponsive Olivia is a blend of sentiment and artifice, true dedication and elaborate self-centredness. We might say of him to a large degree that he is in love with love, with his awareness of himself as an uncorresponded lover, just as Olivia is enamoured of her own grief for her dead brother. Precisely because they are capable of *real* feelings, because their human potentiality, as revealed in the intense poetic quality of their sentiments, so exceeds the common measure, they will have to learn to go in each case beyond their initial attitudes, to accept the experience which life offers, as it always does in these comedies, on terms not exclusively of their own making.

The primary instrument of this transformation is Viola, whose readiness to rely on her own resources in the moment of trial and to allow the currents of life to move and sustain her contrasts with the tensely self-conscious and finally restricting attitudes that prevail at Orsino's court. In her male disguise as "Cesario," and obliged by circumstances beyond her control to carry to another the message of the man she loves, she becomes the instrument by which each of the loves in which she has become so unpredictably involved find their proper object. Both Orsino and Olivia are brought to a recognition that the compulsive force of their passions is such as to draw them finally beyond themselves, demanding from each the acceptance of a fuller, more natural and spontaneous way of living.

Shakespeare's Later Plays: The Achievement in Tragedy

Philip Edwards

The tragedies of Shakespeare explore the dimensions of revenge, loss of love, the vagaries of political power, and even death itself, according to Shakespeare scholar Philip Edwards. Edwards groups Shakespeare's tragedies roughly into tragedies of revenge, tragedies of love, tragedies of political power, and the tragedy of passion represented by *King Lear*. Though each of Shakespeare's tragic heroes must deal with a particular weakness of character or flawed moral decision, these are not the basis of Shakespeare's tragic vision. Rather, what leads to tragedy in each case is the tragic hero's defiance of society and his or her "bid for liberation," in the phrase of Edwards. Edwards, a distinguished editor of Shakespeare's plays, is Professor Emeritus of English Literature at the University of Liverpool.

Shakespeare's tragedies begin and end with Roman themes. The arc goes from the fantastic and gruesome fiction of *Titus Andronicus* of the early 1590s to the spare and craggy study of *Coriolanus* in 1608. In spite of the diversity of tragic subjects, Rome remains a constant preoccupation, inspiring the two major works, *Julius Caesar* (1599) and *Antony and Cleopatra* (1607). These two plays on historical subjects underline the ready transference between 'history' and 'tragedy' and the strong political element to be found in nearly all the tragedies. *Hamlet* (1601), a play directing intense light on the recesses of personality, is all the same a play about the state of Denmark, its government and its relations with neighbouring states. *King Lear* (1605) has the political stability of England at its

From "William Shakespeare," by Philip Edwards, in *An Outline of English Literature*, edited by Pat Rogers. Copyright © Oxford University Press, 1987, 1988. Reprinted by permission of Oxford University Press.

centre. *Macbeth* (1606), drawn like the histories from Holin-
shed's chronicles, is concerned like the histories with rebellion, civil war, foreign invasion, and usurpation. And even in
Romeo and Juliet (1595) and *Othello* (1604), which no one
could call political, the relationship between the individual
and the community is organic, and is essential to the play. *Timon of Athens* (date unknown) combines the story of the hero
with a major political crisis centring on Alcibiades.

Generalizations about Shakespearian tragedy are haz-
ardous, so distinctive is each one in its purpose, its atmosphere, its very language. Of course, all the tragedies contemplate loss, defeat, disappointment, failure, death—but
even here we must be careful if we want to include *Troilus
and Cressida* (1602), for both Troilus and Cressida are alive
at the end of the play. In an endeavour to find thematic
groupings in the tragedies we might begin with revenge, a
major issue in one of the greatest of the plays, *Hamlet,* and
one without much claim to greatness, *Titus Andronicus.* . . .

TRAGEDY OF REVENGE

Titus Andronicus was perhaps a stage rival to the popular
pre-Shakespearian play of *Hamlet* (possibly by Kyd) whose
ghost shrieking for revenge was celebrated. In 1601 Shakespeare, who had just achieved the orderly dignity of *Julius
Caesar,* returned to the wildness of the revenge convention
and remodelled the old Hamlet play. By so doing he composed his most subtle, complex, searching, enigmatic
tragedy, which each successive age thinks the most modern of his plays. But though Shakespeare was revolutionary
in exploiting the potentialities of the revenge theme for
radical doubt and self-questioning, he did not discover
them. Even in the midst of its sensationalism, while 'the
croaking raven doth bellow for revenge', as Hamlet put it,
the revenge play had been concerned with the problem of
justice and the responsibility of the individual in achieving
it. The long life of the revenge play, going back much earlier than Kyd and achieving a new life on the Jacobean
stage, cannot be explained simply by the attraction of the
grotesque horrors it revelled in—ghosts, skulls, insanity,
poisonings, and so on. Some intelligent dramatists, such as
Marston, who wrote *Antonio's Revenge* in 1601, were un-
appreciative of the deeper implications of revenge, but Kyd,
Chapman, Webster, Tourneur, Beaumont, and others make

it clear that the nerve-centre of the revenge play is not the thrill of vindictiveness but the trauma of trying to obtain justice in an unjust and indifferent society. And so it is in Shakespeare's *Hamlet.*

To Hamlet, totally alienated from Danish society, the voice of the Ghost asking for revenge gives meaning to a life that had lost all meaning. His conception of his mission extends beyond killing Claudius into the cleansing of Denmark, and includes what was specifically forbidden by the Ghost, the moral rescue of his mother. Disabling doubts about the authenticity of the Ghost, and about the value of any act (in the 'To be or not to be' soliloquy), alternate with the exultation of conviction, and the impulsiveness of the sword-thrust that kills the wrong man, Polonius. So Hamlet becomes the object of a counter-revenge, Laertes seeking requital for the murder of *his* father. By the last act of the play, after his adventures at sea, Hamlet is utterly convinced of the rightness of his cause and the necessity of killing Claudius, whom he describes as a cancer in society. He sees himself as a humble instrument of heaven, and to fail his duty in removing that cancer would be at the peril of his own soul. But it is too late; Laertes wounds him fatally before he at last kills the king. The Denmark that he had sought to preserve from the odious Claudius passes into the hands of the foreigner Fortinbras. *Hamlet* ends in both vic-

This print depicts a scene from Hamlet, *a revenge tragedy more complex than any before or after.*

tory and failure. The possibility that a man has been picked out to do a deed which society condemns but which a higher, divine authority sanctions is balanced against the possibility that the Ghost led Hamlet into delusion and error, and (to steal Yeats's words) bewildered him till he died.

Revenge has to do with hate. Our second major issue in the tragedies is love, which is the inspiration of four plays: *Romeo and Juliet, Troilus and Cressida, Othello,* and *Antony and Cleopatra.* In each of the plays everything is staked upon a love-relationship which to a greater or lesser extent is unpalatable to society; in each play, though for vastly different reasons, the love fails to abide and ends disastrously.

TRAGEDIES OF LOVE

Romeo and Juliet is Shakespeare's love tragedy of youth as *Antony and Cleopatra* is his love tragedy of middle age. To Juliet, a girl of fourteen, hedged around by nurse and parents and a family feud, comes the liberation of first love— which Shakespeare enshrines in a sonnet shared between Romeo and Juliet when they kiss. The plot moves forward by a simple mechanism of ironic reversals which mark the stages of a clear path of 'responsibility' for the tragic outcome. Romeo's love for a Capulet leads into his killing Juliet's cousin; the Friar's good offices for the lovers lead into the tragic mistiming at the tomb. If there is less than full tragedy at the end, it is not because of too much coincidence and bad luck, but because, for all their impetuousness, the young lovers in their desperately sad conclusion are simply victims—not of fate, but of their elders and betters. There is nothing of that fatal collaboration in one's own destruction which is so marked in the great later tragedies. Intense pity, little terror. 'Catharsis' there certainly is in *Romeo and Juliet,* however, in our feeling that the lovers, completing their union in death as they could not complete it in life, are at least *safe,* and in our feeling that such love as theirs, passionate and sexual though it was, was a dedication to a higher scale of values than obtained in the violent commerce of the worldly society they lived in.

This must surely be the case in *Othello* too. To the wealthy citizens of Venice, epitomized in Desdemona's father Brabantio, Othello is a totally undesirable match; it is against 'all rules of nature' for her to fall in love with a black man, and Othello must have used spells for her to do so. It is a common view that Desdemona did not really know Othello. She did; she knew the Othello who existed before Iago began to twist and corrupt him. She knew, approved, loved; and she committed herself in as definite and courageous an act as is to be found in the tragedies. It was of course a fatal consecration. For Othello, this love, after a career of soldiering, is a miracle of happiness. But Iago was born to oppose happiness. He is the sheerly satanic in man, bound by the acute malevolence that is his nature to wreck and destroy. The strength of the love between Othello and Desdemona is an offence to him. He cannot corrupt Desdemona, but he can corrupt Othello into misconceiving her very goodness:

> So will I turn her virtue into pitch,
> And out of her own goodness make the net
> That shall enmesh them all. (II. iii)

There is no more painful scene in drama than that in which Iago begins his work, crumbling Othello's confidence in his wife's chastity and fidelity and stirring up that unappeasable jealousy which ends in his killing a totally innocent woman. Iago works on Othello's sense of inferiority, his blackness, his foreignness, his ignorance of cultivated society. That Othello has not sufficient faith in Desdemona to withstand the attack is terrible; but the attack is a manifestation of evil that almost by definition cannot be withstood. At any rate Desdemona's dedication of herself is cruelly betrayed. Disowned by her family, she is brutally rejected and ceremoniously murdered by her husband. *Othello* is the grimmest of the tragedies, though in these days a lot of its tragic effect is lost on those who, confident in their ability to deal with such a situation as the play presents, have patronized Desdemona and despised Othello.

In *Antony and Cleopatra* we have once again the old soldier finding a haven in love. But the soldier is now the great sharer of Rome's imperial rule, and the woman is not the virginal daughter of a wealthy citizen. To standers-by Antony's neglect of the claims of office and empire for the seductive sensuality of Cleopatra is simply shameful—

> The triple pillar of the world transformed
> Into a strumpet's fool.

Antony himself veers from protesting that 'the nobleness of life' is within Cleopatra's arms to the sharp disgust at the enchantment that has ensnared him, the 'strong Egyptian fetters'. It seems a straightforward *Either/Or.* The love of Cleopatra means the decline of his power, disorder within the empire, and the abandonment of the codes of honour and responsibility by which he has lived. As he leaves Cleopatra to reassert himself in the affairs of Rome, it might seem that we have a tragedy of choice between love and honour, like the famous choice of Hercules, Antony's supposed ancestor, who came to a fork in the road, one path leading to duty and the other to pleasure. But there is no choice in this play, and no one is free, not even Caesar who, though he seems to have choice, has only drive. Octavius Caesar's progress towards sole rule is remorseless. Shakespeare strongly contrasts the youth and asceticism of this brisk and efficient man with the hedonistic, warmer nature of the older man, Antony. Cleopatra is Antony's only refuge. As he comes to ruin and death the basic question of the play asserts itself as what quality of refuge the love of Cleopatra provides for Antony. It is certain that in military ventures Cleopatra fails Antony again and again. But Antony fails Cleopatra again and again. Her famous question, 'Not know me yet?' after the great row over Caesar's messenger kissing her hand, echoes to the moment of Antony's death. . . .

It takes an Antony to create Cleopatra fully; not to change her but to fulfil the rich complexity of her nature. But there is no possibility that the relationship can prosper, or even survive. Antony's death is a miserable confusion. He is convinced that Cleopatra has betrayed him in the last sea fight. 'The witch shall die!' he vows. To cool his anger Cleopatra sends word that she has died—'and bring me how he takes my death'. On hearing this Antony tries to kill himself, but fails to do it cleanly. As he dies in Cleopatra's arms he does not say one word about their love—only that she should save herself and remember him in his earlier, Roman, greatness. It is not love that is uppermost in his mind at the end, but the past. For Cleopatra, on the other hand, their love is her totality. She has no thought of outliving him, but before she dies there is a stillness in which she can contemplate their love. There is no higher hymn to love in Shakespeare than in the ecstatic imagery of her adoration of the dead Antony.

There was never any future for the love of Antony and Cleopatra in worldly terms. She chokes him like entangling weeds pulling a swimmer down. That is because the world is what it is. 'The holy priests', however, bless her in her very

sexuality, and it is Octavius of all people who utters the
amazing words that even in death she looks ready to 'catch
another Antony / In her strong toil of grace'. A toil is a snare
or trap. The captivation which fetters her 'victims' is a toil of
grace, a captivation which bestows something rare and spiritual, no sooner glimpsed than lost. . . .

We have been looking at tragic heroes in terms of their
commitment to revenge and to love. There is another type of
commitment, to a political course of action, and this brings
together two very different plays in which the hero assassi-
nates the ruler of the state: *Julius Caesar* and *Macbeth*.

TRAGEDY AND POLITICS

Julius Caesar was an anticipation of *Hamlet* in exploring the
problems of an intellectual, a bookish man who is something of a philosopher, who in order to purge and reorder
society undertakes an act of violence against the head of the
state. The texture of the plays is quite different, but each play
illuminates the other. Brutus is invited to join the conspiracy
against Caesar by Cassius, who has a fierce personal and
ideological hatred for the autocratic behaviour of Caesar.
Brutus has no 'personal cause' against Caesar but persuades
himself that it is his civic duty to assassinate the man. In his
high-mindedness he makes political mistake after mistake,
and Shakespeare makes a strong point of contrasting his
public-duty rhetoric with the physical butchery of Caesar.
The old republicanism which Brutus wishes to restore is not
really a political possibility for Rome but in the first place it
is Brutus's great errors of judgement which allow Mark
Antony to take the initiative, exploit civil disorder, and
sweep the conspirators out of existence. Antony, who can af-
ford to be generous at the moment of victory, gives Brutus a
fine eulogy: 'This was the noblest Roman of them all'. He
acted, he says, 'in a general honest thought' and for 'common good to all'. It is the depressing truth. Brutus is the best
man we see in Rome, thoughtful, gentle, altruistic, affectionate, acting for principle and not personal advantage. It is his
personal qualities which make his political career so fright-
ening. It is not alone that he was too 'nice' to succeed in the
rough and tumble of political life, but that his attempt to
phrase political violence within the language of highly prin-
cipled conduct turns him into a pharisaical prig and makes
certain the failure of a political cause which even an Eliza-

bethan could view with a certain sympathy.

In *Julius Caesar, Hamlet,* and *Macbeth* the hero aims at the heart of existing society, intending to change that society by killing the prince or governor. In both *Julius Caesar* and *Hamlet* the endeavour is to restore the moral order of a past society. Macbeth's aim in assassinating Duncan seems entirely selfish. Yet curiously he is impelled by nothing like Richard III's lust for power. Royalty is a misty dream of magnificence, as vague to Macbeth as it is to us: 'the swelling act / Of the imperial theme'. Macbeth and his wife share in a guilty fantasy of becoming king and queen of Scotland. It is a hardened loyal soldier, capable of the bloody suppression of rebels, who is a prey to these strange imaginings, which seem to torment him as much as they give him pleasure. When the weird sisters on the heath hail him as the future king, they have pierced to the secret life of his thoughts. Banquo sees him start with fear. The life of this mental world is

THE RECOVERY OF INNOCENCE

In the years after his greatest tragedies, from 1606 to 1611, Shakespeare again turned to experimentation in terms of dramatic genres. His best plays of this period, A Winter's Tale *and* The Tempest, *are perhaps best described as romances. Like his great tragedies, they are concerned with passions, conflict, and suffering, but unlike the tragedies, they end in reconciliation and harmony.*

Shakespeare's last unquestioned play, *The Tempest . . .* is also concerned with reconciliation. Unlike *The Winter's Tale,* however, it telescopes the complete process of estrangement, suffering, and restored harmony by viewing the earlier stages as past history and concentrating almost exclusively upon the final, resolutive stage in the full development. To do this it takes us away from ordinary life to a magic island on which the normal laws of nature are suspended. Prospero, undisputed master of the island, controls it entirely through the ministration of the spirits whom he has learned to master, and lives with his daughter Miranda—who has no clear memory of any other life—in a state of idyllic simplicity. This change of emphasis, however, should not blind us to the fact that *The Tempest* is as closely connected as *The Winter's Tale* with the passions and conflicts of normal living. The whole point of the early scenes of *The Tempest* is that this abstraction from common reality cannot last. Just as much as the characters in *The Winter's Tale,* as real to Macbeth as the tangible world around him. After the witches have spoken he almost collapses under the pressure of the 'horrible imaginings' in which he sees himself in the act of murder. Later in the play, the dagger which he sees before him in the air—what he calls 'a dagger of the mind'—is 'in form as palpable' as the dagger he then draws from its sheath. After the assassination he *hears* a voice crying 'Sleep no more!' Most terrifying of all these 'palpable' fancies is the bloody corpse of Banquo, sitting in his chair at the feast.

Tempted by the prophecy of the witches and taunted by his wife, Macbeth turns his vivid dream of majesty into reality by murdering the king, Duncan. He is in a state of horror before, during, and after the murder—when, unable to sleep, he says he would rather be dead

Than on the torture of the mind to lie
In restless ecstasy.

Macbeth has to live not only without the glory he thought

those of *The Tempest* are faced with the universal human necessity for maturing; and their attainment of maturity implies at some stage the loss of their original state of innocence, though, as the play proceeds to show, they may find it again—backed this time by a full experience—at the end of their development.

The state of innocence is, even on Prospero's island, a precarious one. He himself, of course, is only there as a result of the envy and ambition of his brother Antonio, and we must not believe that the conditions of a full and civilized life are to be found within its narrow limits. His position, indeed, has been caused by definite and clearly stated deficiencies in the practical order. . . .

Prospero, in fact, has not been able, any more than Shakespeare's more obviously tragic characters, to avoid the existence and development of evil. As always, he is faced by a passion-born excrescence implicit in the nature of things, the effects of which are inevitably disruptive; but though evil impulse of this kind is as clearly present in *The Tempest* as in any of the earlier plays, Prospero is differentiated from Shakespeare's tragic heroes by holding in his hands the weapon of contemplative wisdom, and with it an assurance that, with the help of destiny (more explicitly objectivized than anywhere else in the plays), evil can be mastered.

Derek A. Traversi, "The Last Plays of Shakespeare," in *The Pelican Guide to English Literature.* Harmondsworth, England: Penguin Books, 1955, pp. 274–75.

would come with kingship but also with entire knowledge of what it is that he has done. He cannot avoid facing it, and he cannot face it. 'To know my deed', he says, "twere best not know myself'. His fierce wife succumbs first. The reality which the pair of them created out of their dreams reinvades her dreams, and in her sleep she is forced to re-enact the murder. 'Who would have thought the old man to have had so much blood in him?' Macbeth's fate is different. When he hears 'the cry of women' within, he realizes that his interior, sentient life has gone dead: he cannot even be afraid any more. And when he is told that Lady Macbeth has died, the terrible conviction comes over him that the exterior world is also without life, meaningless, inert.

> It is a tale
> Told by an idiot, full of sound and fury,
> Signifying nothing.

The man whose every experience was made doubly alive by the workings of a powerful imagination now finds only deadness in both imagination and reality.

To body forth the intensity of Macbeth's inner life, Shakespeare gave him a poetry whose metaphoric richness is unsurpassed among the tragic heroes. The power of the poetry draws us in to share this inner life of Macbeth's. We may be reluctant to be so drawn but we have little chance of holding back. The play shows us how a man who is not evil brings himself or is brought to do evil. By the empathy which Macbeth's poetry forces us into, we are made to share his heart of darkness.

THE PASSION OF KING LEAR

Every hero we have looked at makes a commitment—to love, or revenge, or political violence—and this commitment is seen as the key to a new existence. What commitment does King Lear make? He proposes to divide his kingdom between his three daughters and retire from a long life of ruling, looking forward in particular to finding rest in the 'kind nursery' of his beloved Cordelia. He does indeed commit an act, the violent, peremptory act of disowning and banishing Cordelia for not openly professing her love for him, but for the rest of the play, though it is the consequence of his act that he suffers from, he endures rather than acts. *King Lear* is more of a 'passion' than the other tragedies. The closest resemblance is with *Richard II.* Both

plays show us the painful process of the collapse of the
hero's world, and of the self that fitted that world, and the
equally painful process of learning a new identity. The
questioning of himself, his values, the nature of society, and
of the meaning of existence, which adversity forces Lear to
undertake, is not confined to his individual predicament.
The suffering of Gloucester through the malice of his illegitimate son confirms that Lear's bitter experience is not
unique or unrepeatable; and with the tremendous orches-
tration of the storm scenes challenge and protest become a
universal chorus. The outcries of the mad king, the songs
and snatches of the shivering Fool, the manic chatter of
Poor Tom combine into an extraordinary and unsatisfied
interrogation. 'Is man no more than this?' The climax of evil
is not on the heath or in the hovel but in Gloucester's own
castle, where Gloucester is bound to a chair, cross-ques-
tioned and abused by Regan, and has his eyes put out by Regan's husband, Cornwall.

This terrifying scene is the extreme edge of cruelty and
inhumanity in the tragedies, and it is balanced by another
scene in which the power of love is more profoundly shown
than anywhere else in Shakespeare. It is a humble Lear who
emerges from his insanity to be reunited with his daughter
Cordelia. They are defeated in battle and led away to prison.
The prison becomes a symbol of the pressures of the social
and political world from which Lear feels himself totally lib-
erated simply by being with Cordelia.

> Come, let's away to prison.
> We two alone will sing like birds i' th' cage.
> When thou dost ask me blessing, I'll kneel down
> And ask of thee forgiveness. So we'll live,
> And pray, and sing, and tell old tales, and laugh
> At gilded butterflies, and hear poor rogues
> Talk of court news; and we'll talk with them too—
> Who loses and who wins, who's in, who's out—
> And take upon's the mystery of things
> As if we were God's spies; and we'll wear out
> In a walled prison packs and sects of great ones
> That ebb and flow by the moon. (V. iii)

If the transfiguring power of love, which can only exist as an
opposition to the values of worldly society, is never more
shiningly apparent than in this speech, the retribution of the
world is never more cruelly shown than in the ending of the
play. Cordelia is hanged, and the old king makes his final

entrance with the dead girl in his arms.

> Thou'lt come no more,
> Never, never, never, never, never.

The god of Shakespeare's tragedies is indeed a hidden
god. Those who like Albany in *King Lear* expect his inter-
vention or manifestation are disappointed. It is the devil who
is in full view all the time. The witches in *Macbeth*, 'instruments of darkness', tempt and mislead the hero; Othello becomes convinced that Iago is a devil and has brought him to
do an act for which he is eternally lost; Hamlet is deeply
conscious of the traps waiting to ensnare the soul into hell
and damnation. Although the viciousness of Goneril, Regan,
Cornwall, Edmund, and Iago does not exceed the docu-
mented record of human cruelty and malice, there seems no
doubt that in them Shakespeare wanted to portray an operation of evil that is more than a matter of ill will and sadism.
'Is there any cause in nature that makes these hard hearts?'
asks Lear in the crazy 'arraignment' of Goneril. The answer
is no; the cause is supernatural. Evil is a presence lying in
wait below the surface of human life, ready to erupt in the
most unsuspected places, in one's trusted lieutenant, one's
affectionate daughter, one's loyal general, one's own brother.

> Rank corruption, mining all within,
> Infects unseen.

The idea of an indomitable corrupting force in life is strong
also in *Timon of Athens,* a play which Shakespeare seems to
have left unfinished. . . .

The 'tragic flaw', that weakness of character or fatal error
of judgement which since Aristotle's time has seemed a
prime constituent of tragedy, is less important than the
tragic commitment. Within the hero's course there are all
sorts of moral weakness, wrong decisions, and character deficiencies. But these do not initiate the tragic impetus; they
accompany it and direct its course. In his or her consecration to revenge, or love, or political violence, or political re-
sistance, each of the heroes is in some way defying society,
asserting a primordial dissatisfaction with things as they
are. The freedom which each hero seeks is different, leads to
a different kind of disturbance, and ends in a different kind
of failure. But in every single tragedy the audience is left
with a balance of conflicting emotions as regards the hero,
the bid for liberation, and its cost. And in that equilibrium
lies much of the power of tragedy.

THE TRAGICOMEDIES: THE CASE OF *THE TEMPEST*

'Tragicomedy' is not a common classification for Shakespeare's plays, but it is a useful term for distinguishing the later from the earlier comedies. There are two groups: the 'problem comedies' of 1602–5, *All's Well That Ends Well* and *Measure for Measure,* in which there is an extended treatment of serious moral problems with the threatened tragic consequences bypassed, and the 'Romances' of 1608–13, *Pericles Prince of Tyre, The Winter's Tale, Cymbeline,* and *The Tempest,* the highly experimental plays of Shakespeare's last years, in which the tragic crisis occurs but death is averted and loss is miraculously made good. . . .

In the last and greatest of the Romances, *The Tempest,* Shakespeare eschewed the 'anti-dramatic' features of confusion of genres, sprawling narrative, and geographical expansiveness. *The Tempest* is the most tightly knit of all the plays in its unity of tone and action. Yet it contains everything that its straggling fellow plays have been asserting. It too uncreates the reality it creates; by making the whole sequence of events the contrivance of a magician. Prospero's endeavours to bring happy conclusions from the base deeds of men are constantly likened to the endeavours of a dramatist.

The tragic issue which is to be turned to a fortunate conclusion is not this time within the play, except by report; it is the Cain and Abel scenario, brother's hand against brother, by which Prospero was usurped as duke of Milan by his brother Antonio years before. Prospero of course is a kind of usurper himself on his island, having taken it over from Caliban, whom he has reduced to serfdom. Shakespeare preserves an almost maddening fair-mindedness in showing us the rights and wrongs of Caliban, who represents natural man, instinctively poetic and instinctively brutal, longing for independence and manufacturing his own servitude.

Prospero by his art brings his enemies to his island. His idea of building the future lies not in the negativeness of punishment but in uniting Naples with Milan through the marriage of his daughter Miranda with the king of Naples' son, Ferdinand. He makes Ariel bring them together and watches them fall in love.

> Fair encounter
> Of two most rare affections. Heavens rain grace
> On that which breeds between 'em. (III. i)

He arranges an elaborate masque, a 'vanity of mine art', to

convey to them *his* sense of the divine blessing that should fall on this couple. But he brings it to an abrupt conclusion as he remembers the plot of Caliban upon his life. In one of the most renowned speeches in all the plays, he reassures Ferdinand and Miranda that what they have been watching was only a play—and suddenly goes on to say that its sudden end was in keeping with the fleeting and transient nature of everything in the world.

> Like the baseless fabric of this vision,
> The cloud-capped towers, the gorgeous palaces,
> The solemn temples, the great globe itself,
> Yea, all which it inherit, shall dissolve
> And, like this insubstantial pageant faded,
> Leave not a rack behind. We are such stuff
> As dreams are made on, and our little life
> Is rounded with a sleep. (IV. i)

The time-honoured identification of Prospero with Shakespeare, and of this speech with Shakespeare's own thoughts, is very hard to resist. For it is this speech that explains the direction and the seriousness of the last plays, with their perpetual insistence on make-believe, fantasy, improbability. These romantic tragicomedies contain images of life as potent, and to audiences and readers as *true,* as anything in Shakespeare. Yet in general they are not sustained within a prolonged, coherent, and satisfying plot development, but handed to us as the momentary triumphs of the poetic imagination (like the masque in *The Tempest*). Yet the reality of our ordinary life and everyday experience, by the standard of which these moments are mere figments of make-believe, is shown to be as illusory, shadowy, and transitory as the fictions are. Shakespeare balances the 'untrue' images of art against the uncertain 'truths' of reality. His last plays deal with the age-old debate on the relation between art and reality with a brilliance and a lightness of touch that make all attempts at summary sound ponderous and pretentious. He asserts nothing, and offers everything. If you wish, in any way, to take his plays as truth, you have his permission; but he claims nothing for them.

Ben Jonson and the Sensational Jacobean Drama

Eugene P. Wright

While Ben Jonson is certainly the best-known contemporary of Shakespeare, many other fine dramatists followed in Shakespeare's footsteps in the early seventeenth century. According to Professor Eugene P. Wright of North Texas State University, Jonson's career is notable for its range as well as its quality, for it includes comedies, tragedies, satires, and masques. Until the Puritans closed the London theaters in 1642, Jonson was joined by a host of productive playwrights who kept the London stage a vibrant cultural institution. The plays of such writers as John Webster and John Ford tended to emphasize violence and sensationalism, while exploring the psychology of evil. This emphasis also informs many of the best plays of the period.

Ben Jonson (1573?–1637) is second only to Shakespeare as a giant of the period. The two were in many ways very different kinds of dramatists. In his *Essay of Dramatic Poesy* (1668), John Dryden said of Jonson, "If I would compare him with Shakespeare, I must acknowledge him the more correct poet, but Shakespeare the greater wit. . . . I admire him, but I love Shakespeare," a view not uncommon among later scholars.

Jonson's best plays are his comedies, created, in the tradition of [Roman playwrights] Plautus and Terence, to ridicule human foibles. If Shakespeare presented the mystery and complexity of human life, Jonson concentrated on human folly. His *Every Man in His Humour* (pr. 1598), with its well-constructed plot, stands as the first important comedy of humours on the English stage. In this genre, of which Jonson was the major exponent, human foibles are examined as a product of excessive personality traits (which, in medieval times, had been thought to result from an imbalance in the four bodily humours), concentrated in individual characters. A companion play, *Every Man out of His Humour* (pr. 1599), has a more complex plot and suggests that humours are cured by their own excesses. Other early Jonson comedies are allegorical and satiric. *The Case Is Altered* (pr. 1597), based upon a plot by Plautus, is a rather romantic comedy set in modern Italy, but the two other early comedies contain much more satire: *Cynthia's Revels: Or, The Fountain of Self-Love* (pr. 1600–1601) is a complex allegory praising Queen Elizabeth and satirizing some of Jonson's contemporaries, while *The Poetaster: Or, His Arraignment* (pr. 1601) has a Roman setting and contains scathing attacks upon the dramatist's adversaries.

JONSON'S MATURE COMEDIES

The comedies written between about 1605 and 1614 are generally considered to be Jonson's best, most mature comedies. *Volpone: Or, The Fox* (pr. 1606), perhaps the greatest satiric comedy in English, shows the effects of greed upon individual characters and society in general. *Epicoene: Or, The Silent Woman* (pr. 1609), thought by Samuel Taylor Coleridge to be the most entertaining of Jonson's comedies, is not so biting in its satire of humanity generally as *Volpone*; the gulling of the old recluse Morose is all in a kind of fun in which no one gets hurt. Greed, lust, and other human foibles are again satirized in *The Alchemist* (pr. 1610), a play relying upon the medieval belief in alchemy to show how the human desire to solve complex problems with quick, simple answers makes people susceptible to quackery. *Bartholomew Fair* (pr. 1614) utilizes a rather simple, though well-ordered, plot to present a realistic pageant of colorful London characters—a veritable circus of pickpockets, mountebanks, confidence men, religious hypocrites, balladmongers, puppetmasters, and many others. The good fun ends with everyone being forgiven his transgressions.

The late comedies return to the allegorical and satiric form of some of Jonson's earlier plays, with limited success. To this group belong *The Devil Is an Ass* (pr. 1616), *The Staple of News* (pr. 1626), *The New Inn: Or, The Light Hart* (pr. 1629), *The Magnetic Lady: Or, Humours Reconciled* (pr.

1632), and *A Tale of a Tub* (pr. 1633). The plots continue to be developed along the lines of classical comedy and are imaginatively drawn, but the characters remain mere emblems.

Jonson's two tragedies, both on Roman themes, are different in several respects from those of Shakespeare. Jonson, perhaps to display his superior knowledge of classical history, chose as his subjects minor incidents from Roman history; he also took as his sources the original Latin works rather than English translations or dramatic adaptations. *Sejanus His Fall* (pr. 1603), which derives from Tacitus, stretches the unity of time; the play depicts the destruction of the powerful Sejanus by the Emperor Tiberius. The psychological analysis of the tyrant's mind is well done both dramatically and intellectually, leading to the creation of Jonson's great comic character Volpone. *Catiline His Conspiracy* (pr. 1611) uses classical sources and dramatic devices, including a ghost and chorus, to show how mankind's bestial nature shapes political history. Characterization here, however, is weaker than in *Sejanus His Fall.* . . .

Jonson's poetical ability as a dramatist can be seen in the pastoral fragment *The Sad Shepherd*, but it is developed fully in his many masques written throughout his career. The masque is a highly ornamental type of drama written to provide entertainment at courtly functions and celebrations and different from the drama written for the public theater, for the companies of child actors, and for academic purposes. Jonson was the principal writer of masques during the reign of James I, and in these elaborate productions he replaced his satiric wit with his talent for writing carefully crafted poetry. . . . These plays contain neither great character development nor profound ideas, for the purpose of masques was to provide not social commentary but courtly entertainment. What they do show is another side to this prolific and complex writer.

Like many of his colleagues, Jonson collaborated with other dramatists in writing plays. He had gone to jail for his part in writing *The Isle of Dogs* (pr. 1597) with Thomas Nashe, a play now lost. He had better luck with *Eastward Ho!* (pr. 1605), written in collaboration with George Chapman and John Marston. Scholars have been unable to determine with certainty which parts were written by which authors, for the play contains none of the biting satire of Jonson, the psychological analysis of Chapman, or the bitterness of

Marston. The plot is realistic, presenting the virtues and pettiness in the lives of common tradesmen. The moral, if it can be taken at face value, is rather mundane, but the play is a pleasant comedy which presents middle-class London life in the style of Thomas Deloney or Thomas Dekker.

DRAMA AFTER JONSON TO THE CLOSING OF THE THEATERS

Had Shakespeare and Jonson never written drama, the history of the theater during the Renaissance would appear as a continuum from the late Elizabethan period through the early Jacobean period, or almost so. The tradition developed by the University Wits was continued by George Chapman, Thomas Dekker, Thomas Middleton, John Webster, John Ford, and Francis Beaumont and John Fletcher. These men, individually or in collaboration, wrote plays superior to any written for two hundred years or more thereafter. Their relative obscurity is caused simply by their proximity to the greatest dramatists in our culture. Others, such as John Marston, Thomas Heywood, Philip Massinger, Cyril Tourneur, and James Shirley, were good dramatists whose works lie even deeper in the shadows of Shakespeare and Jonson.

George Chapman (c. 1559–1634), perhaps best known in the twentieth century as the translator of Homer who impressed the English Romantic poet John Keats, was a leading literary figure in his day. He contributed both comedies and tragedies in response to the growing demand in London for new plays. His plots are generally more episodic than dramatic and are often exaggerated; his characters are distinctive and sometimes powerful, but seldom are their motives carefully analyzed. His comedies include *The Blind Beggar of Alexandria* (pr. 1596), *An Humourous Day's Mirth* (pr. 1597), *The Gentleman Usher* (pr. c. 1602), *All Fools* (pr. 1604), *Monsieur d'Olive* (pr. 1604), *The Widow's Tears* (pr. c. 1605), and *May Day* (pr. c. 1609). Three others were written in collaboration: *Eastward Ho!* (pr. 1605), with Jonson and Marston, and *The Ball* (pr. 1632) and *Chabot, Admiral of France* (pr. 1635), with James Shirley. The comedies develop interesting characters in usually improbable plots. The vulgarity of some of the subplots in *May Day* seems strange coming from the moral Chapman, but certainly the play offers a realistic treatment of its subject.

Chapman's five tragedies offer an interesting study of the Renaissance view of Stoicism. Drawing primarily on French history rather than English, Chapman created strong heroes placed in stories of political intrigue. The protagonist of *Bussy d'Ambois* (pr. 1604), the best of his tragedies, is a character much like Shakespeare's Hotspur in *Henry IV, Part I*, Othello, Kent in *King Lear*, and Coriolanus. Bussy is a tested soldier out of place in the world of courtly intrigue. His tragedy is as much a result of his surprising passion for a married woman as of political intrigue. In *The Revenge of Bussy d'Ambois* (pr. c. 1610), Bussy's brother Clermont, more of the detached stoic character than Bussy, philosophizes with himself on the subject of morality, revenges the murder of his brother, and dies by his own hand. *The Conspiracy and Tragedy of Charles, Duke of Byron* (pr. 1608) returns to the theme of *Bussy d'Ambois* to show a strong character whose passions lead to his destruction. Chapman's last two tragedies, *The Wars of Caesar and Pompey* (pr. c. 1613) and *Chabot, Admiral of France*, both present heroes who react stoically to the problems which beset them. Chapman's purpose throughout seems to be to use drama to present psychological studies of characters in the manner of Shakespeare before him and Webster after, and while his dramatic structure is often faulted by scholars, he was one of the most popular of the Jacobean dramatists.

Another important dramatist of the late Renaissance is Thomas Dekker (c. 1572–1632), a man whose love of life is reflected in his comedies. He took part in the "war of the theaters" that erupted between Jonson and Marston, writing the comedy *Satiromastix: Or, The Untrussing of the Humourous Poet* (pr. 1601)—the humorous poet being Jonson. Dekker's attack was not vitriolic, but Jonson soon realized that he was far too easy a target and withdrew from the "war." Dekker is best known for *The Shoemaker's Holiday: Or, The Gentle Craft* (pr. 1600), a pleasant comedy using a plot and characters borrowed from Thomas Deloney's prose romance *The Gentle Craft* (1597). Other comedies by Dekker are *The Whole History of Fortunatus* (pr. 1599; commonly known as *Old Fortunatus*), the two parts of *The Honest Whore* (pr. 1604 and c. 1605, respectively), *The Whore of Babylon* (pr. 1606–1607), *If This Be Not a Good Play, the Devil Is in It* (pr. 1610–1612; also as *If It Be Not Good, the Devil Is in It*), *Match Me in London* (pr. c. 1611–1612), and *The Wonder of a Kingdom* (pr. c. 1623). In addition, Dekker collaborated with other writers. His comedies are remarkable for their realistic portrayal of contemporary life and customs in essentially romantic plots. He excelled at the creation of individual scenes, although connections between the scenes are not always adequately provided.

A dramatist known to have collaborated with Dekker is Thomas Middleton (1580–1627), who probably had a hand in writing *The Honest Whore* with Dekker. Middleton's portrayal of London citizens in a decidedly unromantic manner is an interesting cross between Dekker and Jonson. His most important comedies among the many he wrote are *The Phoenix* (pr. 1604), *Michaelmas Term* (pr. c. 1606), *A Trick to Catch the Old One* (pr. c. 1605–1606), *The Old Law: Or, A New Way to Please You* (pr. c. 1618), and *A Game at Chess* (pr. 1624). Generally considered to be his best plays are *A Trick to Catch the Old One* and *A Game at Chess*. His comedies present life as he found it, in all of its coarseness, but his fine poetry and mastery of language attracted the attention of audiences during his day and of scholars since. Middleton also collaborated with Dekker on *The Roaring Girl: Or, Moll Cutpurse* (pr. c. 1610) and probably with Jonson and Fletcher on *The Widow* (pr. c. 1616). He wrote two tragedies in collaboration with William Rowley (1585?–1642?): *A Fair Quarrel* (pr. c. 1615–1617) and his best, *The Changeling* (pr. 1622), plays which contain good ideas well dramatized but which are marred by highly sensational, bloody scenes.

SENSATIONAL PLAYS ABOUT EVIL

The plays of John Webster (1580?–before 1635) are second only to those of Shakespeare in their analysis of the psychology of evil. Scholars have long admired the magnificence of Webster's villains but condemned their motivations as obscure. Modern scholarship has argued that the characterizations in Webster's two best plays, *The White Devil* (pr. 1609–1612) and *The Duchess of Malfi* (pr. 1613–1614), are in fact complex, virtually clinical analyses of psychological disorders. The horrors visited upon the virtuous Duchess of Malfi by her brother Ferdinand, for example, can be traced to the same source as his lycanthropy: his incestuous love for his sister and his inability to achieve his desires or even to admit them to himself. . . .

John Ford (1588–after 1639), like Webster, is known for his use of sensationalism. He explores frustrated love, as many of his colleagues did, but the problems that lead to the

THE FRAGMENTATION OF JACOBEAN DRAMA

The drama of the Jacobean period, from 1603 to 1640, is sometimes charged with being too violent and sensational, lacking the moral cohesion of the best Elizabethan drama. Scholar Alexander Leggatt concedes in the following excerpt that these traits are characteristic of much of the drama of the period. But he contends that the best playwrights of the period make conscious and artistic use of these dramatic elements.

The terms 'Elizabethan' and 'Jacobean' are seductive, inviting a neat contrast between a golden age under a loved and splendid queen and a time of disillusionment and breakdown under an unpopular, neurotic king. But of course the culture of England did not change overnight in 1603. There was a strong vein of satire in the literature of the 1590s, and complaint and disillusion were already in the air. In drama, some of the qualities labelled 'Jacobean' were already in place. The sophisticated violence of Jacobean tragedy would not have been novel to audiences who remembered *Titus Andronicus* and *The Spanish Tragedy*. The tendency for tragedy and satire to converge in dark comedy leading to death was already present in *The Jew of Malta* (*c.* 1589). So, it can be argued, was the uncertainty about the universe in which man finds himself. In *The Spanish Tragedy* and *Doctor Faustus* we see gods, or God, at work and the spectacle is not reassuring. In *Tamburlaine* and *Titus Andronicus* it is hard to be sure what, if anything, is in the heavens. Nonetheless, there are developments that make Jacobean drama distinctive.

To risk a few generalizations: in Jacobean drama virtue is withdrawn and under attack, and much of the energy belongs to vice. Even morally appropriate rewards and punishments do not help us get our bearings, for they are too grotesque to suggest a natural process. Playwrights work for the effect of the moment, even if it means being flippant or sensational. The result is a fragmented vision: at its best, the legitimate reflection of a fragmented world; at its worst, mere writing for effect. The art that Shakespeare consolidated is starting to break apart. In the early years of James's reign a theatregoer who had been unlucky in his choice of plays might have wondered if the dramatic form itself was becoming exhausted. The danger was real; that it was averted can be credited to a number of remarkable playwrights who took the liabilities of Jacobean drama—fragmentation, sensationalism, moral incoherence—and turned them into assets.

Alexander Leggatt, *English Drama: Shakespeare to the Restoration 1590–1660*. London: Longman, 1988, pp. 101–105 passim.

frustration are not the usual ones. Complex plots, as in *The Broken Heart* (pr. c. 1627–1631), lead the audience through a maze of sympathies and emphases. The play begins with a love triangle involving the unhappy heroine, Penthea; moves its focus to her brother, who is murdered by her lover; and ends by concentrating upon Princess Calantha, who stoically receives the news of the death of her two friends and of her father the king long enough to set her affairs and those of the state in order before dying of a broken heart. In his best play, *'Tis Pity She's a Whore* (pr. 1629?–1633), Ford uses the theme of incest, as Webster did in *The Duchess of Malfi*, but in Ford's play incest is much more central to the plot and more explicitly treated. Indeed, so sympathetic is Ford's treatment of the brother and sister, Giovanni and Annabella, whose incestuous love leads to their tragic deaths, that some critics have seen a conflict between the play's apparently moral conclusion (sin is punished) and its inner logic.

Among Ford's other contributions to drama are *Perkin Warbeck* (pr. c. 1622–1632), *The Lover's Melancholy* (pr. 1628), *The Fancies Chast and Noble* (pr. 1631?), *Love's Sacrifice* (pr. 1632?), and *The Lady's Trial* (pr. 1638). All the plays show clear construction and often scenes of intense passion and emotion. *Perkin Warbeck* is generally considered to be the best history play written after those of Marlowe and Shakespeare. Ford also collaborated with Dekker and Rowley on *The Witch of Edmonton* (pr. 1621) and with Webster on *The Late Murther of the Son upon the Mother* (pr. 1624). Several plays known to be by Ford are no longer extant.

The names of Francis Beaumont (c. 1584–1616) and John Fletcher (1579–1625), while they both wrote plays individually and Fletcher collaborated with several other dramatists, are almost always mentioned together because of the great success of the plays that they wrote in collaboration. The one play sometimes assigned solely to Beaumont is *The Woman Hater* (pr. c. 1606), a kind of burlesque comedy; some modern scholars believe that Beaumont was also the sole author of the mock-heroic satiric comedy *The Knight of the Burning Pestle* (pr. 1607). About twenty plays are usually assigned to Fletcher alone, including the pastoral *The Faithful Shepherdess* (pr. c. 1608–1609), a play of excellent poetry and rich imagery. Fletcher collaborated on many other plays with such dramatists as Massinger, Rowley, Middleton, and perhaps even Shakespeare.

Beaumont's and Fletcher's best work, however, is to be found among the plays jointly written by them rather than in their solo efforts. *Philaster: Or, Love Lies A-Bleeding* (pr. c. 1609), one of the finest plays of its day, is a tragicomedy which achieves genuine pathos. The play was acted often during the seventeenth century and returned to the stage well into the nineteenth century. *The Maid's Tragedy* (pr. c. 1611) suffers from sensationalism and sentimentality, but its well-constructed plot and vivid characterization made it a popular play during its day. Both Beaumont and Fletcher were men of good family and good education, giving them a familiarity with men and women of high social standing and a certain contempt for the common man. They were able to write interesting and successful plays which often achieve brilliant effects, but they seldom explored the basic questions of human psychology with the intensity of Marlowe, Shakespeare, Jonson, or Webster.

LOWER RANKING DRAMATISTS

John Marston, Thomas Heywood, Philip Massinger, Cyril Tourneur, and James Shirley are usually ranked somewhat lower than the Jacobean dramatists discussed above, although some noteworthy critics would disagree with this ranking in a given case. Marston (1576–1634) began his literary career as a poet, turned playwright, and then gave it all up to become a priest. He entered the war of the theaters against Jonson with his *Histriomastix: Or, The Player Whipt* (pr. 1599) and was held up to ridicule as the character Crispinus in Jonson's *The Poetaster*, but the battle ended quickly, and Marston collaborated with Jonson and Chapman in *Eastward Ho!* in 1605. He even dedicated to Jonson his most famous play, *The Malcontent* (pr. 1604), the story of a virtuoso cynic. The deposed Duke Altofronto, disguised as the jester Malevole, roams the court commenting upon immorality and injustice. In *The Malcontent*, however, as in Marston's other plays, the characters' motivations are often lost in the vigor of the action.

Thomas Heywood (c. 1573–1641) is usually listed as a major Jacobean dramatist on the strength of volume alone, for he wrote more than two hundred plays wholly or in part, many of which are no longer extant. His plays include chronicle histories, romantic comedies, realistic comedies, allegorical plays, and a number of pageants. The best of his plays are the domestic dramas, the ones in which specific elements of private life are dealt with interestingly and without undue sensationalism. Charles Lamb's description of Heywood as a "prose Shakespeare" is certainly hyperbolic; Heywood was a professional writer turning out plays for actors on proven themes. His best play is *A Woman Killed with Kindness* (pr. 1603), a kind of domestic tragedy on the order of Shakespeare's *Othello*. In Heywood's play, the woman is guilty of adultery but repentant; her husband, controlling his rage and jealousy as Othello does not, banishes his wife to a manor "seven mile off," there to live out her life. When she is near death, he goes to her side and forgives her. *The English Traveler* (pr. c. 1627) presents a similar theme of seduction, repentance, and death from shame. Most of Heywood's plays present the same kind of delicate, thoughtful reactions to sin and a kind of quiet morality. Neither the sin, if that is what it is, nor the morality, if such exists, is analyzed as in the plays of Marlowe, Shakespeare, and others. . . .

Two plays are usually credited to Cyril Tourneur (c. 1575–1626), a poet and dramatist about whose life little is known. *The Revenger's Tragedy* (pr. 1606–1607), regarded by some critics as one of the masterpieces of Jacobean drama, shows the corrupting power of revenge. Vindice, the protagonist, like his predecessor Hamlet, begins the play as a moral man caught up in a plot of lust and murder; unlike Hamlet, however, Tourneur's revenger acts not as a minister of Heaven but as a man who learns to plot and murder with glee. Vindice recognizes at the end of the play that he has been corrupted when he says, "'Tis time to die when we're ourselves our foes." Tourneur's other play (if indeed he wrote either one—there is some question) is also a revenge tragedy, *The Atheist's Tragedy: Or, The Honest Man's Revenge* (pr. c. 1607). As in the earlier play, the dramatist here uses the revenge theme to express Christian virtues. A ghost is employed, as in many earlier revenge tragedies, but this time the ghost does not appear to direct revenge but to urge that revenge be left to God. The play thus offers an interesting addition to the usual revenge theme, but the idea is marred by the rather unrealistic application of reward for a moral life. Because he trusts in the moral order to set things right rather than taking the law into his own hands, Charlemont is rewarded with the same kind of material gain that has caused the villainy in the play. Interesting in the play is the presentation of the new materialism that came to late sixteenth century England.

One of the last dramatists of the period is James Shirley (1596–1666), a professional playwright of whose works more than thirty plays are extant—more than any playwright of the period except Shakespeare and Fletcher. Shirley's plays are consistently competent in structure and characterization, drawing as he did upon the models of his contemporaries over a wide range of themes and plots. Of his six tragedies, *The Cardinal* (pr. 1641) is the best. It has all the trappings of revenge tragedy sensationally displayed, as they had been presented by Kyd and the great writers of revenge tragedy who followed him. There are echoes here of Webster's *The Duchess of Malfi*, but Shirley is content to present the action without psychological probing. He wrote many more comedies than tragedies, the best being *Hyde Park* (pr. 1632) and *The Lady of Pleasure* (pr. 1635). The former is an early comedy of manners which looks forward to the drama of the Restoration. Shirley provides no hint that the pleasures of the aristocracy presented in this comedy would lead to the 1642 Civil War, only a few years away. The latter play presents a similar picture of an aristocracy for whom life is defined by their own pleasures and trivial concerns. The characters play at love in a sensual London, and the morality which is reaffirmed at the end of the play is little more than a witty refusal to sink completely into the mire.

Shirley was at the height of his career when, on September 2, 1642, the ruling Puritan administration proclaimed that "public stage-plays will cease and be foreborne," thus putting an end to the greatest period of English drama the world has known. It had its origins in the ideas and structures of Greek and Roman drama and in the realism of native English drama and life. It was able to grow to maturity because the intellectual and social climate of England was such that citizens were free politically and economically to pursue those ideas wherever they led. That men of rare genius such as Shakespeare and Jonson happened along during the development of drama elevated the achievement to a level that has enthralled succeeding generations, but even without their contributions, the high reputation of Elizabethan and Jacobean drama would be secure. Rarely before or since has literature of any type held such a clear mirror up to nature, and never with such consistency.

Chronology

1341

Petrarch, the first great Italian humanist, crowned poet laureate in Rome.

1353

Boccaccio's *Decameron* published.

1374

Death of Petrarch.

1380s

Chaucer writes *The Canterbury Tales*.

1397

Study of Greek literature initiated at University of Florence.

CA. 1400

Humanism begins to flourish in the Italian city-states.

1434

Accession to power of the Medici family in Florence, Italy.

1453

Fall of Constantinople; many Greek scholars come to Italy.

1455

Gutenberg Bible published using moveable type; the printing revolution begins.

1462

Platonic Academy founded in Florence.

1470

Ficino completes first Latin translation of Plato's *Dialogues*.

1486

Pico's *Oration on the Dignity of Man* published.

1492

Columbus discovers the New World.

1490–1530

The High Renaissance in Italian art; Leonardo da Vinci, Michelangelo, and Raphael active.

1498

Leonardo completes *The Last Supper*.

1504

Michelangelo completes sculpture *David*.

1509

Publication of *The Praise of Folly* by the Christian humanist Erasmus; Henry VIII becomes king of England.

1513

Machiavelli's *The Prince* published.

1516

Sir Thomas More's *Utopia* published in Latin.

1517

Martin Luther posts his ninety-five Theses, sparking the Reformation.

1525

William Tyndale translates the New Testament into English.

1528

Publication of Castiglione's *The Courtier* in Italian.

1534

Rabelais's *Gargantua* published in Paris.

1535

Sir Thomas More beheaded for treason by Henry VIII.

1536

Protestant leader John Calvin completes his influential *Institutes of the Christian Religion*; death of Erasmus.

1542

Publication of Copernicus's *On the Revolution of Celestial Spheres*, which contended that the earth was not the center of the universe.

1545–1563

The Council of Trent, start of the Catholic Counterreformation.

1558

Queen Elizabeth becomes queen of England; rules until 1603; publication of Marguerite de Navarre's *Heptameron*.

1561

Publication of English translation of Castiglione's *The Courtier*.

1564

Birth of William Shakespeare at Stratford-upon-Avon; birth of Christopher Marlowe at Canterbury; deaths of John Calvin and Michelangelo.

1567

Publication of Golding's translation of Ovid's *Metamorphoses*, a major influence on Shakespeare.

1572

Birth of Ben Jonson, Shakespeare's playwriting rival and friend; birth of the poet John Donne.

1576

First public playhouse, the Theatre, opens in London.

1580

Michel de Montaigne, *Essays* (first edition).

1580s

Poems of Sir Philip Sidney widely circulated but not officially published.

1586

Death of Sir Philip Sidney, the most admired Elizabethan courtier and "Renaissance man."

CA. 1587

Thomas Kyd writes *The Spanish Tragedy*.

1588

Defeat of the Spanish Armada, the attempted invasion of England.

1590

Edmund Spenser's *The Faerie Queene* Books 1–3 published.

CA. 1590

Christopher Marlowe writes his hit play *Dr. Faustus*.

CA. **1590–1593**

Shakespeare's earliest plays are written and publicly performed, including *Titus Andronicus, The Comedy of Errors,* and *Richard III.*

1592

The Rose is built in London; plague closes London playhouses for two years.

1593

Christopher Marlowe killed in a tavern brawl.

1594

Shakespeare, *Romeo and Juliet;* Shakespeare's troupe of players is designated the Lord Chamberlain's Men; first record of Lord Chamberlain's Men performing for Queen Elizabeth.

1595

Shakespeare, *A Midsummer Night's Dream.*

1597

Shakespeare, *1 Henry IV;* Sir Francis Bacon, *Essays.*

1599

The Globe built in London; Shakespeare is a major shareholder; death of Edmund Spenser, England's most noted poet; Shakespeare, *Henry V, As You Like It, Julius Caesar.*

CA. **1601**

Shakespeare, *Hamlet.*

1603

Queen Elizabeth dies; accession of James I as king of England; Shakespeare's company becomes known as the King's Men, and begins performing frequently in the royal court.

1603–1606

Shakespeare writes some of his greatest tragedies: *Othello, Macbeth,* and *King Lear.*

1605

Cervantes, *Don Quixote;* Bacon, *The Advancement of Learning.*

1606

Ben Jonson, *Volpone, or the Fox.*

1607

Jamestown Colony (named after King James) is established in Virginia.

1610

Galileo announces his telescopic discoveries.

1611

The King James translation of the Bible is published; Shakespeare, *The Tempest.*

1613

The Globe burns down; rebuilt the next year; John Webster, *The Duchess of Malfi.*

1616

Death of William Shakespeare at age fifty-two, in Stratford; death of Cervantes.

1620

Pilgrims settle at Plymouth, Massachusetts.

1623

Publication of Shakespeare's collected plays in the Folio edition.

1633

Posthumous publication of the poetry of John Donne (d. 1631).

1642

Civil War breaks out in England; English theaters closed down by the Puritans; not reopened until 1660.

1667

Publication of John Milton's epic poem *Paradise Lost,* Books 1–10.

1674

Death of Milton.

FOR FURTHER RESEARCH

STUDIES OF THE EUROPEAN RENAISSANCE

Margaret Aston, *The Panorama of the Renaissance*. New York: Harry N. Abrams, 1996.

Alison Brown, *The Renaissance*. New York: Addison-Wesley, 1990.

E.R. Chamberlin, *Everyday Life in Renaissance Times*. London: B.T. Batsford, 1965.

Gloria K. Fiero, *On the Threshold of Modernity: The Renaissance and the Reformation*. Dubuque, IA: Wm. C. Brown, 1992.

Peter Gay and R.K.Webb, *Modern Europe*. New York: Harper & Row, 1973.

John R. Hale, *Renaissance*. New York: Time-Life Books, 1965.

George Holmes, *Renaissance*. New York: St. Martin's, 1996.

Paul Johnson, *The Renaissance*. New York: Modern Library, 2000.

Charles G. Nauert Jr., *The Age of Renaissance and Reformation*. Lanham, MD: University Press of America, 1981.

Lewis W. Spitz, *The Renaissance and Reformation Movements*. Vol. 1. Rev. ed. St. Louis, MO: Concordia, 1987.

Bard Thompson, *Humanists and Reformers: A History of the Renaissance and Reformation*. Grand Rapids, MI: Eerdmans, 1996.

THE ITALIAN RENAISSANCE

Kenneth J. Atchity and Giose Rimanelli, *Italian Literature: Roots & Branches*. New Haven, CT: Yale University Press, 1976.

Peter Burke, *The Fortunes of the Courtier.* University Park: Pennsylvania State University Press, 1996.

E.R. Chamberlin, *The World of the Italian Renaissance.* London: G. Allen Unwin, 1982.

Leonard Forster, *The Icy Fire: Five Studies in European Petrarchism.* Cambridge: Cambridge University Press, 1969.

J.R. Hale, *Machiavelli and Renaissance Italy.* London: English University Press, 1961.

Denys Hay, *The Italian Renaissance in Its Historical Background.* 2nd ed. Cambridge: Cambridge University Press, 1977.

George Holmes, *Florence, Rome, and the Origins of the Renaissance.* New York: Oxford University Press, 1986.

Charles G. Nauert Jr., *Humanism and the Culture of Renaissance Europe.* Cambridge: Cambridge University Press, 1995.

J.H. Plumb, *The Italian Renaissance.* New York: American Heritage, 1985.

HUMANISM AND THE NORTHERN RENAISSANCE

Roland H. Bainton, *Erasmus of Christendom.* New York: Scribner, 1969.

Otis H. Green, *Spain and the Western Tradition.* Madison: University of Wisconsin Press, 1963–66.

Walter Kaiser, *Praisers of Folly: Erasmus, Rabelais, Shakespeare.* Cambridge, MA: Harvard University Press, 1963.

Donald R. Kelley, *Renaissance Humanism.* Boston: Twayne, 1991.

Margaret L. King, *Women of the Renaissance.* Chicago: University of Chicago Press, 1991.

A.J. Krailsheimer, ed., *The Continental Renaissance, 1500–1600.* Harmondsworth, England: Penguin, 1971.

I.D. McFarlane, *Renaissance France, 1470–1589.* New York: Barnes & Noble, 1974.

Clarence H. Miller, Introduction to *The Praise of Folly.* New Haven, CT: Yale University Press, 1979.

Margaret Mann Phillips, *Erasmus and the Northern Renaissance.* Rev. ed. Totowa, NJ: Rowman & Littlefield, 1981.

M.A. Screech, *Rabelais.* Ithaca, NY: Cornell University Press, 1979.

Katharina M. Wilson, *Women Writers of the Renaissance and Reformation.* Athens: University of Georgia Press, 1987.

THE RENAISSANCE IN ENGLAND

David M. Bevington, Introduction to *The Complete Works of Shakespeare.* New York: HarperCollins, 1992.

Sukanta Chaudhuri, Introduction to *An Anthology of Elizabethan Poetry.* Delhi: Oxford University Press, 1992.

Hardin Craig, *The Literature of the English Renaissance 1485–1600.* New York: Collier Books, 1962.

Philip Edwards, "William Shakespeare," in *An Outline of English Literature.* 2nd ed. Ed. Pat Rogers. Oxford: Oxford University Press, 1998.

Roland M. Frye, *Shakespeare's Life and Times: A Pictorial Record.* Princeton, NJ: Princeton University Press, 1967.

Merritt Y. Hughes, Introduction to *John Milton: Complete Poems and Major Prose.* Indianapolis: Odyssey, 1957.

David Scott Kastan, ed., *A Companion to Shakespeare.* Oxford: Blackwell, 1999.

L.C. Knights, *Drama and Society in the Age of Jonson.* New York: Norton, 1968.

Alexander Leggatt, *English Drama: Shakespeare to the Restoration, 1590–1660.* New York: Longman, 1988.

——, *Introduction to English Renaissance Comedy.* New York: St. Martin's, 1999.

C.S. Lewis, *English Literature in the Sixteenth Century Excluding Drama.* Oxford: Oxford University Press, 1954.

Michael Mangan, *A Preface to Shakespeare's Tragedies.* New York: Longman, 1991.

Russell J. Meyer, *The Faerie Queene: Educating the Reader.* Boston: Twayne, 1991.

Thomas Marc Parrott and Robert Hamilton Ball, *A Short View of Elizabethan Drama.* New York: Charles Scribner's Sons, 1958.

Isabel Rivers, *Classical and Christian Ideas in English Renaissance Poetry.* London: Routledge, 1994.

Derek Traverski, Introduction to *Renaissance Drama*. New York: St. Martin's, 1980.

Brian Vickers, Introduction to *The Oxford Authors: Francis Bacon*. New York: Oxford University Press, 1996.

Gary Waller, *English Poetry of the Sixteenth Century*. Rev. 2nd ed. New York: Longman, 1993.

Richard Willmott, Introduction to *Four Metaphysical Poets*. Cambridge: Cambridge University Press, 1985.

Eugene P. Wright, "Elizabethan and Jacobean Drama," in *Critical Survey of Drama: English Language Series*. Ed. Frank N. Magill. Englewood Cliffs, NJ: Salem Press, 1985.

INDEX

Adagia (Erasmus), 62, 65
Advancement of Learning (Bacon)
  aphorisms in, 145
  metaphors in, 148–49
  as psychological and sociological study, 142, 148
Alberti, Leon Battista, 37–38
Alchemist, The (Jonson), 194
Aldine Press, 23, 100
allegories
  Faerie Queene as, 103
  by Jonson, 194
All's Well That Ends Well (Shakespeare)
  as problem comedy, 191
  as tragicomedy, 191
Antony and Cleopatra (Shakespeare), 179, 182, 183–85
Aphthonius, 85
Areopagitica (Milton), 121
Ariosto, Lodovico, 22, 60, 102
Aristotle
  and civic responsibility, 36
  and education, 64
  on metaphors, 148
  and Scholasticism, 42
Ascham, Roger, 100
Aston, Margaret, 17–18
As You Like It (Shakespeare), 178
Atheist's Tragedy: Or, The Honest Man's Revenge, The (Tourneur), 202

Bacon, Lady Ann, 133
Bacon, Sir Francis
  background of, 144–45
  on recovery of classics, 11
  and science of man, 142–43
  works of
    elements of, 141

  genres of, 144, 145, 148
  metaphors in, 148–50
  purpose of, 141, 142
Baines, Richard, 162
Baker, Sir Richard, 108
Bartholomew Fair (Jonson), 194
Beaumont, Francis, 196, 200, 201
Bellay, Joachim du, 21, 59, 84
Bevington, David, 152
Boccaccio, Giovanni, 12, 20
Broken Heart, The (Ford), 200
Bruni, Leonardo, 36

Cameron, Euan, 14
Canzoniere (Petrarch), 35, 90
Cardinal, The (Shirley), 203
Case Is Altered, The (Jonson), 194
Castiglione, Baldassare, 19, 50
Catholicism, 59
Cereta, Laura, 126
Chaloner, Sir Thomas, 65
Chamberlin, E.R., 47
Chapman, George, 195, 196–97
chivalry, 11
Christian humanism. *See* humanism, Christian
Christianity
  in England under Tudors, 100
  in *Praise of Folly*, 66, 67–69
  in *Utopia*, 72–73, 77
Cicero
  and civic responsibility, 36
  and education, 64
    of governing class, 101
  influence on
    Petrarch, 34
    poetry, 21
classics
  adaptations of, 153–56
  availability of, 36
  education based on, 13

Greek romances, 154–55
imitation of style of, 12
importance of, 18
influence on
  Jonson, 195
  Shakespeare, 182, 183–85
as inspiration, 41, 43
Italy as home of, 32
during Middle Ages, 39, 42
recovery of, 11
use of, in government, 43
Coleridge, Samuel Taylor, 194
Colet, John, 23, 58, 70
Colloquies (Erasmus), 56, 58
comedies, 27
as elements of histories, 174–75
romantic, 154
subject matter of, 78–79
types of
  humours, 193–94
  manners, 203
  romantic, 154, 176–77, 178
  tragicomedies, 186–87, 191–92
Complaint of Peace (Erasmus), 56
Concerning Famous Women
  (Boccaccio), 20
Confessions (St. Augustine), 17
Courtier, The (Castiglione)
as argument for humanist
  values and manners, 19
described, 51–52
purpose of, 47, 49
translations of, 15
as treatise in dialogue form, 19
Crane, R.S., 142
Curtain, the, 25–26
Cymbeline (Shakespeare), 191
*Cynthia's Revels: Or, The
  Fountain of Self-Love* (Jonson),
  194

Dames des Roches, 127
Dekker, Thomas, 196, 197–98,
  200
de Sade, Laura, 35, 89
dialectic, 85
Divine Meditations (Donne), 108
Donne, John
background of, 107–108
influence of Petrarch on, 22
introspection by, 18
as metaphysical poet, 112, 114
poetry of
  love in, 109–10, 111
  religion in, 108, 109, 110

tone of, 114, 115
Don Quixote (Cervantes), 19
drama
and blank verse, 26
Elizabethan
  introspection in, 18
  theaters for, 25–26
  types of, 152–53
forms of, 26, 27
see also comedies; histories;
  tragedies
Dr. Faustus (Marlowe), 157, 199
Helen of Troy, 17, 167–68
importance of, 26
as morality play, 169
themes of
  aspiration, 16–17, 157, 163–65
  classical vs. Christian values,
    165–67, 168–69
  pride, 159, 167
  salvation, 17
  temptation, 17
Dryden, John, 111
Duchess of Malfi, The (Webster),
  198

education
and classics, 13, 24, 42, 100
curricula of, 14, 44, 45
in England, 23–24, 100
and government, 99, 101
importance of, 18, 19
and moral reform of rulers, 43
and Petrarch, 14
in universities, 54
in *Utopia*, 75–76
of women, 20, 125–28, 134
see also Scholasticism
Edward II (Marlowe), 157–58
Edwards, Philip, 179
Egerton, Sir Thomas, 108
Elizabeth I (queen of England),
  129
court of, 153
death of, 27
education of, 20, 127
and *Faerie Queene*, 102–103
and plays of Shakespeare, 26
as writer, 130
Epicoene: Or, The Silent Woman
  (Jonson), 194
Erasmus, Desiderius
background of, 55–56
biblical scholarship of, 56–57
and education, 14

of women, 20, 128
importance of, 56
influence of Lucian on, 83
and More, 57, 62–63
and Oxford Reformers, 70
popularity of, 62
and religion, 56–57, 58
works of, 56–57
  attacks on, 64
  use of Latin in, 60
  see also specific titles
Essay on Dramatic Poesy
  (Dryden), 193
Essays (Bacon)
  aphorisms in, 145
  as psychological and
    sociological study, 142–43
  purpose of, 141
Essays (Montaigne), 136–40
Euphues, The Anatomy of Wit
  (Lyly), 153
Euphues and His England (Lyly),
  153
Every Man in His Humor
  (Jonson), 193
Every Man Out of His Humor
  (Jonson), 194

Faerie Queen, The (Spenser)
  as allegory, 22, 103
  consistency within, 104–105
  as dream, 104
  as epic romance, 102
  influence of *Orlando Furioso*
    on, 60, 102
  language of, 103
  multiple narrative voices of, 105
  Protestantism in, 22
  purpose of, 102, 106
  and Queen Elizabeth, 102–103
fame, cult of, 45–46
Father of Humanism. *See*
  Petrarch, Francesco
Federigo da Montefeltro, 50–51
Ficino, Marsilio, 36–37
Fidele, Cassandra, 126, 134
Fiero, Gloria K., 32
Fletcher, John, 196, 200–201
Florence, 33–34
Ford, John, 193, 196, 198, 200
Forster, Leonard, 88
Frizar, Ingram, 163

Galindo, Beatriz, 126–27
Gargantua (Rabelais), 20, 85

Gargantua and Pantagruel
  (Rabelais), 60
Gill, Roma, 161
grammar, 64
Greene, Robert, 152, 153, 154–55

Hale, J.R., 12, 17
Hamilton, A.C., 104
Hamlet (Shakespeare)
  complexity of, 28
  influence of *Spanish Tragedy*
    on, 26
  as political tragedy, 185, 186
  as revenge play, 181–82
Handbook of the Christian Knight
  (Erasmus), 56
Hazlitt, William, 122
Henry VII (king of England), 98,
  99
Henry VIII (king of England), 57
Herbert, George
  background of, 107, 108
  introspection by, 18
  as metaphysical poet, 112, 114
  religion in poetry of, 108,
    110–11
Heywood, Thomas, 196, 201–202
histories, 26, 27, 159–60, 172
Holmes, George, 28
Hughes, Merritt Y., 116
humanism
  Christian, 54–55
    decline of, 59
    extent of, 84
    and religion, 58, 59, 101
    see also Northern Renaissance
  Italian
    and denigration of Middle
      Ages, 41
    development of, 33–34
    goals of, 11–12
    importance of, 13, 15
    influence on Northern
      Renaissance, 24
Hundred Years' War, 23
Hutten, Ulrich von, 12
Hyde Park (Shirley), 203

irony
  in *Paradise Lost*, 116, 119–20,
    121–22
  in *Praise of Folly*, 67
Italian humanism. *See*
  humanism, Italian

Jacobean drama, 29, 196, 199
James (king of England), 27
Jew of Malta, The (Marlowe), 156, 157, 199
Johnson, Samuel, 111, 113
Jonson, Ben
  on greatness of Shakespeare, 15–16
  influence of Romans on, 193
  satire of, 194
  and war of theaters, 197
  works of, 193–95
Julius Caesar (Shakespeare), 179, 185–86

Katerina Jagellonica (queen of Sweden), 127
Kelso, Ruth, 128
King, Margaret L., 21
King Lear (Shakespeare), 179–80, 188–90
King's Men, 27
Kyd, Thomas
  background of, 26, 163
  death of, 26
  importance of, 152, 156
  influence of classics on, 155–56
  influence on Shakespeare, 180
  and revenge plays, 180–81

Labé, Louise, 127, 130–31
Ladies Peace, 129
Lamb, Charles, 202
languages
  Greek, 100
  Latin
    in education, 14, 24
    importance of, 14–15
    used
      by Erasmus, 60
      by More, 71
      in scholarly works, 35
    veracity of originals, 84
  vernacular
    used
      for poetry, 35
      by Rabelais, 60
      by women writers, 130, 131, 132
    Utopia translated into, 71
Leech, Clifford, 166
Leggatt, Alexander, 199
Lerner, Robert E., 54
Life of Cowley (Johnson), 111
Locke, Anne, 132–33

Lord Chamberlain's Men, 27
Louise of Savoy, 127
Lucian, 83
Luciferi (Vondel), 122
Luther, Martin, 99–100
Lyly, John, 152, 153–54

Macbeth (Shakespeare), 180, 186–88
Machiavelli, Niccolo, 43, 48–49
Maid's Tragedy, The (Beaumony and Fletcher), 201
Malcontent (Marston), 201
Mantuis, Aldius, 100
Margaret of Austria, 127, 129
Marguerite of Navarre, 127–30
Marlowe, Christopher
  background of, 161–63
  and blank verse, 26, 158–59
  death of, 26
  importance of, 152, 156, 158, 159
  influence of Kyd on, 156
  influence on Shakespeare, 26, 157–59
Marston, John, 196, 197, 201
Martz, Louis, 113
Marvell, Andrew
  background of, 107, 108–109
  as metaphysical poet, 112, 114
  poetry of
    love in, 110
    religion in, 111
    tone of, 114–15
masques, 145–47, 195
Massinger, Philip, 196, 201
Measure for Measure (Shakespeare), 191
Medici family, 33–34, 36, 49, 127
Meyer, Russell J., 98
Middle Ages
  classics in, 39, 42
  concept of, as historical period, 41
  English drama during, 25
  insignificance of individual during, 15, 17
  literature of, 11, 22
  morality plays, 25, 169
  sense of history during, 13
  women during, 20
Middleton, Thomas, 196, 198
Midsummer Night's Dream, A (Shakespeare), 176–77
Miller, Clarence H., 62
Milligan, Burton A., 70

Milton, John, 23
Miroir (Marguerite of Navarre), 130
Montaigne, Michel de
  background of, 136–37
  introspection by, 17–18
  reading habits of, 138
More, Ann, 108
More, Sir Thomas
  background of, 57, 59, 70
  and education of women, 20, 128
  and Erasmus, 57, 62–63
Mother Bombie (Lyly), 154
Mulcaster, Richard, 100

Nashe, Thomas, 195
Nauert, Charles G., Jr., 13, 39
Nogarola, Isotta, 126
Northern Renaissance
  development of, 54
    influence of Italian humanism on, 24
  in England, 13, 23–24, 98–99
  and religion, 54–55
Notes on the New Testament (Valla), 57

"Of Masques and Triumphs" (Bacon), 147
"Of Studies" (Bacon), 146
"On Giving the Lie" (Montaigne), 139
On the Family (Alberti), 37–38
"On Vanity" (Montaigne), 140
Oration on the Dignity of Man (Pico), 37
Organon, 64
Orlando Furioso (Ariosto), 60
Ornstein, Robert, 166
Othello (Shakespeare), 180, 182–83
Oxford Reformers, 70

Palmieri, Matteo, 12
Pantagruel (Rabelais), 20, 60, 85
Papal States, 33
Paradise Lost (Milton)
  Adam as hero, 120
  as drama, 116–17
  as epic poem, 116, 117
  irony in, 116, 119–22
  plot of, 116–19
  Satan as hero, 116, 119–21, 122–23

themes of, 23
  aspiration, 16
  creation, 119
Pascal, Blaise, 137
patrons
  importance of, 82
  Medici family as, 33–34, 36
  and Shakespeare, 27
  women as, 108, 127
Pease, Arthur, 65
Pericles, Prince of Tyre (Shakespeare), 191
Petrarch, Francesco
  and concept of Middle Ages, 41
  and education, 14
  essays of, 35
  on imitation, 83
  importance of, 11–12, 21–22, 35–36
  importance of classics to, 13
  influence on Labé, 130
  as medieval man, 35
  and Middle Ages, 13, 40
  poetry of, 21–22
    analysis of, 90–91
    conventions of, 89–90, 91, 93–97
    importance of, 35–36, 88, 89, 91–92, 94
    introspection in, 88
    language of, 90
    women in, 89, 92–95
  prose of, 17, 88
  and pursuit of fame, 45–46
  and recovery of classics, 34
  and religion, 34–35
Philaster: Or, Love Lies A-Bleeding (Beaumont and Fletcher), 201
Pico della Mirandola, Giovanni, 37
Plato
  dialogues of, 42
  influence on
    Castiglione, 19
    poetry, 21
    Praise of Folly, 65–66
  translations of, 36
Plautus, 193, 194
plays
  morality, 25, 169
  mystery, 25
  see also drama; histories
Plutarch, 20, 21
Poetaster: Or, His Arraignment, The (Jonson), 194

poetry
  of Shakespeare, 27
  types of, 21
    epic, 116, 117
    metaphysical
      characteristics of, 111–12,
        113, 114
    narrative, 27
    Romantic, 122
    romantic epic, 21, 22
  see also specific works
Praise of Folly, The (Erasmus)
  attacks on, 64
  definition of Christianity in, 66,
    67–69
  as humanist reform agenda,
    63–65
  humor of, 18–19
  influence of Plato on, 65–66
  irony in, 67
  Scholasticism in, 56
  structure of, 66–69
Praz, Mario, 162
Prince, The (Machiavelli)
  described, 48–49
  purpose of, 47, 48
  themes of
    aspiration, 16
printing press, 12, 23, 100
prose
  forms of, 18–19
  literary devices used, 18–19
  see also specific titles
Protestantism, 22, 24–25, 59
Puritans, 193, 203
Pyritz, Hans W., 89

Quintilian
  and education, 64, 101
  on metaphors, 148
  and rhetoric, 85

Rabelais, François, 20
  background of, 60
  Christian sources of, 79, 80,
    85–86
  classical sources of, 79, 80,
    83–86
  compared to Shakespeare, 81
  lack of moralistic preaching by,
    60–61
  rhetorical and dialectic
    techniques of, 85
  satire of, 81–82
  as syncretist, 79

use of vernacular by, 60
  values of, 80
Reformation, 24–25
Regosin, Richard L., 136
religion
  and Christian humanism, 58,
    59, 101
  and Erasmus, 56–57, 58
  and Northern Renaissance,
    54–55
  Protestantism, 22, 24–25, 59
  and Scholasticism, 45
Renaissance
  birth of concept of, 13
  development of new sense of
    history during, 39–40, 41
  literature of
    importance of, 28
    see also themes
  optimism of, 38
  see also Northern Renaissance
Republic (Plato), 16
Revenger's Tragedy, The
  (Tourneur), 202
rhetoric
  in education, 44, 45, 64
  and Lyly, 153
  and truth, 85
  use of, 148–50
Richard II (Shakespeare), 188–89
Richard III (Shakespeare), 173
Robynson, Ralphe, 71
romances, epic, 11
  Don Quixote as, 19
  Faerie Queene as, 102
  poems, 21, 22
Romeo and Juliet (Shakespeare),
  176, 180, 182
Ronsard, Pierre de, 21, 59, 84
Roper, Margaret More, 127
Rose, the, 25–26
Rousseau, Jean Jacques, 137
rulers
  development of monarchies,
    47–48
  divine right of, 49, 173
  education as means of moral
    reform of, 43
  handbooks for
    Courtier, 49, 51–52
    Prince, 48–49
    Utopia, 71
  New Monarchies, 99
  portraits of, by Shakespeare,
    171, 173–74, 175–76

women as, 127, 128–29

Saint Augustine, 35
Salutati, Coluccio, 36
Satan
  in *Paradise Lost*, 116, 119–21,
    122–23
  seventeenth-century view of,
    121, 122
  and Shakespeare, 190
satire
  Don Quixote as, 19
  of Erasmus, 56
  and Jacobean drama, 199
  of Rabelais, 81–82
  of Romans, 81
  Utopia as, 19, 70, 71
Schanzer, Ernest, 120
Scholasticism
  attacked by humanists, 43–44
    Bacon, 149
  basis of, 45
  described, 42, 44, 63–64, 85
  in *Praise of Folly*, 56, 63
  and religion, 45
Screech, M.A., 78
Seneca, 155–56
Shakespeare, William
  and blank verse, 26
  career of, 26–27
  compared to Rabelais, 81
  education of, 23–24
  histories
    comedy in, 174–75
    development of, 172
    Falstaff, 174–75
    importance of, 26, 159–60
    themes of
      expediency, 175
      pursuit of power, 172, 173
      retribution for sin, 172
  influence of
    classics
      on Greek romances, 155
      on Roman, 24, 179
      on subject matter, 182,
        183–85
    Greene on, 155, 159
    Kyd on, 156, 159, 180
    Lyly on, 153, 154, 159
    Marlowe on, 26, 157, 158, 159
    Peele on, 159
    Petrarch on, 22
  poetry of, 27
  tragedies

devil in, 190
hero's defiance of society in,
  179, 190
importance of, 15–16
works of
  importance of individual
    consciousness in, 28
  see also specific titles
Shirley, John, 196, 201, 203
Sidney, Mary, 127, 129, 133
Sidney, Sir Philip, 22, 59–60
Sigea, Luisa, 127
Smith, Warren D., 166
sonnets, 21, 22, 35–36
Spanish Tragedy, The (Kyd), 26,
  155, 156, 199
speeches, 18–19
Spenser, Edmund
  influence of Ariosto on, 59–60
  on purpose of *Faerie Queene*,
    102
  see also Faerie Queene, The
Steane, J.B., 165
Stein, Arnold, 123
Stoicism, 196–97
St. Paul's School, 100
Switzerland, 23
Symposium (Plato), 36

Tamburlaine (Marlowe), 156–57,
  199
Tarnas, Richard, 15, 42
Tasso, Torquato, 22, 102, 119
Tempest, The (Shakespeare),
  186–87, 191–92
Temple, The (Herbert), 108
Terence, 193
theaters
  Elizabethan, 25–26
  and Puritans, 193, 203
Theatre, the, 25–26
themes
  affirmation of individual, 18
  aspiration, 15–17, 37, 156–58,
    163–65
  classical vs. Christian values,
    165–67, 168–69
  creation, 119
  expediency, 175
  free will, 37
  hero's defiance of society, 179,
    190
  hubris, 16
  individual consciousness, 15,
    17–18, 25, 28, 37, 88, 136,

138–40
morality and power, 48
perfectibility of individual, 37
platonic love, 36–37
pride, 159, 167
psychology of evil, 28–29
pursuit of power, 172, 173
rational man in rational
  universe, 37
retribution for sin, 172
revenge, 180
salvation, 17, 22
temptation, 17
Timon of Athens (Shakespeare),
  180, 190
'Tis Pity She's a Whore (Ford), 200
Titus and Andronicus
  (Shakespeare), 180, 199
Tourneur, Cyril, 196, 201, 202
tragedies, 26, 27
  and Marlowe, 158
  political history in, 179–80
  and Shakespeare, 15–16, 179,
    190
  subject matter of, 78
  types of, 179
    passion, 179, 188–90
    political, 185–88, 197
    revenge, 180–82, 202, 203
      importance of Kyd, 26, 156
    tragicomedies, 186–87, 191–92
Traversi, Derek, 171, 186–87
treatises
  described, 18, 19
  of Erasmus, 56
  on women, 20
Troilus and Cressida
  (Shakespeare), 180, 182
Twelfth Night (Shakespeare),
  177–78
Tyler, Margaret, 132

University Wits, 196
Urbino, 50
Utopia (More)
  Christianity in, 77

citizens in, 72–75
communism in, 74
described, 57, 59
education in, 75–76
government of, 71, 74–75
as handbook for rulers, 71
languages of, 70, 71
and *Republic* of Plato, 16
as satire, 19, 70, 71
as social commentary, 19–20,
  71–74
structure of, 71
war in, 76

Vickers, Brian, 141
Virgil, 21
Volpone: Or, The Fox (Jonson),
  194

Waldock, A.J.A., 120
Waller, Gary, 22, 94
War of the Roses, 23
Webster, John, 193, 196, 198, 200
White Devil, The (Webster), 198
Willmott, Richard, 107
Wilson, Katharina M., 125
Winter's Tale (Shakespeare),
  186–87, 191
Woman Killed with Kindness, A
  (Heywood), 202
women
  education of, 20, 125–28, 134
  during Middle Ages, 20
  opportunities for advancement
    of, 129–30, 134
  as patrons, 108, 127
  portrayals of
    by Greene, 155
    by Petrarch, 89, 92–95
    by Shakespeare, 159
  roles of, 20–21
    rulers, 127, 128–29
    writers, 130–33
  treatises on, 20
Wright, Eugene P., 193
Wyatt, Sir Thomas, 22